TRUMP
Y(F)OU

**PROMISES, LIES, AND CORRUPTION: MY BATTLE
WITH DONALD TRUMP'S FAKE UNIVERSITY**

ART COHEN
with DAN GOOD

To: Corey
Bob.

11/1/21

gatekeeper press™
Columbus, Ohio

TRUMP YOU: PROMISES, LIES, AND CORRUPTION: MY BATTLE WITH DONALD TRUMP'S FAKE UNIVERSITY

Published by Gatekeeper Press
2167 Stringtown Rd, Suite 109
Columbus, OH 43123-2989
www.GatekeeperPress.com

Library of Congress Control Number: 2021940533

ISBN (hardcover): 9781662915437
ISBN (paperback): 9781662915444
eISBN: 9781662915451

CONTENTS

DEDICATION

To my father, Barney, a WWII veteran and the greatest anti-fascist I've ever known. His epitaph, "Never Give Up," inspired me to finish *Trump You.*

To my mother, Hermia, who showered upon me her kindness, hope, and unconditional love to pass on to future generations.

To my wife, Jackie, whose encouragement made the journey of writing this memoir possible.

And my boys, Z and N, whose support and courage helped instill purpose in telling my story.

– Art Cohen

To Suzy and Dean

And those who stand up for what is right

– Dan Good

INTRODUCTION

Trump University is no joke.

The for-profit education scam—which was operated out of hotel ballrooms—centered on business honcho and reality TV star, Donald Trump, who promised to share his real estate secrets. As it turned out, Trump University wasn't an actual university and didn't feature much input from Trump besides promotional materials and snazzy videos preaching "success."

Before it was shut down in 2010, TrumpU shattered the lives of thousands of student-victims.

Including mine.

Yep, I got suckered out of a lot of money—I'm embarrassed to say how much—and ended up suing Trump personally in 2013, serving as lead plaintiff in one of two federal class-action lawsuits. At the time, Trump's oft-teased political ambitions seemed like a pipe dream.

With the legal saga still ongoing two years later, Trump decided to run for president, leaving me locked in a court battle against the potential leader of the free world. When the Trump University lawsuits threatened to derail his race for the White House, Trump defaulted to his corrupt impulses to pollute and undermine the rule of law, paving his illegitimate path to the presidency.

Trump vowed to never settle the cases: "I'm not a settler." But weeks ahead of trial, Mr. Never-Settler, then the president-elect, ended up agreeing to a $25 million settlement, the most expensive legal defeat of his career.

All these years later, TrumpU seems quaint—but in fact, it foreshadowed the devastation, bloodshed, and corruption that defined Trump's presidency. He operated the federal government similarly to Trump University by stocking Washington with his "hand-picked experts," misinforming the public with a flurry of lies, tricking unsuspecting people into losing everything, then spending years avoiding accountability for his criminal activity.

As lead plaintiff against Donald Trump, I witnessed a secret conversation in December 2015 between Trump and his attorney that reflected Trump's corrupt intent, his impulse to do anything and attack whomever he believed was a roadblock. During that hot-mic conversation, Trump showed his tendency to speak in code. Directives were easy to miss to the untrained ear, but they represented subliminal calls to action to his supporters and enablers. His not-so-veiled language to a mob in Washington on January 6, 2021 incited an insurrection at the U.S. Capitol. Fueling the deadly uprising—a stain on our country's democracy—reflected an extension of the tactics he used throughout the Trump University ordeal.

This memoir reveals never-before-shared details of the legal saga that come from private conversations, notes, and recollections. I've also obtained fresh interviews with some of the key people associated with the Trump University legal battle. Their quotes are interspersed throughout the book.

I aimed to present this material in an entertaining, thoughtful, and courageous manner. I strove to tell this story—the story that Donald Trump never wanted you to learn—as truthfully and unflinchingly as possible.

I wasn't involved in national politics when I sued Donald Trump. I only hoped to right a wrong for thousands of scammed students and get our money back. I didn't expect to find myself stuck in a battle of wills with the man who would become President of the United States.

As with so much in Donald Trump's professional life, Trump University began with promises and lies—one giant con . . . .

CHAPTER 1

THE ART AND THE DEAL

I was in a vulnerable place.

I found myself jobless in early 2009 after my consumer electronics company went through a forced sale. I'd poured my life into Aerielle, Inc. You might remember our "AudioBUG" FM transmitters, ladybug-shaped devices that aired music from portable devices over a car radio. After Apple's iPod became all the rage, we developed, manufactured, and licensed products for major retailers and brands such as BestBuy's Dynex, iriver, Kensington, SanDisk, XMRadio, and Delphi. Later, we looked to expand our wireless music transmission offerings with our own i2i brand working seamlessly with the debut in 2007 of the new iPhone.

Everything was going well . . . until it wasn't. The consumer electronics industry was hit hard by the 2008 recession. Our major investor wanted to restructure the company and install new management. I was out as CEO in 2009.

I wanted to find something new—and fast. It wasn't a great time to be unemployed. The national economy was tanking. To top it off, Silicon Valley isn't a cheap place to live. I worried about providing for my wife and two sons. At age 44, I found myself at a crossroads, an inflection point in my career. After spending five years as a CEO, I wanted to do something different and carve a new path.

AN INTRIGUING OPPORTUNITY

And then, I came across a "special invitation" in the mail and a full-page ad in the *San Jose Mercury News* promoting an opportunity.

"Don't think you can profit in this market? You can. And I'll show you how," proclaimed the advertisement's headline, underneath a photo of real estate developer Donald Trump. The ad promised the opportunity to "learn from Donald Trump's hand-picked experts."

"He's the most celebrated entrepreneur on earth. He's earned more in a day than most people do in a lifetime. He's living a life many men and women only dream about. And now he's ready to share—with Americans like you—the Trump process for investing in today's once-in-a-lifetime real estate market."

"Come to this **FREE introductory class,** and you'll learn from Donald Trump's handpicked instructors a systematic method for investing in real estate that anyone can use effectively. You'll learn foreclosure investing from the inside out. You'll learn how to finance your deals using other people's money. You'll learn how to overcome your fear of getting started."

The ad featured a guarantee attributed to the man himself: "I can turn anyone into a successful real estate investor, including you."

Why not me?

THE OLD COLLEGE TRY

Donald Trump was a name I trusted. I grew up in Philadelphia, less than 100 miles away from Trump's home base in New York City, so I was familiar with his success as a real estate developer and as the author of the 1987 bestseller *The Art of the Deal.* I'd made the hour-long drive to Atlantic City, NJ a few times, and his last name was splashed across his casinos, T-R-U-M-P, in flashing lights.

I considered the name "Trump" synonymous with success and wealth. At least that's what it meant for me back then, anyway. During the mid-eighties, while a student at Drexel University, I was one of the co-founding members of the DUsers—widely acknowledged as the first Macintosh users group. I was invited to a Hollywood-style event called "Going National," hosted by Drexel on its campus. There, I met the legendary Steve Jobs, co-founder of Apple. His inspiring talk that day imagined future computers using artificial intelligence (AI) to have conversations with the dead; not literally, but using inputs known about, for example, Abraham Lincoln. The AI would bring "Lincoln" to life so you could have a modern-day conversation with him as if he were alive today. Jobs' talk inspired me to lead a team tasked during a competition with imagining the personal computer of the year 2000. The contest, sponsored by Apple, had us competing locally and nationwide. We were one of five national finalists and invited to Cupertino, CA. There, we were to present our vision to an impressive panel: science-fiction writer Ray Bradbury, futurist Alvin Toffler, education writer and historian Diane Ravitch, computer pioneer Alan Kay, and Apple co-founder Steve Wozniak. A team from the University of Illinois at Urbana-Champaign won the competition—they envisioned a tablet device that sounded an awful lot like the eventual iPad.

During a luncheon, I got to sit at a table with Bradbury, and we began talking. He was amiable. He told me how his writing career didn't take off right away—he kept at it, day by day, year by year, and eventually success and fame found him. I love science fiction, and *Fahrenheit 451* is one of my favorite books. Besides my father, Bradbury probably inspired me more than anyone else as a writer, something I enjoy doing in my spare time.

CALIFORNIA DREAMIN'

The "Project 2000" contest was beneficial in another way—it allowed me to connect with Apple employees and give them my résumé. By 1989, I was moving to California as an Apple employee. I worked as an engineer at Apple until the mid-nineties, during the time before Steve Jobs returned to the company. I left to join a company called General Magic, where I worked on product and project management. During my time there, I bumped into a French-born computer programmer who said his wife came up with an idea about selling stuff from around the house online. Everyone laughed about it. I guess Pierre Omidyar got the last laugh; his creation AuctionWeb was later renamed eBay and became one of the world's leading ecommerce companies.

I bounced around several tech companies in Silicon Valley, including Corrigo, Oracle, and Philips Semiconductors. At one point, I tried my hand at law school, taking classes at night—Philips was picking up the tab. Classes were challenging, and my head wasn't in it. It was a big commitment, and I only ended up going for one year. My passion remained with high-tech.

After moving to California, I didn't keep close tabs on Donald Trump—I wasn't aware of his casino empire cratering or his amassing massive debt. Even as he weathered tabloid headlines and marriages and affairs and divorces, I didn't have a reason to doubt his business success. My father had a positive attitude toward Trump, too. He was a lawyer and was always impressed by Trump's business savvy. He passed away in 2006.

I never watched much of Trump's reality TV show, *The Apprentice*, where participants would compete in challenges for a chance to work at one of Trump's companies for a year. In a way, Trump University was a complement to the show—another opportunity for regular, everyday people to learn The Donald's secrets.

Real estate intrigued me. I had previously owned a rental property. With so many foreclosures on the market (this was at the height of the housing bubble) and strong property values in Silicon Valley, there were many opportunities. The "special invitation" I received in the mail contained two VIP tickets for a Preview Live Event on April 29, 2009, at the Fremont Marriott Silicon Valley. I went with my wife. I wanted her to check out this opportunity, too.

'WE TEACH SUCCESS'

My Trump University education began in a ballroom at a hotel off Interstate 880, adjacent to marshland along the southern edge of San Francisco Bay.

The 90-minute Preview Live Event featured many references to Donald Trump, from banners to handouts to an introductory video. The video opened with a title screen—*Donald Trump Welcomes You*—against an image of skyscrapers. Majestic, regal music played in the background, paired with the Trump University coat of arms, a lion.

Trump himself appeared on the screen. wearing a blue suit, white shirt, and lavender tie. He's sitting in front of a bookshelf.

"At Trump University, we teach success. That's what it's all about—success. It's going to happen to you," he says, looking into the camera lens.

A voice-over is matched with Trump Tower shots in New York City and other images highlighting Trump's real estate empire. "Donald Trump is without question the world's most famous businessman. As a real estate developer, he has reshaped the New York skyline with some of that great city's most prestigious and elegant buildings. Now, Donald Trump brings his years of experience to the world of business education. With the release of Trump University, he makes the very best of America's business education available to you, and others like you who seek a life of success, fulfillment, and prosperity."

Trump returns. "If you're going to achieve anything, you have to take action. And action is what Trump University is all about. But action's just a small part of Trump University. Trump University's about knowledge, about a lot of different things. Above all, it's about how to become successful."

Trump continues speaking to the interviewer. "And we're going to have professors, and adjunct professors, that are absolutely terrific—terrific people, terrific brains, successful, the best. We're going to have the best of the best. And honestly, if you don't learn from them, if you don't learn from me, if you don't learn from the people we're going to be putting forward, and these are all people that are hand-picked by me, then you're just not going to make it in terms of the world of success. And that's OK. But you're not going to make it in terms of success.

"I think the biggest step towards success is going to be, sign up for Trump University. We're gonna teach you about business; we're gonna teach you better than the business schools are going to teach you, and I went to the best business school. We're going to teach you better. It's going to be a shorter process; it's not going to involve years and years of your life. It's going to be less expensive, and I think it's going to be a better education. And it's going to be what you need to know. It's not going to be a lot of different theory that doesn't matter and will never be put to use. It's going to be what you need to know. So, we're going to teach you business, we're going to teach you life, we're gonna teach you salesmanship, and we're gonna teach you what you need to know. And we're gonna also make sure that no matter what you do, as I said before, you're going to love it. Because if you don't love it, it's never, ever going to work."

I was transfixed. I wanted to learn Trump's secrets. I wanted to take part in an educational process that wouldn't take years and years of my life. I wanted to find *success*. Success is difficult to define, but Donald Trump, by any measure, had led a successful life.

Seeing Donald Trump so excited further piqued my interest. And the fact that he put his name, his brand, his reputation on this opportunity meant he took it seriously.

The next step on the road to success was a three-day "Fast Track to Foreclosure" real estate retreat for $1,495, where I could learn other real estate secrets not included in the preview seminar. I was in. I put the charge on my credit card.

MENTOR FOR LIFE!

"Go home today and write yourself a check for a million dollars. Someday you're gonna be able to cash it," James Harris told us.

James was slick and brash, a loud talker with straw-colored hair and blindingly white teeth—the whitest white you've ever seen. He was a walking TV infomercial with his demonstrations and promises of added value, a can of Red Bull personified. He wanted to let us know how successful he was, and he had the Rolex and tailored blazers to show it. Think Alec Baldwin's "Always Be Closing" speech in *Glengarry Glen Ross.*

Oh, have I got your attention now? Good.

He seemed sincere and friendly, somebody who was going to have your back. He promised to be part of my team––someone I could call and reach out to, someone who'd accept your Facebook invites (he accepted mine).

James made real estate sound fun and lucrative by breaking it down to its basic elements, giving a high-level view of capitalizing on market trends, of embodying a lifestyle. *Success*—there was that word again. He talked about his jet-set lifestyle and personal connection to Donald Trump.

He tapped into your emotions, sucking you in and homing in on a personal level, getting a feel for our real estate backgrounds and work experiences and motivations. *You wanna do better for yourself . . . you wanna do better for your family . . . .* He had the ability to single you out and make it seem like he was talking to you directly, to you alone, even when you were in a crowded room.

Which made him such an exciting instructor for my "Fast Track to Foreclosure" event, held May 8-10, 2009. In the Sheraton Palo Alto Hotel ballroom, James was in his element, a master craftsman under the blasting air conditioning and artificial lights.

His colorful nature was reflected in the email he sent us ahead of the program, encouraging us to invest—the text was written in six different colors. Six! It started in navy, then switched to green, red, darker red, royal blue, back to navy, black, more red, and navy again. The first section, in navy, welcomed us into the Trump family.

I hope you understand that you are now with the "Best of The Best" in the Real Estate Industry . . . .

You are now going to become a "TRUMPSTER"!

Say WOOOHOOO!

Real Estate is the quickest, most least resistance path to WEALTH that you and your family could ever be involved with . . .

And the best part is . . .

You now can say that you are a "TRUMP GRADUATE"! (use the name . . . you are in the family now)

After including details about paying for the program, James closed his email with a personal touch.

I feel blessed to have met you all and want to say "Thank You" for your energy, passion and commitment to the TRUMP LEGACY . . . .

We NEED you to be successful!

I want to see you all on the next "Trump Video/Commercial" with your "Success Story"

Your Mentor For LIFE!

Mentor For LIFE. That had a nice ring to it. During the program, James tantalized us with stories of investment opportunities that lay ahead—connections that could lead to opportunities to invest in Trump properties at discounted prices before they were on the "public" market. He was adept at explaining different foreclosure techniques, a crucial area in the market at the time, given the economic downturn.

James also made a live phone call about a potential deal during the seminar. He wanted to show us "how it's done." If that's how Donald Trump does it . . . .

BEST OF THE BEST

I filled out a detailed financial statement, a chance to put my real estate investment prospects on paper, and I had a one-on-one interview in which we discussed my financial situation. The process was thorough. They really cared about me.

James addressed every question raised by the crowd, giving us enough information to consider opportunities involving certain types of real estate transactions. He deflected the questions he couldn't answer. I attempted to ask questions a few times, and he promised he would "get back to me" on the complicated ones. As we reached the third day, I forgot about the questions I was going to ask.

By that point, Harris focused on my need to connect with a mentor, someone who would guide me through my first few deals. One needed to sign up at the Gold Elite Level to receive a mentor. As the Trump University staff described it, the mentor would be an expert in real estate and someone, like James, who'd worked directly with Donald Trump. The "best of the best" enrolled in that program, James assured us. He said Gold Elite members would become part of the "family" with himself and other Trump University mentors.

But entering that family came at a high cost—$34,995. It was *a lot* of money. But with a few deals, the price would pay for itself, and then some. That "discount" offer was only in place that day. If we didn't act now, the price was liable to increase. James urged us to call our credit card companies and extend our lines of credit if needed.

I used my American Express card to pay for the program. If I could learn even a few of Donald Trump's secrets, it would be well worth the investment.

Near the end of the three-day seminar, we filled out questionnaires rating our experience. I listed my real estate experience as a beginner. I rated the quality of the presentation 4 out of 5, and the usefulness of the information 5 out of 5.

In terms of James' exceeding my expectations as a subject matter expert who presented the material clearly: 4 out of 5. "Note: I already had very high expectations! He did a great job!" I wrote. My suggestions for improving the seminar: "Have lunch sandwiches brought in—make 45 min lunch."

On topics that I'd like to see covered in future Trump University seminars, I wrote, "Provide PowerPoint presentations to those who join GOLD ELITE."

Would you attend another Trump University seminar? Yes.

Would you recommend Trump University seminars to a friend? Yes.

How could Trump University help you to meet your goals? "Mentoring key to success," I wrote.

For completing the "Fast Track to Foreclosure" training, I received a "Certificate of Accomplishment" awarded by Trump University, a document crudely resembling a diploma stating that I had completed the course. It featured the facsimile signatures of Donald Trump (listed as the Chairman of Trump University), Michael Sexton (President of Trump University) and Harris's signature in black pen scribble.

It was impressive seeing my name on the same piece of paper as Donald Trump's. I believed in Donald Trump. I believed in his university. I thought I was going to learn from the best.

It's so embarrassing now, looking back at how gullible I was. I can't believe I fell for it. But like I said, I was in a vulnerable place, in between jobs in a shaky consumer electronics space. After getting pushed out of my electronics company, I was coming off of a lot of stress and pressure. My self-esteem was in the gutter. I wanted to find something new and make my family proud, to uncover a path to a new leadership role, and the seminar seemed compelling.

CHAPTER 2

LETDOWN

I was getting antsy.

After plunking down nearly $40,000 for the Gold Elite Program, I wanted to meet my mentor and start learning the tricks of the trade. But the mentorship program didn't kick off right away.

While I waited, I took advantage of other Trump University opportunities. That June, I attended another seminar, a Quick Start retreat held in Las Vegas that covered fundamental investment techniques. I was disappointed that it wasn't held at Trump's hotel—it instead was held at a location off the beaten path. A man named Chris Goff was the course instructor. He taught everything at the service level . . . he wasn't as slick or engaging as my previous instructor, James Harris, but he also stressed his connections to Trump and how he could help in deal-making. I never followed him up on that offer. I was more interested in meeting my mentor!

At the urging of Trump University staffers, I set up a limited-liability company that I could use for transactions: AJZN Property Group, LLC. I named it after my family's initials. This venture was personal for me, something that reflected our shared goals and dreams. I set up a 1-800 number, designed a company logo, used Vistaprint to create the business cards, and took out newspaper ads promoting my new venture, all of which cost roughly $1,000-$1,500.

I also subscribed to additional online services for $34.95 a month—access to listings of properties on Trump University's website. I put those charges on my credit card, too.

I spent a lot of time on administrative tasks necessary for making a transaction, and I wanted to be spending more time on actual transactions. One technique that intrigued me was "lease to own," which required the least amount of up-front capital. But it's tough to achieve *success* if you're not selling, right? And I needed my mentor to help me sell.

INTERNAL ALARMS

After months of waiting, and after tackling the necessary administrative tasks, I was matched with my mentor: Kerry Lucas. Kerry was based in Florida, not California. But he told me he had deep connections to Donald Trump and real estate connections in California, and he discussed my goals with me. I was excited to work with him! The mentorship was considered the most valuable aspect of my Gold Elite membership.

Kerry and I talked on the phone, and he gave me advice on research materials. He flew to California for hands-on mentoring from July 19-21, 2009, the chance for me to shadow him and soak up his knowledge.

Kerry was amiable. I took a photo shaking his hand—he was middle-aged and fit, wearing an Air Force cap, polo shirt, and jeans. I like taking photos with people I meet, and here I was with the mentor who was going to help me unlock my potential in the real estate world.

The properties we visited were single-family homes in need of repair with owners who were supposedly stressed enough to take an "option" deal that would give the option-holder some rights of first refusal to lease the property while repairing it, then selling to another person without owning the title. But there were legal snags at every turn, and Kerry was recommending hiring an attorney.

That was a red flag for me—that would mean more money out of my pocket.

"Don't you know an attorney that works for Trump that can help us with these 'simple' questions?" I asked. All I got was crickets.

As we visited the properties, Kerry connected me with real estate professionals, but at the properties, these local licensed agents were doing all the work, talking about the neighborhoods, and what needed to be done to the properties to make them more viable for resale. They were showing me aspects of the houses that needed repair. Kerry was mostly walking around, agreeing with the local pros, and talking about which supplies we'd need at Home Depot.

I didn't need tips on what to buy at Home Depot.

It was odd. I asked Kerry questions, hoping to get as much information from him as I could . . . he taught me about receiving compensation for referring buyers to brokers. But Kerry wasn't acting like someone who was "the best of the best" and hand-picked by Donald Trump. And with all the red tape, I faced the creeping realization I might not be able to do "options to sell" deals—and the real estate brokers may not want to share anything with me.

Kerry also kept bugging me for a positive review. "I need a good review to get paid," he told me. I never gave him one. My internal alarms were sounding, and the noise was piercing.

MY WORST FEARS REALIZED

Kerry did connect me with the real estate professionals, and I hoped there was an opportunity with them. I sent the agents leads in the ensuing weeks, hoping I could start making money as a finder's fee. My optimism was crushed on Sept. 2, 2009, when I received an email from one of the real estate agents Kerry matched me with: "We have consulted with the Department of Real Estate, California Association of REALTORs, and a local Real Estate Attorney. There is no way we can sign any type of agreement that provides an unlicensed REALTOR from getting compensation [sic] due to the 'success' of a transaction. We will either have to find a way to pay for all leads or look for other avenues. Our Broker refuses to allow us to do business with an unlicensed agent."

This was bad.

I spent nearly $40,000 in large part to shadow my mentor, and the only salvageable advice my mentor gave me turned out to be illegal.

Everything he told me had been worthless.

I tried to make sense of it all. When I talked further with the real estate salesperson who sent the email, I asked him about his relationship with Kerry and Trump University. He said there was no financial connection and that Kerry had connected with him over the phone before meeting him when he came out to California.

I tried to reach Kerry after his visit, too, but he became distant. He made it clear that he came out for one visit only, and all other communication would be via phone, at best. Some year-long mentorship this was . . . . To be fair to him, he wrote that his father was in hospice and later died and that he was handling that estate. I lost interest in dealing with him anymore. It wasn't getting me anywhere, and my issues went far beyond him.

THE FINE PRINT

Maybe I could get a refund? Even a partial refund could clear this up. I checked the fine print on my agreement. Students had three days to cancel after signing up for the Gold Elite Program. THREE DAYS.

A student had 72 hours to reconsider a $34,995 bill.

I didn't pay enough attention to the fine print when I signed the agreement. I didn't pay enough attention to a lot of things. I was excited to be joining Trump University and blinded by the pursuit of *success*. But after three months, I had no success to show for my Trump University enrollment, only sunk costs and anguish.

PICKING UP THE PIECES

It was a dark time for me, one big crushing dose of reality. On top of getting dumped from my consumer electronics company, I was now out tens of thousands of dollars.

Seeing my Trump University and real estate pursuits were going nowhere, my wife suggested I find other work or start a different venture. I tried to refocus my angst, hoping to ignore the embarrassment and sting of being scammed. When I was angry, I'd occasionally play poker at a poker house in San Jose called Garden City. I figured I could try to win back the money I'd lost. I had some limited success with that—I even came in first place in a tournament there. I think I still have the jacket and trophy around somewhere.

But I found more satisfaction with a theater startup in Cupertino that my wife and I opened in November 2009 called Bluelight Cinemas, a discount premium theater with five screens that served as a community venue. The theater helped me build business and personal relationships in the city and local schools, some of which I've maintained to this day. It also enabled me to apply my technical know-how to take the theater from the 35mm-film generation to the new digital video and sound era. New connections with Hollywood allowed me to pursue my *Star Trek* passion. With that, I was able to host actors from the original and "Next Generation" *Star Trek* TV and movie series. Nichelle Nichols (Lieutenant Uhura) celebrated her 82nd birthday at Bluelight Cinemas, meeting and greeting fans. It was such a thrill connecting with her—she was so charming. She helped break down barriers with her role. Martin Luther King, Jr. had encouraged her to stay on the show. The on-screen kiss she shared with William Shatner (Captain Kirk) during a 1968 episode of *Star Trek* was the first interracial kiss on television. I was also thrilled meeting Gary Lockwood, who starred in my favorite childhood sci-fi film, *2001: A Space Odyssey*. Meeting with him gave me bragging rights of then being just two degrees of separation from Elvis Presley. Lockwood had befriended Presley in his early acting years. Gary and I shared poker stories, and I soon learned of his photographic memory, which he demonstrated by looking at a $1 bill for no more than five seconds and repeating the serial number back to me backward.

A few years after launching Bluelight Cinemas, I had the chance to meet another sci-fi actor at a conference: Thomas Wilson, whose most famous role was "Biff" in the *Back to the Future* trilogy—a character whose self-absorption was inspired by Donald Trump. But where I felt dissatisfied by my connection with Trump, Wilson was wonderful, and I value the autograph he gave me more than anything I got from his character's real-life inspiration.

It felt good to contribute and bury myself in a new endeavor after getting entangled with Trump University. I remained hopeful I could turn real estate transactions through Trump University. Still, the licensing issues were a major sticking point, and without any help with capital, any deal would be extremely challenging.

My Trump University experience was a dark cloud hovering over me. The money was gone, and I tried to come to grips with the fact that I wasn't getting it back. That wasn't an easy process. I spent months researching Trump University, seeking answers and trying to understand how I had been so foolish. I was vulnerable at the time I encountered Trump University, sure. But what did I miss? How did this happen?

Through my research, I read about Trump University receiving a D- rating from the Better Business Bureau, and how the state of Maryland barred Trump University from calling itself a "university"—regulatory entities had started hearing complaints and cracking down on Trump's institution. The New York Department of Education also demanded that Trump University remove "university" from its title, a request that Trump University ignored for years. The term "university" usually conveys a level of accreditation, a standard of learning required for matriculation. In this case, the "university" at Trump University meant nothing. I wish I had known that before I enrolled.

On June 2, 2010, I received an email notifying me that Trump University was changing its name to The Trump Entrepreneur Initiative. The name change came a few months after a San Diego-area woman, Tarla Makaeff, filed a class-action lawsuit against Trump University, claiming she spent nearly $60,000 on Trump University seminars and opportunities and got nothing of value in return.

"Tarla was a really charismatic person, very smart, articulate, and energetic. She was someone who clearly wanted to do everything she could to make this work— and it didn't because it was a scam."

AMBER ECK
HAEGGQUIST & ECK, LLP PARTNER AND TRIAL ATTORNEY
CO-LEAD COUNSEL IN CLASS ACTION AGAINST DONALD TRUMP AND
TRUMP UNIVERSITY

In her lawsuit, Makaeff compared the preview seminar to "an infomercial," highlighted how the speakers urged attendees to increase their credit card spending limits, addressed mentors giving advice that was illegal, the high-pressure sales pitch to get attendees to enroll in the Gold Elite Program, and how mentors "quickly disappeared" after the three-day shadowing program . . . the same types of issues I encountered. Makaeff wrote that she was taught to post anonymous "bandit signs" —signs on the side of the road promoting house sales—until she was contacted by the District Attorney's Office informing her that "those techniques could subject her to hundreds of thousands of dollars in fines, a misdemeanor charge, and up to six months in jail." And I thought Kerry's advice about working with the REALTORS was bad!

Makaeff's class-action suit covered anyone in California, Florida, and New York who purchased Trump University seminars from April 30, 2006, to the present. She suggested that the number of victims of Trump University nationwide might number into the tens of thousands. I was one of those victims.

After I learned about Makaeff's lawsuit in 2011, I contacted the law firms involved to ask if I could join the class. The lawyers said yes. I hoped the lawsuit would have a clean and quick resolution, that I could get my money back and move on with my life.

More than two years after enrolling at Trump University, I was finally joining a legitimate class. My education was finally beginning.

CHAPTER 3

THE BEGINNING

Trump University was ridiculed from the beginning.

"Proving again that his megalomania knows no bounds, Donald Trump is plotting the establishment of, we kid you not, Trump University," the Smoking Gun website wrote in August 2004 after publishing a copy of The Trump Organization's application with the U.S. Patent and Trademark Office for Trump University.

"Perhaps he can lecture on the importance of having a rich father. Or maybe he could offer a somber Founder's Day reflection on how he actually managed to lose money operating a casino."

The application listed the venture's aims: "Educational services in the nature of conducting online courses in the fields of business and real estate."

At the time of Trump University's founding, Donald Trump was on an upswing due to his popular reality TV show, "The Apprentice," which debuted that January. But even though Trump's star was shining brighter, his casino business was in debt to the tune of $1.8 *billion*.

Trump's rises and falls were epic. From the heyday of his casino empire during the 1980s and best-selling book *The Art of the Deal* to economic peril and personal drama—he endured marriages and affairs and divorces and scandal. He slapped his name and image on any product he could—from an airline (Trump Shuttle) and bottled water (Trump Ice) to Trump

Steaks, Trump Vodka (he's a teetotaler), clothing, cologne . . . and then there was Trump University.

A UNIVERSITY . . . IN NAME

The new educational venture was officially announced in May 2005 at a Trump Tower news conference. It came with a website launch and a crest featuring a lion. Squint your eyes, and it all looked legitimate enough (as it turns out, it wasn't). Michael Sexton, a management consultant described as "an expert in accelerating the foundation and growth of early-stage companies," was selected to serve as Trump University's president.

The faculty included business and entrepreneur professors from top schools like Northwestern, Dartmouth, and Columbia University— respected figures who brought a level of credibility to the venture.

Not that everyone was buying it. *Doonesbury* cartoonist Garry Trudeau, a longtime Trump critic, pounced at Trump University. A comic from June 7, 2005, features the characters Zonker and Boopsie speaking about the program.

"Trump University? That's an actual university?" Boopsie asks.

"Practically—it's an online school. Trump hired some legit Ivy tweed-heads to teach under the Trump brand," Zonker says. "The web site is really classy. Portraits of the founder, a coat of arms, even a university motto . . . 'Greed est bonum'" (a loose translation of "Greed is good," the message of the Trumpian corporate raider Gordon Gekko, played by Michael Douglas in the movie *Wall Street*).

"Wow, part Latin—that is classy," Boopsie says.

At its onset, Trump University courses (they ran $300-500 each) were online only, and the program featured CD-ROMs, seminars, and consulting services, but no grades or degrees. So, it wasn't an actual university under the New York State Education Department's criteria. A state education official reached out to Trump's team in 2005 to express concerns with the use of the term "university." Trump University could avoid further scrutiny if it abided by two conditions:

1. Trump University's place of business and corporate organization needed to be located outside of New York

2. It could not run live programs or other live training in New York.

According to legal filings, Sexton suggested that Trump University would create an LLC in Delaware and merge the New York operation into the Delaware entity and end the live programs in the Empire State. But none of those things happened, and Trump University continued to operate out of Trump's 40 Wall Street building. And then the bait-and-switch began in earnest.

FREE MONEY! BUT NOT FOR YOU.

Turn on the TV in the middle of the night in 2006 or 2007, and you were liable to see infomercials that promised you wealth. Free money! Grants! Property rehab! Business development! You could learn more at a free seminar coming to your area, so *sign up now* because space was limited.

The infomercials were the handiwork of National Grants Conferences, or NGC, a company run by Boca Raton, Florida residents Mike and Irene Milin. The Milins had found a well-worn model—wealth generation seminars—that made them rich and also left a trail of ruin for people who paid $999 or more, hoping to find free money for themselves. The couple had previously reached settlements in numerous states regarding fraud and deceptive marketing . . . a new wave of allegations would follow with NGC.

But for Michael Sexton, NGC was "the best in the business." That's what he said, anyway, when asked by *The Sacramento Bee* in 2006 about NGC's investigations and lawsuits in multiple states. Despite the complaints and criticisms surrounding NGC's business practices, Donald Trump licensed his name and image to the company for a traveling seminar series devoted to "wealth creation" under a venture branded Trump Institute.

Trump Institute seminars strongly mirrored other NGC events with Trump branding added. Live events featured a video of Trump, and attendees could pay $1,399 or more to attend additional "wealth-building" opportunities (it was later found that they could receive course materials that were at least partially plagiarized from a mid-1990s real estate book). Donald Trump also participated in an infomercial to promote the Trump Institute. "If you're smart and if you work hard, and if you love what you do and if you don't give up, you have not quit, you can make a lot of money," Trump said in the infomercial.

"I'm teaching what I've learned. And I'm real." The message of the seminar: you too can become Donald Trump. But many attendees didn't feel satisfied, and after they forked over their money, it didn't seem to get them any closer to becoming The Donald.

Within a few years, Trump Institute and the partnership with NGC faded away. But the venture gave Trump and Sexton a model they could use to generate millions of dollars, a model they could exploit. Why charge attendees $1,399 when you can charge between $10,000 and $35,000? Against that backdrop, by 2007, Trump University began hiring seminar leaders and offering live events of its own, building on the Trump Institute model with a focus on hotel conference room crowds across the country. Seminar leaders would try to upsell year-long "mentorship" packages, and then the money would REALLY be rolling in. And it did. All told, Trump University would take in more than $40 million.

'RUN FAST AND KEEP RUNNING'

Complaints against Trump University started emerging following each subsequent round of live events. Some of the students would get buyer's remorse after a few days or weeks, then come across the fine print—giving you only three days to request a refund—and become irate; others would attend numerous seminars, looking to unlock value, before throwing in the towel.

One after another, websites featured screeds and warnings from people who signed up for Trump University only to realize the scam when it was too late.

One woman from Michigan claimed she and her husband spent $19,000 on a mentor program and "canceled immediately," but since they paid by check, they'd had trouble getting their money back. "We'd been lied to, deceived, promised the person with 'authority' would call us back immediately (doesn't matter when you call, they are never in) and told there was a glitch in their system and our refund was being processed.

"Does this sound like Donald Trump is an honest man concerned with helping you build wealth?"

Another unhappy customer from California wrote that she "never would have paid if I had known that the info given to me was not true . . . I can't believe Donald Trump would allow such misbehaving to be associated with his name. Run fast and keep running where they are involved!"

Another commenter on a customer complaints website classified Trump University "a well-designed scam using the name of Donald Trump who apparently doesn't care how much more Americans get hurt this year and the next ones by a weak economy. Instead, he's using it to take advantage of you."

Trump Organization tried to brush the complaints away, arguing that most students were satisfied with the services. But the truth wasn't as straightforward. Since the events didn't stay long in any one place, and since the experience played to its participants' hopes and fears, the situation's full scope took time to emerge. For those—like me—who struggled to get a return on their Trump University investment, we felt like *we* did something wrong, that our failure was a reflection of not trying hard enough; a reflection of our internal failings. We felt like we were the problem rather than the victim, which we were.

As wave after wave of complaints continued rolling in, the Better Business Bureau refused to accredit Trump University and gave it a D-minus rating. Which, I found out later, infuriated Donald Trump to no end.

THE WILL TO WIN

Investigations and litigation started picking up in 2010, the same year Trump University changed its name to Trump Entrepreneur Initiative, and Tarla Makaeff filed her class-action lawsuit. Texas AG Greg Abbott—

who'd later, as the state's governor, become a staunch ally of Trump—began investigating Trump University, bringing an end to the live events in the Lone Star State (after that investigation ended, Trump happened to donate $35,000 to Abbott's campaign).

Maryland also barred Trump University from calling itself a "university." And in early 2011, six years after New York state officials first noted concerns with Trump University, an investigation from New York State Attorney General Eric Schneiderman's office kicked off, growing out of a broader look at for-profit education platforms.

The for-profit education push was guided behind the scenes by Karla Sanchez, who was the Executive Deputy Attorney General of Economic Justice, and Jane Azia, Chief of the Bureau of Consumer Frauds and Protection. Tristan Snell says he was handed the Trump University case on his second day working for the office as Assistant AG and told to see if there was "something here." So, he spent the next month or so calling New Yorkers who'd attended TrumpU programs.

"I would literally just say hello, and I would immediately get responses like, 'Oh my God, that was the worst rip-off,' 'Oh my God, they took my life savings,'" Snell said. "People cried when I called them because they were so upset or so happy that someone was finally looking into it.

"People volunteered themselves, without prompting, as witnesses to testify. They didn't care about the consequences of trying to attack Trump. Even at that point, he was considered to be kind of a scary guy to go after. So, that was how it started."

FOLLOWING THE PAPER TRAIL

Snell presented his findings to his higher-ups, including first deputy Harlan Levy. There was definitely *something here*. Snell became the de facto guide of the investigation, which moved to third-party discovery, in which the AG's office pursued documents and information from sources outside of The Trump Organization, including bank records.

"We had all this heartfelt testimony from our consumers, but then we were able to corroborate it by the biggest thing of all—the transcripts of the seminars themselves—which the Trump people, I still believe that they had them, or they did have them and just deleted them to try to cover up the evidence," Snell said.

As Snell was sifting through emails supplied by The Trump Organization, he found numerous references to an outside vendor who'd transcribed TrumpU seminars. Unfortunately, like many others tasked with aiding The Trump Organization, that vendor was still owed lots of money.

"It took a lot of work to track him down, but I did. And when I got him on the phone, he was very skeptical about speaking with me," Snell said. "I just happened to ask him, 'Were you ever paid back? Were you ever paid what you were owed there?' And he was like, 'No, actually, I wasn't,' and his entire tone suddenly changed, like I had flipped a switch. And suddenly it was like, 'You know what, if you give me a Dropbox link, I will send you the documents.' Within 48 hours, he sent me over 200 transcripts."

FOLLOW THE MONEY

To keep student-victims quiet, and to shake down vendors, Trump brought in a favored fixer—his attorney Michael Cohen (no relation!). Michael Cohen would "play hardball," and those who "squawked enough" or threatened to report TrumpU could expect a check, Snell said.

Michael Cohen also screwed over small business owners owed money by Trump University, telling unpaid vendors that TrumpU "only had $1M in cash to meet all its liabilities, which came to $5M, so they had to take twenty cents on the dollar, or sue the company in bankruptcy, which would only drag out the inevitable and waste even more money and time," he wrote in his memoir *Disloyal*.[1]

The New York AG's office was also able to obtain financial records showing that Donald Trump personally profited from TrumpU to the tune of $5 million from about $42 million in gross revenue. For Snell, following the money revealed that Trump University was nothing more than a get-rich-quick scheme.

"The whole enterprise was not about building something bigger, or building a truly great company that was going to outlast him. It was about cash flow for him in the immediate present," Snell said.

"Donald Trump was actually signing checks out from TrumpU directly to himself for $500,000 a pop. Those were the only checks that he would sign. All of the other checks were signed by (The Trump Organization CFO) Allen Weisselberg.

"He was not reinvesting any of the profits, which is what a better business would do.

"If you're trying to build something bigger than yourself that lasts, and you're sucking every dollar out of the business as soon as you make it, you're just a shitty businessman."

'THEY WERE SUCH ASSHOLES'

Even so—despite the documents and financial details and heart-wrenching statements by victims—the New York Attorney General's Office hesitated in bringing a lawsuit over Trump University. Donald Trump was a bully and media magnet who had bent the system to his advantage at every turn. And a lawsuit would put AG Eric Schneiderman on a collision course with The Donald.

---

[1] When reached by phone for further comment in May 2021, Michael Cohen said, "Please don't ever call my home again."

Schneiderman, youthful and fit, presented a conundrum for the Trumps. Trump's family liked to buy influence in New York City, and Schneiderman operated in some of their social circles.

Like Donald Trump, Schneiderman fashioned himself something of a smooth operator and lady's man (years later, his reputation and career came undone after he was credibly accused of physical abuse by four women, accusations he later apologized for). He was also a master media manipulator, able to play to TV networks or major newspapers to promote his cases, which got under Donald Trump's skin.

During his office's two-year investigation into Trump University, Schneiderman—according to Trump and people in his orbit—downplayed the investigation in private conversations as "very weak." At the same time, he kept hitting up the Trumps for political donations. In September 2012, Schneiderman hosted Kamala Harris, then California's attorney general, for a fundraising event. Trump donated $5,000 himself at the time and $6,000 total for Harris. At the same time, Ivanka would donate $2,000 (the donations would become a curious footnote during the 2020 presidential election when Kamala Harris was running as Democratic candidate Joe Biden's VP pick against Trump).

Settlement talks between the New York AG's Office and Trump's team in 2013 sputtered. "They wouldn't even counter," Snell said. "Their intransigence and just pigheaded stubbornness was a lot of what pushed Schneiderman to actually go forward with it. I don't think he would have (otherwise). That case was very settleable if they had tried . . . if they had been more polite. But they were such assholes."

In August 2013, Eric Schneiderman moved forward with Snell's work, suing Trump Entrepreneur Initiative LLC/Trump University, Donald Trump, and Michael Sexton in state Supreme Court in Manhattan and seeking $40 million, Trump University's revenue (my counsel was also able to confirm that figure). The suit noted that Donald had a 93 percent stake fed through two companies: DJT University Member LLC and DJT University Managing Member LLC. The lawsuit also highlighted how the real estate scion "netted about $5 million in profit" through the scam.

"Trump University's day-to-day operations were directly managed by Donald Trump's closely held holding company, The Trump Organization, and almost none of the formalities of a separate corporate existence were observed by Trump University or the limited-liability companies through which Donald Trump purported to hold his stake in it. Trump University could not even issue its own checks, and it never held a board meeting," according to Snell and Schneiderman. Trump's team pushed back against the lawsuit, suggesting it was a means for Schneiderman to increase his visibility and acquire political capital, or a means of payback because the Trumps hadn't donated more to him.

"Eric feels he can get political capital by taking on Mr. Trump to fight the perception that he is a weak and incompetent attorney general. It's nothing more than a cheap publicity trick," Michael Cohen (again, no relation!) told the *New York Post* at the time the lawsuit was filed.

In interviews, Schneiderman suggested that Donald Trump would be motivated to settle the case out of a desire to avoid bad publicity—but his sole purpose in everything was always to win, not to save face. He didn't care about the means or the cost required. The dirt never bothered him. Instead, he craved publicity of any kind, even when it was negative. Publicity fed Trump's need to be relevant, to be in the limelight. His desire to be relevant foreshadowed his persistence to exaggerate, to hyperbolize, and to lie.

Trump was going to do everything he could to prevail, as I'd learn, even if it skirted the lines of legality or decency. Settling the cases would have been easy for him, and it would have probably saved him money while also helping Trump University victims avoid so much needless suffering. But Donald Trump needed to find a way to win, and he didn't have one yet.

CHAPTER 4

LEAD PLAINTIFF

I didn't set out to become a lead plaintiff or personally take on Donald Trump. It's a stressful, demanding role. I just wanted my money back.

Tarla Makaeff's 2010 lawsuit, *Makaeff v. Trump University, LLC*, already had a lead plaintiff attached to it, along with named plaintiffs in Sonny Low, J.R. Everett, and John Brown. The attorneys chose those named plaintiffs strategically. Low lived in California, Everett in Florida, and Brown in New York. Makaeff's class-action suit covered residents in only those states—that's where the law firms located the bulk of the Trump University student-victims. A handful of other named plaintiffs in other states didn't have similar statutes to California, New York, and Florida regarding elder law and fraud and, therefore, could not join the class certification.

Since the Makaeff case came first, she was the canary in the coal mine. She faced Donald Trump's wrath more directly than any other plaintiffs, enduring an anti-defamation counterclaim and more direct attacks (she successfully defeated an anti-SLAPP, or Strategic Lawsuit Against Public Participation, suit—basically just a way to intimidate her). The situation dragged on for years and gave her anxiety. She worried Trump would ruin her, both financially and emotionally.

The motion to extend, adding additional causes of action to the original Makaeff complaint, was not allowed due to time constraints for filing amendments. That amendment would have allowed a federal statute to enable the complaint to include a national class action.

In a hearing when Judge Gonzalo Curiel denied the motion to add to the Makaeff complaint, he also implied nothing was preventing a new complaint from being filed that would not stain Makaeff's current complaint. There needed to be another lawsuit and another lead plaintiff to cover all students, including those of other states. The attorneys also wanted to file the case under the RICO (Racketeer Influenced and Corrupt Organizations) Act—it's often reserved for mafia cases and other organized crime. It reflects offenses committed as part of an ongoing criminal organization.

Instead of suing Trump University again, the attorneys planned to file the new lawsuit directly against Donald Trump. It was a compelling strategy. Trump, who owned 93% of Trump University, could no longer hide behind his fake university's corporate veil. Like mobsters that create corporations to conduct their fraudulent activities, Trump's corporate shield was cracked, which left him vulnerable to personal liability. Trump's greed to own it all was his Achilles heel that opened him to a RICO.

PIT BULLS AND HONEY BADGERS

To think, the court battle against the eventual president began with a phone call to a law firm with only four attorneys. Tarla Makaeff reached out to multiple firms seeking representation, but they passed. Then she called the offices of Zeldes Haeggquist & Eck, where she spoke with attorney Aaron Olsen—the law firm saw the truth that victims like Makaeff had a legitimate class-action claim, and that there were potentially dozens, or hundreds, or maybe even thousands of people just like her. Olsen and senior partner Amber Eck, along with others, began interviewing other Trump University victims. They later enlisted Rachel Jensen of Robbins Geller Rudman & Dowd, the country's largest plaintiff's class-action firm, for an assist with the Makaeff case. Eck had previously been a partner at Robbins Geller, where she litigated class actions. It's common for law firms to team together on class-action lawsuits because of their size and scope.

Jensen—a superstar in consumer law—deposed Trump in 2012 for the Makaeff case.

"I think the lawsuit is trying to hurt the brand, and I honestly look forward to winning this case and suing your law firm for as much as we can sue them for, and we will be doing that. We have a 97 percent approval rating. Harvard doesn't have a 97 percent approval rating. And we will be suing your law firm for as much as we can possibly do. That I can tell you," Trump told her during the deposition.

"OK," she responded.

"And you individually," he fired back. But instead of belaboring the point or getting rattled, she came back to her question, declining to yield any ground.

Due to the RICO angle, Jason Forge of Robbins Geller joined the Makaeff case in 2013. Forge was a pit bull—as a prosecutor, he conducted the trial that brought down Congressman Randy "Duke" Cunningham, the largest bribery scheme in congressional history.

Eck and Forge were named co-lead counsels, but there were many attorneys involved with the cases, the best of the best. Eck would serve as a point person for Trump University victims, hearing their stories and keeping them updated on developments. Forge loved diving into case studies.

Another attorney on the case, Patrick Coughlin, was affectionately nicknamed "honey badger" by Forge because of his relentlessness—like the thick-skinned animal, he wouldn't quit, burrowing, climbing, and withstanding animosity as he pursued his target.

After I joined the class in 2011, I kept in close contact with the attorneys. They all did a great job of explaining the nuances of the case to me and would drop me quick emails to keep me up to speed. They thought my story resonated—being out of my company and looking for a new opportunity, the desire to make money on real estate, my owning the movie theater, it was believable. It would connect with a jury if the matter ever went to trial. So in 2013, two years after I first joined the class of Trump University student-victims, they asked me if I'd agree to take on the lead plaintiff role for the national class-action RICO suit against Donald Trump.

"Let me think about that," I said. I had questions about the time commitment and potential risks. This was *Donald Trump* . . . the attorneys explained that they would cover all costs and how I would be required to participate in hearings, approve drafts of legal filings, and sign off on any settlement offers.

I weighed my options. I would be putting myself out there in a way that felt uncomfortable to me. As a businessman, and as someone who enjoys maintaining his privacy, I was ashamed that I fell prey to the Trump University scam. I didn't want people to know about it. I didn't talk about it to most of my friends and relatives. Those I did open up to were surprised. "You got scammed by that? Come on!" my in-laws had said. That was the attitude: How dumb could you be? You got tricked by Donald Trump? It didn't feel good to relive that trauma (it still doesn't).

At the same time, serving as the lead plaintiff could offer a sense of control. *OK, I got scammed, but now I can help get my money back and help others do the same.* All the bad energy could get erased. Having a sense of control meant the decision on a settlement was on my shoulders. *Yes, I will do this.* I discussed the situation with my counsel and said I wanted everyone to get at least half of their money back. I wouldn't accept a settlement offer under 50 cents on the dollar.

We ended up doing quite a bit better than that. But it took a long time.

OPERATION DISCOVERY

We signed an engagement agreement that set everything in place. The next step was the discovery. If you're not familiar with the legal world, this may sound exciting—but in actuality, it sucks up a lot of time. It can be very intense, while—in paradox—it's simultaneously very boring. Discovery involved poring through *years* of emails, photos, and phone records. The attorneys wanted *everything*. Every communication. Every document. Everything my "mentor" Kerry Lucas shared with me.

I think Kerry Lucas' incompetence[2] was a fortuitous reason why I made a solid lead plaintiff. It felt like I had a strong case. I think it also helped that I was on the younger side (a number of the Trump University victims were seniors), and I was located an hour away from San Diego by plane if I needed to appear for a meeting or hearing in federal court. Ultimately, my experience of getting screwed by Trump University was reflective of other students' experiences. I was meticulous and understood the legal world due to my business experience, and I hadn't made any public statements about Trump University.

Tarla Makaeff participated in a video interview recorded at the time she signed up for a TrumpU package, with Trump University reps standing by. She spoke favorably about Trump University, and Trump's counsel could play that video in court. They would use it against her. It was similar to the reviews they had us sign after the "fast track to foreclosure" events, where we had no reason *not* to be excited. Clearly, they did an effective job convincing us that this could be a great opportunity. If they hadn't, we wouldn't have spent tens of thousands of dollars. Donald Trump and his attorneys kept quoting this 98% statistic. Trump University had a 98% approval rating among students, but that only applied to students when they signed up for gold or silver packages. It'd be like reviewing a meal at a restaurant before the food arrives. I'd love to know the approval rating for TrumpU students one year later.

It was painful to learn about the other Trump University victims, especially senior citizens who'd lost their life savings. Like me, these people bought into the myth of Donald Trump and thought that he would help them succeed . . . we trusted Donald Trump and quickly learned to regret it.

When it happened to me, I felt like maybe I didn't work hard enough or that I missed something. It brought about a lot of self-reflection with my ego in the gutter. *I screwed up.* Maybe, I thought, I didn't follow the process properly—that others would succeed where I failed. But learning of the

---

[2] Kerry Lucas was contacted by phone in July 2021 but did not respond to multiple requests for comment.

thousands of other victims, I quickly realized it wasn't just me. We weren't the reason why we failed—we were ripped off. We were scammed. Trump University wasn't something I could have fixed or succeeded at, no matter what I did. The odds were slanted, so there was no way of winning.

"This Trump university scam had a severe impact on a lot of victims' lives. Some of them lost their houses, lost their retirement funds, and went through divorces. Some of them faced depression, anxiety, were suicidal, or financially devastated. It was really disturbing. And they felt that they'd really been betrayed by Donald Trump.

A lot of them would tell me, 'How can he sleep at night after taking advantage of me and all these people? How can he do this?' He really was betraying his biggest fans."

AMBER ECK
HAEGGQUIST & ECK, LLP PARTNER AND TRIAL ATTORNEY

Those slanted odds became evident after my counsel, through discovery and lots of effort, was able to obtain copies of the Trump University playbooks—documents outlining the TrumpU guiding principles and practices—as well as generic scripts for instructors to follow. Paydirt! It was all about profit, profit, profit. The playbooks documented every step of the marketing and recruitment process, from targeting potential student-victims to setting the venue's temperature (no more than 68 degrees). It also included tips for handling the media—"Reporters are rarely on your side and they are not sympathetic," a stance that wasn't all that far removed from Trump's eventual calls of "fake news" for unflattering coverage—and guidelines for actions to take if an attorney general arrived at a seminar location: "If an attorney general arrives on the scene, contact April Neumann (Trump University's director of operations) immediately. By law, you do not have to show them any personal information unless they present a warrant; however, you are expected to be courteous." *How many legitimate universities tell their employees how to respond if an attorney general appears?!*

The scripts—which Trump's team failed to initially produce, despite my attorneys' numerous requests—unlocked the patterns behind the seminars. With the scripts in hand, you couldn't effectively argue that the problem was one or two rogue lecturers. The scripts showed that they were *trained* to spin stories about Trump and prey on people's vulnerabilities.

Going through all the records again took me back to 2009, reliving the seminar where I was inspired by James Harris, the carnival barker who spoke of his close personal connection with Trump . . . the contract gave attendees only three days to back out and get their money back. No control. Why would someone sign a contract like that? It's because Donald Trump had a reputation, at the time, of somebody successful. Maybe a little shady, sure; over the top, of course; but this guy was an international and reality TV star. His name was synonymous with wealth and opportunity. And even if he'd had some missteps along the way, he usually came out on top.

I guess I was a sucker for trusting Donald Trump. But so were more than 6,000 other people who signed up for Trump University (thankfully, the bulk of the student-victims only signed up for seminars, although many, like me, signed up for more expensive packages; victims ended up spending roughly $6,000 on average).

Among Trump University's live-events students, only a handful voiced support for the "education" they received, and those who did turned out to be close supporters of Trump or people who had business connections with his business or family. There was nothing to show for what anyone "learned" at TrumpU, and even if there was, even if someone did magically learn meaningful real estate tips from Trump University, it wouldn't negate the reality that most students (like me) were ripped off with nothing to show for it.

My time as lead plaintiff came with lots of second-guessing and regret. I could have used the money I spent on Trump University for my children's education. For legitimate investments. For improvements on my house. Instead, I flushed it away. But I was going to get it back.

PIERCING THE CORPORATE VEIL

The key to the lawsuit was the RICO designation. A RICO claim must allege: "(1) conduct (2) of an enterprise (3) through a pattern (4) of racketeering activity."

What made the RICO case possible was the corporate structure of Trump University. Donald Trump himself owned 93% of Trump University, meaning, in essence, he *was* Trump University. Entrepreneurs set up limited-liability companies, in part, to protect personal liability, to separate them from any legal issues that are brought against the company. But Donald Trump and Trump University were one and the same. He appeared in Trump University promotional videos and advertisements. He lent his name, brand, and reputation to it. He was front and center. The image presented—whether or not it was valid—was that there was no one else in the Trump Organization that had any involvement, as far as you could tell, with Trump University (outside of Michael Sexton, who was seemingly working in tandem or consultation with Donald Trump). Donald Trump was organizing Trump University and handpicking everybody. Or so it seemed.

My counsel, in the lawsuit, highlighted the ways Donald Trump embedded himself within the structure and operations of Trump University:

- Providing the initial operating capital and holding an approximately 93% ownership stake;

- Creating and approving marketing and advertising materials, which featured his name, likeness (in most), and voice (in the Main Promotional Video);

- Selecting both the original name of Trump University and, five years later approving the change to the name of The Trump Entrepreneur Initiative;

- Regularly reviewing financial records; and

- Negotiating and authorizing others to negotiate significant contracts, such as the lease for the Enterprise's headquarters.

Through Trump University, he was able to make somewhere upwards of $5 million personally, which incensed me. He took millions out of the venture without ever being engaged to make it succeed, and he used his reputation not to share his secrets, but to prey on people who believed in him. All he cared about was how much money he could take from us without investing his time or care. But he also lacked adequate protection from the corporation, proving he's not as smart as he likes to say he is.

Our efforts to "pierce the corporate veil" infuriated Donald Trump, especially since RICO judgments come with treble damages, meaning if we won at trial, he'd be on the hook for three times the actual damages, plus legal fees. So instead of the roughly $40 million that Trump University's student-victims paid, he could wind up being forced to pay more than $120 million himself. And that was a hefty total, even for a self-described billionaire like Trump.

But despite numerous challenges and objections from Trump and his legal team, the RICO complaint stood firm. On February 21, 2014, the same day the class was certified for Makaeff, meaning she was representing a group of people who suffered a similar type of harm as she did, Judge Gonzalo Curiel made his decision. Trump's motion to dismiss my complaint was denied. *Cohen v. Trump* could proceed. Which meant I'd be front and center.

CHAPTER 5

COHEN'S DEPOSITION

Breathe.

Listen.

Pause.

Think about your response.

Don't say anything beyond what you were asked to answer.

Breathe.

On May 29, 2014, I sat for a deposition with Donald Trump's lawyers (my counsel, attorneys Amber Eck and Jason Forge, were also present for the hearing). The first deposition hearing was all about getting the class certified. Trump's legal team hoped to undermine my ability to represent a class of over 6,000 people I've never personally met.

To represent the class, my experiences needed to be similar to other class members. That doesn't mean that everyone needed to feel the exact way I did about their Trump University experience—a few people believed they got something out of it. No, it meant they took similar Trump University classes like I did, received similar course materials, watched similar videos, learned of Trump University in similar ways, and had similar outcomes after signing up for the program.

Attorney Nancy Stagg, then of Foley & Lardner, LLP, took my deposition at Robbins Geller Rudman and Dowd's LLP law offices in San Diego. Stagg was representing Trump, and Jill Martin was there from The Trump Organization.

Ahead of the deposition, I noticed that Martin had viewed my profile on the social media website LinkedIn . . . it gives you an alert when someone looks at your profile, and there she was. I knew they were digging into information about me and learning more about who I was. Which wasn't unexpected, but it also felt intrusive. I suddenly realized that Donald Trump's people were checking on who I am.

Those clues, and the fear that the case could put me in the public spotlight, caused me to become more protective about what I posted online. I didn't want people to be able to stumble onto my social media accounts and try digging up dirt on the guy who's suing a celebrity real estate guy. Not that there was much, if anything, to find; it just made me uncomfortable.

Breathe.

PREPARING FOR A FIGHT

There was a lot of planning and preparation that went into my deposition. My attorneys and I reviewed documents and prepared for the type of questions that the opposing attorney would potentially ask. My attorneys didn't want to have any written notes or documents with me. Any notes or documents could be requested following the deposition by the deposing counsel and used as evidence.

Ahead of the deposition, my counsel sent me a timeline of the case to refresh my memory, as well as a list of tips to keep in mind. I studied the tips, making sure I had them memorized. Like this one: "Pause before answering all questions. Even when the answer is obvious, if you hurry your answers to easy questions, you tend to hurry answers to more difficult questions that require more thought." My attorneys always wanted me to pause purposely before answering all questions, even when all it required was a simple "yes" or "no." I needed to wait to give my attorneys time to state any objections they wanted for the record. Sometimes they would state objections and then say I could then answer the question. My attorneys' advice is a typical deposition protocol; however, nothing about a deposition is natural. A deposition is not a conversation. Listen carefully to the question and answer no more than what the question asks explicitly. Never guess. If you don't know the answer, respond that you don't know or can't recall. Avoid colloquial terms such as "I think" or "I might." Rachel, Jason, and Amber coached me on answering the questions I was asked without volunteering additional information and only sticking to facts—if I started presenting my unfounded beliefs, it would undermine my credibility.

Another tip that stood out to me involved the interrogating attorney ruffling papers or sitting silently for 30 seconds, or a minute or more. During a typical conversation, we're inclined to fill the silence. But in a deposition hearing, I was under no obligation to fill the silence and potentially say the wrong thing.

I flew down to San Diego the night before the deposition and had a nice meal. I made sure of that. I have Type 1 Diabetes, also known as juvenile diabetes, meaning my body doesn't produce insulin. So on top of breathing and remaining calm and pausing during the hearing, I also had to keep my stress in check since stress can impact one's blood-sugar level. I made sure I had a good breakfast before the deposition, so my blood-sugar level wouldn't drop too low, and I brought my insulin needed before having lunch. Since it was a video deposition, I didn't want to be in the middle of the hearing sucking on hard candies or chewing raisins.

Of course, I could have easily at any time said, "Look, I need to take a break," and it wouldn't have been a problem. And that's how I planned to handle any situation where I wasn't feeling right. If my blood-sugar level was off during the deposition, it could cloud my thoughts and cause me to say things that were unclear or inarticulate—which in turn could jeopardize my chances of serving as a class representative.

Breathe.

A VERY ODD CONVERSATION

I arrived for the deposition; the office had a special floor set aside for depositions in order to provide a sense of privacy. I wanted to abide by the rules, standards, and structure of this very odd conversation. I tried not to be defensive. I also made sure to pause before answering. If my counsel wished to raise an objection to a question, I needed to allow them the chance to respond before I began answering.

The deposition began, and I think it went pretty well for a while. The designation of on and off the record was fascinating, like a traffic light switching back and forth in synchronization. There would be a sticking point, and Jason Forge would request to go off the record. Nancy Stagg would agree, we'd go off the record, discuss one quick issue, then come back on the record. That happened when I was asked about whether I'd taken a deposition before—I had, as a witness in a personal injury suit which had absolutely nothing to do with me and seemed utterly irrelevant to the matter at hand. I tried to cite attorney-client privilege, and Jason went "off the record" to discuss with me that I could provide a little bit more clarifying information.

When I didn't know the answer to something, I made sure to say so. I said, "I don't recall" 29 times during the hearing. If I wasn't sure about answering a question and wanted to buy myself extra time, or if I wanted to hear the query again for clarification, I asked Nancy Stagg to repeat the question.

Needing clarification is not unusual, given the awkward circumstances of answering questions under pressure. I knew that she scrutinized the meaning of every mannerism, and each word I uttered. That was her job.

A SLIP OF THE TONGUE

When I did feel comfortable about a question, I made sure to answer clearly. "I did not have the expectation that Donald Trump was going to be teaching directly. That would not be reasonable to expect at that time. I did have the expectation that the people who were teaching it were people who had worked with Donald Trump, because they said they did, and also had experience with Donald Trump. So that was my expectation," I said.

"Who told you that?" Stagg asked.

"James Harris," I responded, recalling the name of my seminar leader.

I answered questions about my "mentor" Kerry Lucas and Trump University experiences, and my communication with the attorneys handling the case. In one slip of the tongue, I referred to the Makaeff case as the "Madoff case," as in Bernie Madoff, the investor who ripped off his clients in a massive Ponzi scheme. Whoops! Guess I had fraudsters on the mind after spending so much time focused on Donald Trump. "Excuse me," I said.

Stagg tried, unsuccessfully, to bait me by bringing up my satisfaction with the introductory seminar that led me to sign up for the Gold Elite Package. My counsel raised objections to the questions, then I was required to answer.

"At the time I thought I got value. Today, I thought . . . today, I feel I was . . . I was misled. I was cheated, because the information that was provided was not directly from Donald Trump, you know. He had nothing to do with the program, yet he used . . . yet he said that he did," I said.

CORRECTING THE RECORD

Things were going fine until about two hours into this very odd conversation (not counting off-the-record breaks), when I was asked about my reasons for suing Donald Trump. "In general, I was looking to recover my loss because I felt that a fraud had been perpetuated against me," I said.

"What do you say the loss is?" Stagg asked.

"The investment that was made in money and time, effort, interest fees. Whatever is named in the complaint."

Stagg focused on one word: time.

"I'm trying to understand, in your mind, what you're seeking when you say you're looking for recovery of your investment time," she said. "Do you have an amount of time involved? Is it just the time while you were in the courses? Is it time you spent doing exercises?"

Hmm. How should I quantify that? How could I explain five years of my life and tens of thousands of dollars flushed away? How would I feel satisfied in a resolution?

"It was the time that I spent in the courses, it's the time that I spent with Mr. Lucas, it's the time that I invested in setting up a corporation, it's the time that I'm spending with you here today and traveling here. It's all the time that's involved around the Trump University unfortunate experience."

As soon as the words left my mouth, my attorney Amber Eck jumped in. "We've been going about two hours. Can we take a quick break?" The attorneys discussed the situation, and we went off the record from 11:50 to 12:09.

Then Jason Forge took me out of the room.

"OK, now we have to correct ourselves here," he said. "We can't be talking about soft costs, only hard costs, the cost of the program. We can't be talking about the time it took to go to the class and so forth. You're not going to recover those costs. We're only going after the hard costs. That's it. And that's what makes the class action work. So that's what we're focused on."

Oof.

Forge obviously had a point, and he understood this legal world so much better than I did. I know he wasn't happy about my misspeak . . . it's the feeling like when a parent is disappointed in you, this unspoken weight you carry that you want to be perfect and not let them down . . . I felt so small in that moment. I tried to refocus, to manage my stress, to keep everything in check.

Breathe.

I made sure to clarify as soon as we came back on the record.

"What I'm trying to recover for the entire class is the investment that every student has made into it," I said. "That meant the money for classes. And if by chance there's . . . you know, as a class, we're awarded additional compensation for peoples' time or whatnot, that's fine. But the most important thing is that all the students get their money back."

Stagg pressed me over whether I decided to change my testimony after talking to my attorneys.

"I did. Because they felt that I was not clear." She tried to hammer my word choices, to pick apart my statements, but she didn't get far.

FIREWORKS

A little after 12:45 p.m., Stagg said she was going to conclude the deposition for that day. And that's when the fireworks began.

While Stagg suggested that my counsel would need to wait until the conclusion of the deposition—whenever that would be to ask me follow-up questions and clarify any of my comments, Jason Forge argued that they were allowed to ask me questions now based on the deposition that had just happened.

"Your objection is noted, but I am going to ask questions based on the questions you asked," Forge said. "So I'm just letting you know . . . ."

"No, I don't think . . . we're not finished with the deposition," Stagg said. "So I have a two-hour limit . . . ."

"Right."

"And if you want to ask questions, I get to keep going until we're done. You don't get to stop and ask questions . . . ."

"I am going to ask questions," Forge said.

"No. No. No. That's not how it works," Stagg said.

I found myself in the middle of these two opposing forces pushing against each other . . . I felt the urge to grab some popcorn and watch, because there was absolutely nothing I could contribute to the conversation, even though the conversation involved who got to talk to me next. It got to be so intense that the court reporter asked both sides to slow down—it was tough for them to keep up.

Stagg suggested going off the record.

"No, we are going to stay on the record," Forge said, ensuring that the conversation continued to be documented. "If you want us to call Judge Gallo, we can call Judge Gallo."

"Let's call Judge Gallo," Stagg agreed.

The attorneys continued to discuss their stance. Forge argued that the class certification deposition only featured two hours of questioning, how "there was no need to ask more than two hours' worth of questions related to class certification issues." Forge looked to forge ahead with his questions, but Stagg said she was moving to suspend the deposition as she pursued a protective order—and that if my attorney continued with his questions, that it would be a sign of prejudice, an error that would undermine the entire case.

She continued to suggest that the sides wait for Judge Gallo, but he was in a settlement conference at the time. Eventually the court reporter suggested they should stop.

"I would rather not be put in the middle, because I feel uncomfortable, one attorney says yes, one attorney says no. I would rather get guidance from the judge," the court reporter said.

The sides continued bickering, not budging an inch, with Amber Eck and Jill Martin also weighing in. Eventually Forge asked the court reporter and videographer if they'd like a 45-minute break—without them, the deposition could not continue—so we took a recess. I made a point to take advantage of the hard stop for lunch. Had to make sure my blood sugar was steady. And I was hungry. My counsel ordered lunch and we ate in a conference room. During the break in the official proceedings, the attorneys were finally able to connect with Judge Gallo. Witnessing those fireworks represented my first chance to watch Forge and Jensen in a live battle making arguments before the judge. It was fast and furious, and when my counsel won the argument, there was a genuine feeling of elation among us.

YES OR NO

We came back from break (I made sure I didn't have any lettuce stuck in my teeth) and Jason Forge began questioning me. His questions were lightning quick. Speed round! He asked me a series of clarifying questions and asked them in a manner that made it very clear about what he was asking for. A chance for some cleanup work.

He asked me about a few paragraphs of text and whether they were consistent with the Trump University advertisement I saw in 2009 that featured lots of empty promises: "I can turn anyone into a successful real estate investor, including you."

"That's correct," I said.

He peppered me with a series of yes and no questions—the themes of the seminar, the presentation I viewed, questions about the complaint, about Trump University's shaky status as a "university," and my questions consisted of "yes" or "no."

He circled back to that damages question I'd been asked about earlier.

"Are you seeking any damages that are unique to you, or are they the same type of damages for all members of the class?"

"The same type of damages for all members of the class," I said.

Forge breezed through his questions, and then Stagg asked me a few more questions, and that was that. The deposition hearing was over.

Afterward, he thought I did very well, even with the misspeak about retribution for time. He was happy. And that made me happy.

READY FOR MORE

I had a follow-up deposition in June 2015 with the same attorneys. For the second deposition, I was ready, and I knew what to expect. It was easier. It was also shorter. I think they realized they weren't going to get anything out of me.

At one point, Stagg asked me about my email addresses. "Tell me all the email accounts that you looked through to collect documents to produce for discovery in this case," Stagg said.

Oooh. Um . . . "I'd prefer not to give all my other business email accounts. I'd like to take a break," I told her. I didn't want my personal information published. I didn't know where this was going. I pleaded with my counsel.

"Provide them. It will be confidential," Forge said. "You can provide them. We can designate this portion, at least on a preliminary basis, confidential."

Fine. I provided my email addresses, but I wasn't happy about it (luckily, while my name was thrown out in public, my email address was never divulged—that turned out to be an unwarranted concern). I still felt vulnerable and open about everything . . . I wasn't trying to bring attention to myself. Publicity wasn't beneficial for the case, my family, or me. I had two small kids at home. That feeling of vulnerability was unsettling. It gave me a deeper appreciation and respect for Tarla Makaeff. Trump and his lawyers dragged her through hell.

During my second deposition hearing, I got the sense that Nancy Stagg was frustrated. She was flipping through pages a lot, not saying anything, uncomfortable moments of silence in which a few minutes seemed like an hour. I remember thinking, "When are you going to ask a question?" as she shuffled through folders and documents without saying a word. She was silent for a minute or more at a time. As my counsel instructed me, I remained silent—which wasn't easy. But my goal wasn't to have a conversation with her, it was to answer her questions, and if she wasn't asking questions, then I had nothing to say.

The second hearing ended with a whimper. No fireworks, no added drama, no notable cleanup needed.

Exhale.

SOFT COSTS AND HARD TRUTHS

Following the deposition hearings, there was a lot of work to be done. We received a copy of the transcript from the stenographer and the lawyers, and I had to read what was written to make sure it was accurate and make any necessary corrections. That took hours and hours. At one point, I was keeping track of all my time, and then I just said, "Oh, forget it." Those were the soft costs I couldn't mention in court, the time, stress, and frustration I couldn't quantify. I had to face the fact that even if I eventually received financial compensation from this mess, Donald Trump had taken something from me that I would never get back. He'd made me more closed, cynical, and jaded, and less trusting, fueling a cycle of shame and self-doubt.

As I look back at my deposition hearings, it's interesting to consider the journeys of the two Trump defense attorneys, Jill Martin and Nancy Stagg. Martin has been with The Trump Organization for more than a decade and is entrenched with the company. Her name was listed on arbitration documents for Essential Consultants, LLC—the company that Michael Cohen, Trump's longtime attorney and fixer, used to pay adult film star Stormy Daniels (real name Stephanie Clifford) to keep her quiet ahead of the 2016 election. And in 2019, Martin was named The Trump Organization's chief compliance officer, dealing with conflicts-of-interest rules.

Nancy Stagg, meanwhile, along with her colleague Benjamin J. Morris from Foley & Lardner LLP, were substituted as counsel of record on Dec. 18, 2015, by Daniel Petrocelli and David Kirman of O'Melveny & Myers LLP—a powerful international law firm with deep ties to media and entertainment companies. This was about a week after Trump participated in a deposition hearing for the case that gave a private view of him—one that made me very worried.

Years after representing Donald Trump in court, Nancy Stagg apparently wound up disenfranchised by him and increasingly criticized him on social media. As the 2020 presidential election neared, her Twitter feed carried more and more posts promoting Trump's challenger, Democratic candidate Joe Biden. "The contrast between Biden and Trump could not be starker—counting the days until we can replace Trump with Biden," she wrote. Stumbling onto her social media feed was both surprising and far too familiar. Trump alienates lots of people, including some who've operated on his behalf.

CHAPTER 6

THE CLASS CERTIFICATION

It was a make-or-break moment.

From discovery and legal maneuvering to my first deposition, all of our efforts set the stage for an October 2014 class certification hearing in my case against Donald Trump.

Judge Curiel would decide whether to grant class certification, whether I was a suitable class representative, and whether my counsel was adequate to represent the rest of the class members and me. Curiel was the third federal judge with the United States District Court for the Southern District of California to handle Trump University matters after Makaeff filed her lawsuit. The first was Judge Irma Elsa Gonzalez, who was appointed to the bench by President George H.W. Bush and who in 2012 was preparing to retire. The next judge to take the case was Cathy Ann Bencivengo, a President Barack Obama appointee, who handled the matter into January 2013, at which point Judge Curiel took over.

If he rejected the motion for class certification, the class was effectively dead. And if myself or my counsel were not certified, it would significantly change our path forward (and potentially mean my removal from the case).

OUR PROPOSED CLASS

In June 2014, months ahead of the hearing, we filed class certification documents outlining the stakes: "If Plaintiff can prove his allegations, he and the rest of the proposed class will prevail. If not, Trump will prevail. What this means is that this case can be litigated one time for thousands, or it can be litigated one at a time by thousands."

Our proposed class included anyone who purchased a live event from Trump University throughout the United States beginning in 2007. In the Makaeff case classes, only people from three states—California, New York, and Florida—could be included. The class in my case, if certified, would ensure that Trump University victims in any state would be covered as a single nationwide class.

It made sense to certify a nationwide class. Can you imagine the legal fees and time involved with fighting thousands of lawsuits, one after another? (Come to think of it, Donald Trump could . . . he's been doing precisely that for decades.)

As my counsel wrote, "Trump's integral involvement was **the selling point** for Trump University." Without the name *Trump* attached to the courses, why would anyone sign up? If the seminar were called "James Harris' Fast Track to Foreclosure," I certainly wouldn't have thought about attending or spending my money. The only reason I was excited to participate in was the hope of learning some of Donald Trump's secrets—his strategies for success. We included lots of evidence supporting our arguments about Trump University—marketing materials, the "Playbook," PowerPoint presentations, and scripts.

PEEK BEHIND THE CURTAIN

We felt confident that our class certification would prevail based on the classes being certified in Makaeff—even if those classes didn't cover every student nationwide—as well as the Ninth Circuit reversing Trump University LLC's anti-SLAPP motion, in which the panel noted, "Trump University's advertisements promise that enrolling in **Trump University is 'the next best thing to being [Trump's] Apprentice.'"**

That anti-SLAPP ruling was important because it allowed us a peek behind the curtain, so to speak, about how we might expect the Ninth Circuit to view and handle other Trump University matters. The Ninth Circuit panel reversed a 2010 ruling by Judge Irma Gonzalez that Trump University LLC was a private figure—as a limited public figure, Trump University had to prove "actual malice," that Tarla Makaeff's criticisms of Trump University were made with a reckless disregard for the truth. They failed to do so, and after a years-long court battle, she succeeded in defeating the defamation counterclaim, which allowed her to recoup legal fees and other costs. Notably, regarding Makaeff's previous positive comments about Trump University, the appeals court wrote, "victims of con artists often sing the praises of their victimizers until the moment they realize they have been fleeced."

In laying out Makaeff's proposed reimbursement, our attorneys painted a chilling portrait of Trump that has proven to be prescient:

"Seeing the procedural history laid out below is almost depressing in its stark demonstration of just how easily someone with means can use our system to oppress someone without. At every turn of this litigation, Trump University ("Trump") chose the most punishing path. The vindictiveness of Trump's counterclaim is self-evident inasmuch as Trump did not file it until after Ms. Makaeff had sued Trump, and Trump relentlessly pursued it at a cost that far exceeded any amount of money it could have hoped to extract from Ms. Makaeff even if its counterclaim were meritorious, which it was not. Trump's scorched-earth tactics were designed to, and did, send a message: stand up to Donald Trump and you will suffer."

The court ordered Trump University to pay Makaeff $790,083.40 in fees and $8,695.81 in costs—a hint at the financial toll he could face if the cases ever went to trial, especially considering RICO with its treble damages.

THE BEST BITE OF THE APPLE

Trump's team countered with opposition in response to our class certification application, which was expected. Both sides resembled bidders in a never-ending auction—whenever one side would weigh in, the other side would respond, back and forth, back and forth, a well-choreographed dance that was both brilliant and cumbersome, resulting in lots and lots of legal filings.

They argued that we were attempting to "get a second bite at the apple. Cohen now seeks to certify a nationwide class against Donald J. Trump in the same court, on the same facts, alleging the same fraudulent misrepresentations, with largely the same Class Members." *We wanted the best bite of the apple! Attempting to certify a nationwide class after seeing other classes certified wasn't improper, just a way to streamline our legal approach and ensure that we include all victims in one class.*

"When Mr. Trump started saying, 'Oh, we got 98% all fives,' that's a fallacy. It's not really a true evaluation. On my evaluation, I did not give a good review. I put down threes instead of fives, and because we had to put our names down, they asked me afterward if I would be willing to change my scores. And I said, 'Why would I change my scores?' I found out later that they got paid more money with higher scores. I kept refusing. I said 'No, I won't change the score.' They called me over and over again, two or three times a week, about changing the scores. I said, 'No, I won't change the scores.' So then when it came to the trial time, Rachel Jensen and Jason Forge told me that my evaluation could not be found."

-JOHN BROWN
NAMED PLAINTIFF IN MAKAEFF/LOW CLASS ACTION LAWSUIT

Another well-worn argument they used involved Trump University student evaluations being mainly positive—this was the same claim Trump himself has made ad nauseam, that 98 percent of the reviews were glowing, which may have been true. I filled out one of them myself! But those reviews students provided at the time we signed up for our packages and had no bearing on what happened after that point. Up until the iceberg, I'm sure reviews of the Titanic's maiden voyage were positive, too.

A significant point of focus for Trump's legal team involved a statute of limitations, that somehow too much time had passed. The federal statute of limitations for RICO is four years from the time the victim discovers his or her damages. Still, Trump's team argued that the statute of limitations should only cover the four years since someone signed up for a Trump University course, meaning anyone who'd signed up before Oct. 18, 2009, should not be included in the class. That included me. If Judge Curiel agreed, I wouldn't be able to serve as a class representative.

They also argued that "all the facts as to whether TU was a 'university' were available to or known by Cohen as of July 2009." Basically, that I should have known shortly after first meeting my mentor that Trump University was committing fraud. According to their thinking, I should have known, based on online reviews and a few critical news reports, that Trump University was a scam, and it was up for me to inform myself of the truth, but it wasn't their fault for perpetuating a scam. *SURRRRE* . . . . In all honesty, the earliest I recognized the truth, and I'm sure many other students were in the same boat, came after the Makaeff case was filed in April 2010. There were undoubtedly some TrumpU victims that complained earlier than that. Until seeing Makaeff's lawsuit, I still assumed that I did something wrong, not that I was a fraud victim. And our suit in October 2013 was filed long before the statute of limitations would have expired. It was just another "Hail Mary" attempt by Trump's team, another way they tried to quash our case. I hoped the judge would see through it all.

Weeks ahead of the hearing, we received some promising news out of New York, where state Supreme Court Justice Cynthia S. Kern found Donald Trump personally liable for Trump University continuing to operate without a license after being warned about it back in 2005. "It is undisputed that Mr. Trump never complied with the licensing requirements" for Trump University, Justice Kern wrote. The AG would decide damages later. The temperature was rising for Trump as he fought a multi-faceted legal battle. These litigations against Trump and Trump University were not going away as easily as he'd hoped.

CLASS IS IN SESSION

After all the legal filings and posturing, Judge Curiel's class certification ruling was upon us. Even though it was procedural in nature—I didn't appear in court myself—his order had major ramifications.

First came size and commonality. Thousands of Trump University victims had a similar experience: being drawn to live events under the guise of learning from Trump's "hand-picked experts," then being upsold packages that were virtually worthless.

On the point of commonality, Judge Curiel agreed that the threshold had been met, writing, "Plaintiff has introduced evidence that Defendant's marketing campaign repeatedly made at least the two representations that Defendant was integrally involved in Trump University and that Trump University was an 'actual university.'"

OK . . .

The next requirement was typicality: whether my experiences as lead plaintiff were typical of other Class Members. Judge Curiel believed they were.

OK . . .

After that came adequacy, to show that my representation was suitable to protect the interests of the class—which, of course, it was—the same attorneys who were approved to represent the class in the Makaeff case.

OK . . .

Regarding the statute of limitations argument, a key focus from Trump's counsel, Judge Curiel shot it full of holes.

"The Court has found a nucleus of common issues and is not convinced at this point that the inquiry into whether the individual Class Members in this case knew or should have known about the fraudulent scheme as alleged in the present action will require individualized determinations or may depend on facts peculiar to each class member's case," he wrote.

OK . . .

Judge Curiel also ruled that class-wide litigation would reduce legal fees and streamline the legal process.

OK . . .

Judge Curiel granted our class certification motion, appointed me as the class representative, and Robbins Geller Rudman & Dowd LLP and Zeldes Haeggquist & Eck as class counsel.

OK! We hit the royal flush. Everything we hoped for—a resounding legal victory!

Trump's attorneys filed an appeal, naturally, but in February 2015, a panel of three judges denied a petition to appeal the order granting class-action certification.

CHAPTER 7

MEETING TRUMP

My day in court with Donald Trump came on March 12, 2015.

Four of the named plaintiffs from the Makaeff case—Tarla Makaeff, Sonny Low, John Brown, and J.R. Everett—along with myself were required to attend a mandatory settlement conference. This was the first time I'd be meeting all of them.

I flew down to San Diego the night before and made sure to eat a hearty breakfast that morning. Ahead of the conference, my counsel sent the other plaintiffs and me a set of instructions.

Among them: "Always speak respectfully to Judge Gallo (address him as Judge or Your Honor), regardless of how Donald Trump talks or acts." *Regardless of how Donald Trump talks or acts.* It's a shame that a caveat like that had to be added, but my counsel wasn't quite sure what Trump would say or do in court with us present. And if he did say something, they didn't want us responding.

A Mandatory Settlement Conference is a less formal type of a hearing— it's not structured like a usual court proceeding where the plaintiff and defendant are seated at their respective tables with the judge presiding and everyone silent unless asked to speak by the judge. It isn't a trial, and there aren't any witnesses called.

TO SETTLE OR NOT TO SETTLE?

Prior to the March 2015 mandatory settlement conference, my counsel drafted a global offer to settle the cases. They called for 1.25 times the amount that victims had spent, arguing, correctly, that our negotiation position was stronger after the nationwide class certification—especially due to the potential for treble damages because of the RICO complaint. As a class action, we argued our settlement case to the defendants, Trump and Trump University, and the court. In a class action, the court had to approve any settlement ultimately approved by both parties. There were a lot of reasons, on both sides, that a settlement was advantageous. A trial would be bitter and messy and damaging. The longer things continued, the higher the legal fees. And for Trump, 1.25 times the total damages was better than the three times he'd be forced to pay if we won at trial.

In addition to the potential for treble damages from my RICO case, the Makaeff class certification also came with the potential for additional damages and statutory penalties for elderly Class Members, such as $15,000 in penalties for each senior in the Florida subclass.

If the case went to trial, it could have the potential to financially ruin Donald Trump. And that's not even taking the hit to his reputation into account. RICO was troubling for Trump because it was often associated with gangsters. And although he loved to operate like a mobster, he didn't want the Trump name associated with RICO.

But Trump's team rejected the settlement offer—he wasn't ready to appear vulnerable or give in. Trump was playing a different game than we were.

By March 2015, Trump was toying with the idea of running for president, something he'd considered as far back as the 1980s. I discussed his presidential ambitions with the other lead plaintiffs the day of the conference. If he wanted to run for president, we figured, he wouldn't want the Trump University legal saga hanging over his head—a settlement would be the easiest way for him to make the whole thing go away.

A TRUE TRUMP LIVE EVENT

The plaintiffs and our attorneys met outside the courthouse at 7:30 a.m. and walked in together about 10 minutes later, a team, a unified front. We entered the courthouse through a special entrance to make sure we wouldn't bump into members of the press . . . no need to bring any extra attention to the matter.

We entered the courtroom and sat with our attorneys. Each side would sit in Judge Gallo's chambers to discuss our positions as far as potential settlements.

And there was Donald Trump, in person, the man who'd taken up so much of our time and energy and effort. He was tall but underwhelming, nervously pacing about, never taking a moment to sit down. His combover and excessively long tie reminded me of a child trying on his father's clothes.

There was a time when I would have been awed to share the same room with him—but not anymore. I'm used to seeing or meeting high-profile people like Steve Jobs and Steve Wozniak, who built great things, or Ray Bradbury, who moved people with his writing, or Larry Ellison, who built a hugely successful business in Oracle, and is among the world's wealthiest people. Donald Trump wasn't self-made, didn't build great things, didn't write his own books—or read them, we'd later learn—and wasn't among the world's richest people. Heck, it wasn't even clear if he was a billionaire.

WHAT I WANTED TO SAY

Trump was talking to his longtime bodyguard Keith Schiller. A former New York City police officer, Schiller spent decades by Trump's side. Schiller was a gatekeeper and confidant, one of the few people that Trump trusted. As Trump spoke to Schiller, all I overheard him saying was something about "RICO"—Racketeer Influenced and Corrupt Organizations, the law at the center of our lawsuit. Trump had RICO on his mind and his lips.

65

> "I remember being there in the courtroom with him and looking over at him, glancing at him a couple of times, and realizing how impatient he was about things. It was clear to me that he wanted the proceeding to move faster and the judge wasn't moving fast enough for him. I hadn't met him of course, but I thought that he was perhaps more of a reasonable kind of person, and I suddenly realized when we were in the courtroom that he was unreasonable, and he was impatient, and probably impulsive."
>
> -JOHN BROWN
> NAMED PLAINTIFF IN MAKAEFF/LOW CLASS ACTION LAWSUIT

I felt an urge to go over and talk to Trump. It may sound weird, but I wanted to take a picture with him—it's something I enjoy doing with people I meet and would have been a nice complement to my photo with my Trump University "mentor" Kerry Lucas.

I would have told Trump, "Look, why don't you settle this case? You can look like a hero, just settle it with the students. If you didn't know who the teachers were and everything, maybe those decisions were being made further down the line. You could settle the case without admitting fault, and blame the situation on things that were out of your control, and say you're sorry, and pledge to reimburse everyone's money, and that would be that. You'd look like a hero."

That's what I wanted to tell Donald Trump. I wanted to stick it to him a little bit, sure—but at the same time, why not settle? I was still pretty naïve at the time. I still felt, deep down, that Donald Trump had a conscience. If he had settled the case and showed some humility, I think it would have allowed many people to bury the hatchet and put Trump University behind us. It would have for me, anyway.

Who doesn't make a mistake? But life is defined by how you own up to your mistakes and learn from them. America is all about second chances.

Trump clearly couldn't own up to his mistake, and as we'd see later, he didn't learn anything from it.

TWIDDLING OUR THUMBS

Trump and his attorneys went into Judge Gallo's chambers first, so we continued to sit in the courtroom, and Schiller stayed behind in the room with my attorneys and fellow plaintiffs. Finally, Jason Forge went over and said, "You know, you probably should leave." Schiller agreed and left the courtroom so we could talk amongst ourselves.

We sat, twiddling our thumbs for half an hour or 45 minutes before Trump's team came back out, and then Judge Gallo called us in. Somebody from New York Attorney General Eric Schneiderman's office was in Judge Gallo's chambers, too—that state case was still ongoing, and any settlement would involve Schneiderman.

Judge Gallo wanted to know an absolute number we were seeking.

"First, we need to know how much money Trump University officially received from students," my counsel said. We had a sense that the total was about $40 million.

We spoke about trying to reach a settlement at some point in time. But in terms of $40 million, "That's a lot of money, maybe even for him," Judge Gallo said of Trump.

THE TIES THAT BIND

When we walked out of the courthouse no closer to a settlement, I went to lunch with the plaintiffs and our attorneys Amber Eck, Jason Forge, and Rachel Jensen, and it gave me a chance to connect more deeply with the other plaintiffs from the Makaeff case. Before that, we'd communicate over phone or email, but we were all together, unified against a common foe, commiserating over our shared experiences. We discussed the classes we'd taken and our journeys with Trump University. While the general chain of events was similar, each of us faced slightly different factors in our signing up since seminars were held in different states at different times.

After spending so many years burying my shame, it was therapeutic to talk with people who understood where I was coming from. Serving as lead plaintiff is a lonely, isolating experience. But it felt a lot less lonely that day.

THE SETTLEMENT 'OFFER'

At one point after the class was certified, I was talking to Jason Forge about settlement offers—remember, my stance was that I wouldn't accept anything for the class unless it meant we'd recover at least half of our losses.

I asked him if Trump's team had made an offer.

"They did. The offer was ridiculous. It was terrible," Jason said.

> **"The unrealistic refusal to actually face the facts was part of what ultimately undid him. Because if they had treated this seriously, any half-decent white-collar attorney could've made that matter go away quietly."**
>
> -TRISTAN SNELL, NEW YORK STATE ASSISTANT AG, 2011-2014

"Well, what did they actually offer?" I asked. I was expecting him to throw out a low-ball dollar figure like $5 million, which would have worked out to less than $1,000 on average for each Trump University victim, even though some like me had spent more than $30,000.

"Instead of money, they were offering free rooms to Trump's hotels and resorts as compensation to students."

"Really?"

"Yeah. It was so bad that we didn't even bring it to your attention. We just dismissed it."

Free room vouchers. Donald Trump still saw us as suckers who would continue to bow down and exalt him even after Trump University had ripped us off. Thousands of peoples' lives were upended because they believed in Donald Trump, and still all he could think about was himself—T-R-U-M-P.

If I had any doubts about the type of person Donald Trump was and what he thought about others, he erased those doubts when I learned about the settlement offer. That moment showed me how cold, ruthless, and indifferent he was about human suffering, even if he was responsible.

He doesn't care about people. We were nothing to him, which made his next move all the more troubling.

CHAPTER 8

THE POLITICIAN

Donald Trump gave a thumbs up and waved, and then he rode down an escalator at Trump Tower to make his big announcement.

June 16, 2015, and the man I sued was now running for president.

Trump's speech that day was incendiary and spiteful, his true self projected onto the national political stage. "Our country is in serious trouble. We don't have victories anymore. We used to have victories, but we don't have them," he said.

His comments about Mexicans drew the most attention—"They're bringing drugs. They're bringing crime. They're rapists. And some, I assume, are good people"—but his statements on wealth were also troubling. As he spoke, he remained the defendant in an ongoing civil RICO class-action lawsuit in which we accused him of defrauding thousands of people through fraud and racketeering.

"There is so much wealth out there that can make our country so rich again, and therefore make it great again. Because we need money. We're dying. We're dying. We need money. We have to do it. And we need the right people," he said, in lines that could have been pulled from his late-night infomercials or Trump University marketing videos.

He also highlighted how he was able to build his wealth. "I made it the old-fashioned way. It's real estate. You know, it's real estate."

I tried to establish wealth through real estate, too . . .

'DOWN THE DRAIN'

During the speech, Trump suggested his net worth was $8,737,540,000—and yet, he was pushing back against me getting my $35,000 back.

"We have losers. We have people that don't have it. We have people that are morally corrupt. We have people that are selling this country down the drain," he said. Morally corrupt? Selling this country down the drain? Sounds familiar . . .

My counsel brushed off the announcement. Donald Trump, president? *It's not going to happen,* they said. *It's nothing to worry about.*

That was the thinking at the time—Trump wasn't a serious political candidate; he was too erratic and scandalous and petty and flawed, a coastal elite who had little in common with middle America. Who would vote for him? Someone else, maybe Jeb Bush or Ted Cruz or John Kasich, would wind up with the Republican nomination, and Trump would use the race to fortify his national profile, and when he dropped out, he'd host a TV show or find a new con. That was the thinking at the time, anyway.

PROMISES MADE, PROMISES BROKEN

I hoped he wouldn't succeed in hoodwinking the public like he had Trump University's student-victims. His promises sound nice, like the ones I heard in the video at the introductory seminar I attended: "That's what it's all about—success. It's going to happen to you." But I knew the value of Trump's word. My lawsuit was centered on the notion that Trump's promises, at least in the case of TrumpU, were worthless.

Now he was promising to build a wall on the U.S.-Mexico border, and repeal Obamacare, and bring new jobs to the country. If he were so inept or corrupt in overseeing a real estate education program that carried his name, how could he possibly succeed as president?

A POLITICAL ELEMENT

The presidential run poured kerosene on everything.

We were still waiting for Trump to sit for a deposition in *Cohen v. Trump*—it was initially supposed to occur by July 2015 but was pushed back amid some housekeeping measures—and here he was deciding to run for the highest office in the land?

It meant more attention on the Trump University legal battle. More public scrutiny. More media coverage.

But it also brought a partisan element to what had been an apolitical process. The lawsuits occurred because we believed we were ripped off by Trump University and Trump himself—not because we disagreed with his political viewpoints. And they were filed years before he announced his candidacy. But Trump has a way of casting everyone who opposes him as an enemy, and now we were enemies against one of the world's most visible and vengeful people, someone who'd be hitting the campaign trail and telling his supporters whatever came to mind. It also meant that finding a jury would be more difficult because identifying jurors who didn't know about Trump University was plausible. However, not knowing about Trump running for president was much more challenging.

THE WHOLE TRUTH

Within a few weeks of announcing his presidential run, Trump got some bad news regarding his case against me: his financial details and net worth, something he'd spent his entire career inflating, were fair game. It wasn't enough for Trump to stand up and suggest his net worth was $8,737,540,000. He'd have to reveal those details under oath.

"Donald Trump has to put his mouth where his money is," Dareh Gregorian wrote in the *New York Daily News*.

Judge Curiel's order followed an earlier order by Judge Gallo in which the magistrate judge—who handled administrative matters in the *Makaeff* and *Cohen* cases—ruled that Trump's profits and financial details were non-discoverable. Judge Gallo had suggested that Donald Trump's net worth was publicly available "through a simple Google search." Judge Curiel disagreed, writing, "Publicly available figures of Trump's wealth have been the subject of wild speculation and range anywhere from $4 to $9 billion.

73

Simply stated, Plaintiffs are entitled to answers made under penalty of perjury."

Our interest in Trump's finances centered on intent—did he have a reason, a need, a motive to commit fraud? Understanding *why* the fraud occurred could prove valuable to our case. This was about more than simply forcing Trump to reveal his financial details (although, as a presidential candidate, all of that information should be fair game anyway). Luckily, Judge Curiel agreed with us.

STANDING UP TO TRUMP

Even as the Trump University cases lingered, and even though Trump's run was considered *nothing to worry about,* I started to worry as he inexplicably shot to the front of different polls among Republican presidential candidates during the summer 2015. Reputable polls, too— ABC/*Washington Post*, Morning Consult, Quinnipiac University, CNN/ORC, Emerson College . . .

Trump drew people to him the same way I'd been drawn to him years earlier. His straight talk could be exciting and fun. He didn't sound like other candidates. He was going to help you live the life you wanted.

But his straight talk was a bunch of gibberish, a way to trick you into giving him your time, or your support, or your money or your confidence (hence the term "con man"). By the time he became a serious presidential contender, I'd spent the better part of half of a decade trying to recover what he'd taken from me. I continued to trudge on because I believed in justice and right and wrong, that people should be held accountable for their actions, especially if those actions result in thousands of people losing their life savings.

It would be nice to get the money back, of course. But for me, the court battle meant something more profound. Someone had to stand up to this guy. I guess it was going to be me.

MONEY MAN

Ahead of Donald Trump's deposition, which wound up happening in December 2015, my attorneys secured depositions from people in his orbit, including Allen Weisselberg, the shadowy CFO of The Trump Organization. Where Donald was constantly in the news, Weisselberg operated largely in the background. His ties to the Trumps date back to Donald Trump's father Fred—he started working for the family's company in 1973.

Weisselberg sat for a deposition with Jason Forge on June 24, 2015 in New York City, stating that he served as Trump's eyes and ears for his investments "from an economic standpoint." Despite not having an official title with Trump University, Weisselberg was tasked with overseeing TrumpU's financials.

"I wanted to make sure that the money wasn't being spent in a way that was not advantageous to our investment. So I wanted to be sure I was on top of things to make sure the money was being spent properly. So I'd ask for budgets once a year. And then we wanted to make sure that they would adhere to those budgets.

"And I went one step further. I said I wanted also to sign checks because I didn't want to find out a year later that there was something they could have done better and save money as related to Donald's investment.

"So I set up a control where I would sign checks just to make sure that money wasn't being spent, you know, in a way that wasn't advantageous . . . to the company." That control, he explained, gave him a "good feel" for the company's day-to-day operations.

"Did you regard Trump University as basically any other investment that Mr. Trump might have?" Forge asked.

"Just one more investment," he said.

Just one more investment . . . it was such a cold and flippant answer. Trump and his ilk had claimed that Trump University was meant to help people achieve their dreams. But there was no deeper goal, no desire to give back, no benevolent aspirations for Trump to share his secrets. It was only about money.

The money man confirmed that only two people—he and Donald Trump—signed checks for Trump University. Forge reinforced the relationship between the two men. "Throughout the time that you were overseeing these things at Trump University, as with all of the other of Mr. Trump's investments, you were acting on Mr. Trump's behalf, correct?" my attorney asked.

"Yes, of course," Weisselberg said.

"And you were ultimately ... you're subject to his ultimate control, correct?"

"Yes."

Weisselberg claimed he did not receive any extra compensation or bonuses for his work involving Trump University. He said he made $450,000 in annual salary and that his yearly bonuses could reach $400,000. He testified that he reduced his bonuses around the time of the 2008 financial crash. "I wanted to set an example for my company," he said. "My kids are grown and I don't have the same needs I had many years ago. So I was fine with what I was making. I had no problem with it."

The deposition was easy to overlook, even for people like me who were so closely connected to the TrumpU cases. My lawsuit wasn't against Allen Weisselberg; it was against his boss. Weisselberg's deposition appeared typical for a business executive. He confirmed some details and was guarded about others but seemed generally candid. He was the guy in the background following orders and doing things by the book . . . er, books.

SLIPPERY

My attorneys also hoped to depose James Harris, the Red Bull can personified who hyped up his phony connections to Trump during my "Fast Track to Foreclosure" event in 2009. My counsel had been aiming to depose him for three years, first through the *Makaeff* case. He'd been served with seven different subpoenas. SEVEN! A deposition was scheduled for April 23, 2015, but Harris didn't appear, and attempts to contact him through his relatives were unsuccessful. And to think, Harris once described himself as my *Mentor For LIFE*. The guy was slippery.

But with the discovery deadline in the case already passed (outside of Trump's deposition, which was allowed to go past the deadline), Judge Gallo denied our extension request. James Harris was going to slip away again.

We hoped Trump, now a presidential hopeful, wouldn't be so lucky. His deposition—the one that would make my stomach turn—was fast approaching.

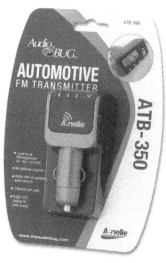

I founded the consumer electronics company, Aerielle, Inc., presenting at the Consumer Electronics Show (aka CES) in Las Vegas, 2008

This popular car FM transmitter was a product for mp3 and iPod products, 2006

Branded iRiver FM transmitter manufactured and designed by Aerielle Inc., 2006-2009

Licensed Aerielle technologies to Kensington branded FM transmitter, 2005-2009

With Nichelle Nichols (Uhura) from the original Star Trek and Marc Cushman, author, in the background, 2014

Art Cohen and Oliva D'abo meet at Bluelight Cinemas, 2016

I worked with Sean Kenney (original Captain Pike from Star Trek) for four years, 2012-2016

Art Cohen with Barbara Luna, Marc Cushman and Sean Kenney and Garrett Wang @ Bluelight Cinemas, 2015

With Ray Kurzweil, founder of the Singularity University—a bonafide university dedicated to improving the quality of health and longevity @ Bluelight Cinemas, 2010

Gary Lockwood played roles in the original Star Trek series as well as 2001: A Space Odyssey, 2013

Meeting Steve Jobs @ Going
National—inspired me to
join Apple, 1985

DUsers Computer Club was the first Macintosh User club in the nation. It also sponsored the
first-ever Macintosh Computer Fair, Called MacFair, where 30 developers and accessories
manufacturers attended, 1985

Apple Design the Personal Computer
of the Year 2000 contest, 1988

With Steve Wozniak—signing my original
Macintosh mouse and taking Segway lessons,
1988 & 2004

Steve Wozniak personally
engraved mouse, 1988

Meeting with Ray Bradbury, 1988

Top left- Photo with myself in from center, to my left, fellow Drexel student Scott Brown and to my right Smita Bhatia. Behind me left to right, Apple VP Del Yocam, Drexel Professor Jeff Popyack, Author Alvin Tofler, Apple's Steve Wozniak, Apple VP Jean-Louis Gasse, Author Ray Bradbury, and Director of Encyclopedia Britanica, Diane Ravitch, 1988

Judges Bios for Design Personal Computer of Year 2000, 1988

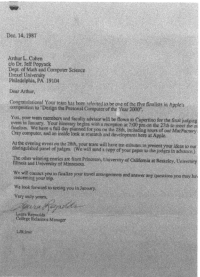

Design Personal Computer of Year 2000 Contest Description, 1988

Letter from Apple notification of top five winners in national competition, 1988

My father, a WWII veteran who managed to persevere the barrage of V2 bombs while in London, died on D-day precisely 63 years later. His memory and stories continue to live with me. He rests in peace as the world struggles with the many issues—fascism and nationalism he fought long ago, 2003

Letter received from Mayor Goode of Philadelphia recognized our honorable mention award for a nationwide computer design contest, 1988

Art Cohen on flight to San Diego for first deposition, 2014

Hotel Room in San Diego before the 1st deposition, 2014

Hotel Room desk where I prepared and reviewed for 2nd deposition, 2014

CHAPTER 9

TRUMP'S DEPOSITION

Video of Donald Trump streamed into my home, and I couldn't believe what I was hearing.

But this wasn't his latest incendiary campaign speech—it was his video deposition for *Cohen v. Trump* on December 10, 2015. Two-plus years after I filed my lawsuit, and after I'd already endured two deposition hearings, it was finally Trump's turn. It was a small pittance for the man who wanted to be the next president.

The deposition hearing occurred at Trump Tower—the same building where he made his campaign announcement months earlier. Instead of standing in front of a row of U.S. flags and speaking to a crowd of friends and family members, he was sitting at a table in a nondescript conference room in front of a blackboard covered by a wrinkled sheet, as though it had just been taken out of the packaging for the first time but never washed or ironed. The day before the hearing, a company ran tests to make sure the feed worked, and I was given a log-in and password with which to watch the video feed.

ONLY IN AMERICA

Trump pursed his lips and tapped his fingers together, checking his watch as the hearing began as if he had somewhere else to be.

He did, in fact, have somewhere else to be. After the hearing, he was headed to Portsmouth, New Hampshire, to speak at a New England Police Benevolent Association meeting.

Only in America could someone leave a deposition hearing in a fraud case to accept a police group's endorsement.

He wore the same outfit at the court hearing and New Hampshire speech, but at some point, he added a U.S. flag pin to his navy blazer, as though it magically brought out his patriotic side.

He asked for a hard stop at 5 p.m.

The deposition came at a precarious time for his campaign. Days earlier, in the wake of a horrific shooting in San Bernardino, California, carried out by a radicalized Middle Eastern couple, Trump called for a ban on Muslims entering the United States, the latest in a series of xenophobic and hateful policy announcements from his campaign. The suggestion drew lots of backlash. But it also garnered support from his followers.

As I watched the deposition, I checked emails at certain points, but mostly I was communicating by text with lawyers. If I saw something notable, I'd text Rachel Jensen: *why don't you ask him this?*

While three lawyers from my team were present, other attorneys were also watching the video feed remotely. I prepared popcorn at one point, the kernels *pop, pop, popping* during a lull in the action. But at other times, I listened intently, watching the video for trial purposes. I never expected that other people would want to watch the video or that it would mean something more.

TRUMP'S OATH

The hearing got underway just after 10 a.m. Eastern Time—7 a.m. Pacific Time, where I was located—with Trump pledging to tell the truth, the whole truth, and nothing but the truth. *Surrrre.* Was it possible for him to tell the truth at this point? With Trump, there was the truth, and the truth as he believed it, and those things didn't seem to align.

Trump sat beside his attorney Daniel Petrocelli at the hearing, with Petrocelli leaning into and out of the video frame. With his slicked gray hair and firm voice, Petrocelli was a pro, someone with experience handling high-profile cases and high-profile clients.

At the opening of the hearing, Petrocelli aimed to designate the transcript confidential, arguing that "obviously we don't want this transcript getting into the hands of the media." Trump's team trying to avoid media coverage? That was a new strategy for him . . . .

While he would fail in keeping the transcript from release, the video was another story. It was odd to watch the video to get this private view of someone who was on the news every night.

Where my deposition hearings were halting and jerky, a strange form of communication that involved deliberate pauses for my counsel to weigh in and deep thoughts before answering, Trump's deposition was more conversational. Where I was instructed to pause and think about each answer, Trump seemed to blurt out whatever thought crossed his mind at that moment.

Petrocelli stayed silent for minutes at a time as Trump answered questions. Petrocelli would grow heated at other points, lobbing his own criticisms at Forge or telling Trump not to answer.

"Every time he opens his mouth, he lies. You can't believe him on anything."

-SONNY LOW
LEAD PLAINTIFF IN LOW V. TRUMP UNIVERSITY CLASS ACTION LAWSUIT

Trump was on the defensive almost immediately, peppering his answers with vitriol. "You're not gonna get anything; you're just trying to waste a lot of time," he told Forge when asked about the things he would look for when reviewing résumés. This guy thought he was above everything, that this was all beneath him, that he couldn't be bothered to answer questions. That approach surprised me. By that point, we'd all seen him being abrasive in interviews or on the campaign trail, but I expected him to act professionally during a deposition hearing. Would he be evasive? Probably, yeah. But I didn't think he would insult and criticize my attorney and decline to answer questions. That's not how a deposition works—for people like me, anyway. But this was Donald Trump, someone who'd been handed every opportunity in life and still seemed to go out of his way to hurt people because he felt like the world owed him something.

OF MICE AND MENTORS

My attorney, Jason Forge—who could be heard but not seen on the video feed—was handling the deposition, and he made an important distinction early in the hearing: this was not Trump's first legal rodeo. "I'm not going to waste time going over the ground rules of depositions because you've been deposed several times before, right?" he asked.

"Yes," Trump said.

He was a business expert with decades of experience in court proceedings. And also someone prone to argue about anything and everything.

Since the promise of "mentorship" was such a central part of the Trump University fraud, as well as a theme of Trump's reality TV show *The Apprentice,* Forge asked Trump about his own definition of mentor. "I think it has many definitions," Trump said. "It depends . . . some of the best tips that I've ever received, I was with somebody for minutes . . . you don't have to spend a lifetime with somebody to be a mentor. But I've received very good for short, and I've been with other people for long periods of time, and I haven't learned anything."

Trump admitted that he didn't have a working definition of the term "mentor."

"Was your father your mentor?" Forge asked.

"Yeah, he was my mentor," Trump responded. But as the questions continued about his father—someone Trump both respected and hated—Trump grew heated and reversed course.

"He didn't mentor. He was my father. It's not . . . he didn't mentor. He was my father. I worked for my father. He was my boss. He wasn't a mentor. He was my boss. I mean, you could call it mentor if you want, but he was my father. He was my father. He was my boss. I worked for him for a period of time. Then I left, and I went out on my own."

Ooh. Trump's bitterness with his father was a well-worn topic, and Forge, with an innocuous line of questioning, got underneath Trump's skin. Forge continued prodding and poking through a basic line of questioning.

"How about your kids? Have you taught your kids the real estate business?" Forge asked him.

"Yeah, I have," Trump said.

"Have you served as a mentor to them?"

"I think I served as a father to them . . . more than a mentor. A mentor is a much lesser position . . . I was a father to my children."

"Well, have you taught them the real estate business?"

"I've helped them to learn it, yeah."

As Forge continued to ask about Trump's mentoring his children, Trump was already breaking, turning eight shades of red and fuming. If this was a heavyweight boxing match, Forge had drawn first blood, opening a cut over Trump's eye.

"Oh, come on. Give me a break," he said. "These are ridiculous questions. This is a filibuster for seven hours."

I kept going back to the advice my counsel had given me ahead of my depositions. One of the tips: "Do not attempt to persuade the interrogating lawyer of the correctness of your position; it will never succeed." Trump's goal was always to win—and he planned to "win" the deposition, even if his definition of winning didn't match reality.

STILL FIXATED ON RICO

That "desire to win at any cost" covered his legal challenge against me, too.

Soon after a recess for lunch, the conversation turned to my lawsuit. "It's the most ridiculous lawsuit I've ever seen, I will say that, especially as a RICO lawsuit," he said as he glanced at a packet of papers in his hand. "But that's OK. That's up to you. You'll see how we do." His focus on the RICO designation was notable. It wasn't enough that we sued him personally— just like our mandatory settlement hearing months earlier, Trump was fixated on RICO.

RICO.

RICO.

RICO.

Forge, the RICO expert, deftly focused on Trump's argument that the lawsuit was the "most ridiculous" he'd ever seen. This was someone who'd sued journalist Timothy O'Brien for defamation for $5 billion—yes, with a "B"—for reporting in his book *TrumpNation* that Trump's net worth was hundreds of millions of dollars, not billions (Trump's ludicrous lawsuit against O'Brien was dismissed, and an appeals court affirmed the dismissal).

"I did very well in that lawsuit. Unfortunately, we can't prove damages, so that's OK," Trump said of the lawsuit against O'Brien.

"Donald Trump would tell people what he thought they wanted to hear, even if it wasn't true, especially if it would benefit him or his family or his company. He didn't really care if he was taking advantage of other people who trusted him. He really only cared about himself and his profits and his ego."

- AMBER ECK
CO-LEAD COUNSEL IN CLASS ACTION AGAINST DONALD TRUMP AND
TRUMP UNIVERSITY

"Hold on," Forge responded. "Your testimony was you did very well in that lawsuit?"

"We were doing very well. And, frankly, the biggest problem with that lawsuit is we couldn't prove damages," Trump said.

"No, your testimony you just gave is that you did very well in that lawsuit; right?" Forge asked.

"I lost the lawsuit, but I made a very good point with that lawsuit."

"So you lost the lawsuit."

"Yes, but I'm glad I brought that lawsuit. I made a very good point with that lawsuit." He looked almost wistful as he said it, the way someone would talk about an ex-girlfriend or a perfect sunset or their childhood pet. *I made a very good point.* Most people would have been ashamed by the outcome of the lawsuit—it was embarrassing and also elevated reporting he deemed damaging. In Trump's view, the consequences and facts didn't matter; he was going to make any legal challenge he wished, and if he felt like he won, that was enough to declare victory.

HOW QUICKLY HE FORGOT

As Trump was asked about details involving Trump University, his main argument came into focus: "You're talking about many, many years ago."

I wish I could have come so unprepared to my depositions . . .

Forge homed in on Trump's memory, calling back to a controversy from weeks earlier, after Trump mocked a *New York Times* reporter's disability during a campaign rally. You know the moment—Trump held his hands close to his torso and writhed, a clip that's been played again and again over the years.

After facing a wave of backlash, Trump released a statement: "Despite having one of the all-time great memories, I certainly do not remember him." How did someone with "one of the all-time great memories" so easily forget so many details about Trump University?

93

"Do you remember saying that you have one of the all-time great memories?" Forge asked.

"Yes, I said that," Trump said.

Forge was baiting his target.

"And do you believe that's true? Do you have one of the all-time great memories?" Forge asked.

"I have a very good memory, yes," Trump said, trying to sidestep the question. Forge stayed focused on his line of questioning.

"Do you believe you have one of the best memories in the world?"

"That I can't tell you. I can't tell for other people, but I have a good memory."

"You've stated, though, that you have one of the best memories in the world?"

"I don't know. Did I use that expression?"

"Yes."

"Where? Could I see it?"

"I can play a video of you reporting it."

"Did I say I have a great memory or one of the best in the world?"

"'One of the best in the world' is what the reporter quoted you as saying."

"I don't remember saying that. As good as my memory is, I don't remember that, but I have a good memory."

I don't remember. Tough to argue you have a great memory if you can't remember anything . . .

"So you don't remember saying that you have one of the best memories in the world?"

"I don't remember that. I remember you telling me, but I don't know that I said it."

"Do you recall saying that you have one of the all-time great memories?"

"I think that was the expression I used."

"And you stand behind it?"

"Yes, I have a great memory. I have a very good memory."

If you say so, Donald . . .

A DIFFERENT LOOK

About half an hour into the hearing, Trump pulled his reading glasses out of his blazer pocket and put them on to read the text on the page in front of him. The brown-rimmed glasses rested below the bridge of his nose. I'd never seen him wearing glasses before . . . it wasn't a common sight.

And where occasionally on the campaign trail, he'd pull out his glasses for a moment to read a passage of text aloud then take the glasses off, during the deposition, he kept the glasses on for minutes at a time. Occasionally, he would twirl the ends in his fingers, spinning the glasses in a circle as though he were operating a hand crank.

I felt that Trump didn't like wearing his glasses much because he didn't want to show any physical weakness, that it was a lot for him to show that his eyes weren't as powerful as they used to be. Glasses were a reminder that he was getting older and not, as he believed, a physically superior specimen. He was just a guy who had a lot of privileges that others didn't.

As Trump wore his glasses, Forge had him look at Trump University LLC's operating agreements, Trump University Member LLC, and DJT University Managing Member LLC. He flipped to the final pages of each, barely hiding his disdain as he confirmed the signatures on each document were his. He reached into his pocket to pull out a dispenser of Tic Tacs, giving a deep exhale, phewwwww, before shaking mints into Petrocelli's hand and tossing a Tic Tac into his mouth hole. He held the Tic Tac in his open mouth as he studied the documents in front of him. Without these documents showing his personal ownership stake in Trump University, the RICO case likely wouldn't have gone very far.

"Just out of curiosity, why did you hold your ownership interest in Trump University LLC through two different companies?" Forge asked.

"I don't know," Trump said. "The lawyers do that."

"You don't know why?"

"No. The lawyers set it up that way."

THE NAME GAME

Forge kept hammering Trump on his inability to recall anyone, other than Michael Sexton, who'd been attached with Trump University live events. My counsel asked Trump whether he could identify a single live events instructor.

"You'd have to give me a list," Trump said. *Ooh.*

So, Forge did exactly that. He started reading a list of names.

"Johnny Harris."

"Too many years," Trump said.

"Tim Gorsline."

"Too many years." Trump looked down.

"Mike Dubin."

"It sounds very familiar. Names . . . the names sound familiar, but it's just too many years."

"Darren Liebmann."

"The name sounds familiar, but it's too many years."

"Johnny Burkins."

"I don't know." Trump's eyes darted about.

"Johnny Horton."

"Too many years."

"Tim Voss."

Trump sneered as he responded to Forge. "Again, you can go through this whole list. And I'm sure you'd like to so you can take this for a long time, but these are . . . some of those names sound familiar to me, but it's too many years ago.

"Chris Goff." He was the person who ran my Quick Start retreat.

Trump glanced at Petrocelli, perturbed, hoping for a lifeline so he'd avoid having to answer. Petrocelli didn't say anything. With his attorney declining to step in, he looked down and shook his head. "Are you going to go through a whole list of names?" he asked Forge.

"You're the one that said, 'Give me a list,'" Forge responded.

Trump held up his index finger and paused. "You're right," he said, with a bemused smile on his face.

All in all, Forge asked Trump about 48 different names, a few of them repeated. He couldn't place a single one. He answered "Too many years" again, and again, and again, to dramatic effect. He could barely look up as Forge read the names.

"How many more do you have? How many more names do you have?" Trump asked.

"Mr. Trump, you're the one who wants to get through this quickly. Just answer the questions and we'll get through it quickly," Forge told him.

"You're not going to get anything through quickly. You don't want to get anything through quickly." Trump started pouting as he was asked about new names. "Same answer to your harassment questions."

Oh, this was harassment?

When asked about the list of names minutes later, and whether any of them were real estate or business experts, Trump claimed that he was the victim of "time harassment."

I found it galling that Trump—after stalling on the case for so many years and making us wait for any semblance of closure—would bring up time. During my first deposition hearing, I was sweating bullets because I suggested that Trump University victims should be compensated for their wasted time. And here was Trump, claiming *he* was a victim of time harassment because he was being asked about a list of names. C'mon, man.

MY REAL-TIME REACTION

"Stunning he can't remember," I texted Rachel Jensen as I watched him brush aside the list of names.

"Not surprised!" she responded.

"He claims he has a brilliant memory and then cannot recall one instructor's name that he hand-picked? His combination of him claiming a good memory and then not recalling should be replayed at trial. To a lay person, makes him look like a liar," I typed furiously on my phone, suggesting that Forge should ask Trump his definition of "hand-picked."

Forge obviously made sure to cover the "hand-picked" angle, too, highlighting the second part of the Trump University ruse that the instructors were selected by Trump himself.

Forge read directly from Michael Sexton's deposition in the case brought by New York State Attorney General Eric Schneiderman: "None of our instructors at the live events were hand-picked by Donald Trump."

Forge asked whether Trump had any reason to dispute Sexton's testimony.

"No, that's correct," he said, before Petrocelli could voice his objection. "I looked at résumés and things, but I didn't pick the speakers," Trump added.

Trump, in his admissions, was proving our entire argument that the Trump University promotions and marketing were deceptive and factually inaccurate—he didn't pick anyone associated with Trump University live events other than Sexton. He had no way of knowing if there was any value in the programs being offered. It almost felt too easy.

About two hours into the deposition, it was time for a lunch break so he could make his calls. Trump stood, stepped away from the table, unclipped his microphone, held up the microphone for emphasis, placed it on the table, then walked away to get on the phone. His lunch break wound up stretching for nearly an hour.

CHEESE!

I had to chuckle when Trump was handed a printout of a photograph—my picture standing beside my "mentor" Kerry Lucas from the summer of 2009.

He was asked if he recognized anyone in the photograph. He shook his head. "This is a very bad picture," he said. "You can't even see the faces." He declined to put his glasses on, saying he didn't need them. He was supplied a different copy of the photo and asked whether either of the people in the photo—my photo—is a Trump University student.

"Was, you mean?" Mr. Petrocelli asked.

"Was," Forge responded.

"I don't know," Trump said. "Maybe one of them is Mr. Cohen."

Ding ding ding ding.

BUT HER EMAILS

When asked about his use of emails, Trump found a way to criticize the Democratic presidential front-runner, Hillary Clinton, who'd been investigated for using a private email server during her time as Secretary of State.

"Mr. Trump, throughout the discovery in this case, we haven't received any emails that were sent to or from you. Did you not use email when you were . . . during the years 2005 through 2010?" Forge asked him.

"It's possible," Trump said. "I send very few emails. I send very, very few. I'm not . . . unlike Hillary Clinton, I'm not a big email fan."

I rolled my eyes. Trump didn't take much of anything seriously, and he certainly wasn't taking this deposition seriously.

OFF THE RECORD . . .

As I watched the video feed, two things stood out to me:

1. The feed continued when sections of the hearing were labeled on or off the record. The only times the feed cut out were for extended breaks, such as lunch.

2. For someone with so much experience with lawsuits, Trump didn't have a clear understanding of "on" and "off" the record.

Going "off the record" in an official capacity required a discussion among the attorneys and court stenographer. There was a process.

Trump would start making a point by saying "off the record" and start talking about all the calls he needed to make during breaks, as though his words weren't being recorded (they were, on both the video feed and in the court transcript). From watching his liberal use of on and off the record, I got the impression that it reflected the way he operated with cozy media outlets where he decided what was "reportable."

Trump also seemed to have trouble making up his mind. Did he want to speed through the deposition or stretch it out with breaks?

"This is the longest deposition I've ever done in terms of no break," he said. "So I need breaks because I have to make some calls."

"No problem," Forge told him. "We haven't taken a break because you want to get through this."

"We do, but breaks are very standard, so . . . ."

". . .We'll do one more," Forge said.

WINNING AND LOSING

At times, watching the video feed from home, it wasn't easy to recognize which parts of the video were part of the official proceedings and which were not. During a break, Trump, with his arms folded, asked my counsel when they thought the trial would begin. "August," Rachel Jensen said.

"August, all right," he said. He gauged my counsel's interest in putting the Makaeff and Cohen trials together; something Judge Curiel had rejected.

"Well, the judge didn't want to do it, but . . . he might revisit it," Jensen said.

"Would you wanna do it? Would you rather have them together?" Trump asked, curious.

"In federal court we need a unanimous jury. They typically sit between six and 12 jurors—you need six to reach a verdict, and they typically seek some alternates. Whoever's remaining at the time they deliberate, every person's vote counts."

-AMBER ECK
CO-LEAD COUNSEL IN CLASS ACTION AGAINST DONALD TRUMP AND TRUMP UNIVERSITY

"I think everybody would probably want them together," she responded.

"I'd like 'em together. I think it probably makes more sense."

He then started asking about the jury pool in federal civil trials. At least six jurors are required to reach a verdict, but normally, eight or nine jurors are empaneled in case someone has to drop out.

"This could be a long trial, I'd imagine," he said. Trump also asked whether the jurors had to be unanimous or if only a majority was needed. "You mean you have to get a unanimous jury victory to win? Now I know why you wanted to stay in state court," he said, incorrectly.

"We were never in state court," Jensen tried to correct him.

"Originally you wanted to be in state court."

No . . . .

"You mean if I get one juror, I win the trial?" he asked.

Petrocelli corrected him: "They don't win."

"Meaning they don't win," Trump said. "Wow, I like that. I like those odds."

"So do I," Petrocelli said.

Trump tried to goad Forge. "I like those odds, Jason . . . . You like 'em?"

The exchange was telling for a number of reasons. He had an odd fixation on the jurors, as though he'd be able to flip at least one of them. The way Trump talked down to Forge spoke volumes, too. Forge was a studious, relentless legal force who'd put away California Rep. Randy "Duke" Cunningham in what's considered the largest bribery scheme in congressional history. He wasn't intimidated facing down corrupt politicians—even those running for the highest office.

LIE, LIE AGAIN

Jason Forge was great at using non-sequiturs and throwaway lines to craft his arguments in real-time, to get Trump to say things that were telling. It was impressive to watch. At one point after the lunch break, Trump suggested that he wouldn't want instructors he'd never met to say that they met him, but that he didn't think it would have any impact on students.

"But you agree that encouraging instructors to lie to students sets a bad example?" he asked.

"I wouldn't do it," Trump said. Not that it sets a bad example, but he wouldn't do it.

Forge stayed on the line of questioning.

"I just don't like something that's not truthful," Trump said, without a hint of irony.

"But I'm just asking, do you believe that would set a bad example for the instructors?" Forge asked.

"I don't think it would have any impact on the students, no. I think it would ... it might actually incentivize the students and it might make the students feel better about themselves because they've taken the class. So, I think, if anything, it might have a positive impact, but I still wouldn't authorize it."

Wait. What? Might it incentivize the Trump University students to get fed lies? Might it make them feel better about themselves? Six years and $35,000 later, I could honestly say that the lies only incentivized me to take legal action and that the situation definitely did not make me feel better about myself. It made me feel about as valuable as my Trump University "education," one that was centering a lot more on legal insight than real estate know-how.

FANTASY QUEST

I watched intently as Jason Forge harnessed and shaped an argument that the appeals court made in striking the anti-SLAPP lawsuit against Tarla Makaeff—how victims of con artists are often supportive of their victimizers until they realize they've been conned. Notably, regarding Makaeff's previous positive comments about Trump University, the appeals court wrote, "Victims of con artists often sing the praises of their victimizers until the moment they realize they have been fleeced."

Trump made his argument again about how Trump University students were so positive in their reviews as they signed up for packages. Forge took the conversation in a place I didn't expect, highlighting an appearance Trump made on ABC's "This Week" months prior, in which Jon Karl asked Trump about his previous praise of Jeb Bush: "He is exactly the kind of political leader this country needs now." Or a 2012 quote from Trump about Hillary Clinton: "She's a terrific person, works hard, and I think she does a good job." He called George Pataki "the most underrated guy in American politics." And of Rick Perry, Trump called him "a very effective governor, Texas is lucky to have him." As a presidential candidate, he was now trashing the people he once praised.

Trump argued that his past comments came in his context as a businessman, not a politician, and how they reflected his need to potentially help him do business—a means for getting what he needed. That Trump's glowing praise wasn't actually reflective of his later feelings about someone. Petrocelli bristled against the tactic, telling Trump not to answer and telling Forge to "please move on."

OK. Forge did move on to highlight a section of text from Trump's aptly named book *The America We Deserve* in which Trump's ghostwriter wrote, "The education industry is delivering less for more money and claiming no ground has been lost. It's fraud, pure and simple." *Ooh, nifty.* Forge asked whether Trump believed that the scenario represented fraud.

"I would say it's . . . no, it's not fraud," Trump said.

"(Trump) had a great lawyer, Dan Petrocelli, representing him, and he's done a number of high-profile cases, but I am very confident that Mr. Trump is uncoachable. And there's no way that Dan prepared Mr. Trump to give some of the answers that he gave. But the fact of the matter is he's in charge, whether it's in a deposition or in any other context, and no matter how high ranking the lawyer is, no one's going to tell him how to answer a question."

-JASON FORGE, LEAD COUNSEL FOR RICO CLASS ACTION SUIT, TO CNN

"OK, it's not fraud," Forge said. "So, this statement in your book is not accurate?"

"It's not accurate, yes. It's trying to get a point across."

Forge pressed on that point, asking Trump if he believed in playing to people's fantasies.

"I see nothing wrong. Sure, you want to . . . life, you want to . . . you want to play to something that's positive and beautiful. And you can use the word 'fantasy' if you want. Or I could use the word 'fantasy,' but, sure, you want to play to something that's beautiful and good and successful," Trump said.

Trump also suggested how "innocent exaggeration," i.e., lying to Trump University students, might not always be so bad. "It depends on the materials," Trump said. "The instructors have great materials to work with. It depends on the materials they use. It depends on the books they've been given. It depends on a lot of other information."

GETTING FRUSTRATED

The bickering between Forge and Petrocelli—and by extension, Trump—grew heated as the deposition wore on that afternoon. As Trump spun his bullshit, because that's what it was, about how he "heard good things" about Trump University courses and failed to directly answer my attorney's questions, Petrocelli took offense with Forge's editorializing and asides, which were typical for a deposition. I saw Petrocelli's over-the-top responses as a reflection of his client's inability to hold back himself.

Forge was hammering Trump about Trump University reviews, going back to his line of commenting about Trump's positive statements regarding Jeb Bush and George Pataki.

"I instruct you not to answer," Petrocelli told Trump, holding his hand in front of Trump.

Trump smiled with the side of his mouth, proud that he wasn't going to do what Jason Forge wanted him to do. His attorney said no, so *nanny boo, you can't catch me.*

As Trump continued smiling, the happiest he'd looked all day, Petrocelli accused Forge of getting frustrated.

"I'm not getting frustrated," Forge said.

Petrocelli had enough. "Time out. We're taking a break right now. Let's go." As Petrocelli stood, Trump continued staring at Forge. "We've been going for over an hour. We're going to take a break," Petrocelli continued.

"An hour? We've been going for two hours . . . Two and a half hours," Trump said, glancing at his watch.

"Let him cool down," Petrocelli said.

"Are you OK? You're not frustrated, are you? You're not frustrated . . . Don't get frustrated," Trump said to Forge.

As Petrocelli and his client unclipped their microphones and walked off-camera, Petrocelli sounded hostile toward my counsel.

"Jason, don't do that again. Don't talk to my client," Petrocelli said.

Forge chuckled as he answered. "Dan, don't wave your finger at me. OK, buddy?" he said.

Petrocelli issued a warning. "Don't do that again . . . You're really an amateur." He also directed his attention at my other attorneys present. "You two, stop snickering or I'm going to call it out on the record," he said. *Ohhh* . . . .

"Dan, I don't know if your blood sugar got low or something, but you're out of control right now," Forge said.

Petrocelli slammed the door behind him as he left the room, and the videographer announced that he was going off the record at 3:45 p.m. ET. But the camera stayed on and the video feed continued broadcasting. What I witnessed next would haunt me for years.

CHAPTER 10

THE HOT-MIC MOMENT

The video feed continued, but at first, I didn't understand what I was watching.

Minutes after the heated deposition exchange with my counsel Jason Forge, Donald Trump and his attorney Daniel Petrocelli returned to the room where the deposition was being held. Trump sat at the table with the wrinkled sheet as his backdrop and angled his swivel chair toward Petrocelli. He had one leg crossed over the other.

As other people buzzed around the room, and as the video feed continued broadcasting into my home 2,500 miles away, Trump and Petrocelli spoke—a 13-minute hot-mic moment. I watched on in horror as Trump said the quiet parts out loud.

MAKING IT PERSONAL

Their conversation first focused on the need to complete the deposition at a later date.

"By the time we are finished here we'll only have two hours left, and we'll worry about it another time," Petrocelli said. "Maybe when you're in LA next."

But Trump wasn't interested in that topic. He was intent on discussing the case, his face growing redder and redder as he spoke.

"They made it personal," he said, speaking in hushed tones that were difficult to hear in some spots—he notably did not clip on a microphone until after the personal conversation ended and the deposition continued. "I had a corporation. Y'know, every one of my friends who's a lawyer says, how could it be so personal?"

"The judge did not care much about your personal interest," the attorney told Trump.

"And you're shocked by that?" Trump asked.

"I am . . . That's what made me feel the judge had it in for you," Petrocelli said. "We're gonna take another look . . . ."

"There is a reason for a corporation," Trump said. "Is there something you can do about it? Because if you could win that, we'd win the case."

"Exactly right. Exactly right. You're the only reason this case is going on . . . ."

"What can you do about it?"

Petrocelli exhaled. "We have one more shot at it." Petrocelli was discussing a legal challenge they could mount, something they were entitled to do. In Trump's eyes, the case should have involved his company, not him personally.

'THE SPANISH THING'

Trump remained fixated on his personal involvement, which was due to Trump himself owning 93% of Trump University.

"I've got hundreds of cases and I never get sued," he told Petrocelli.

Petrocelli tried explaining the situation in a way that would appease Trump. "Because they are saying you are personally involved in making false statements, and they can't prove that. That's the only reason," he said.

Trump remained inquisitive. I tried following the conversation but the audio was choppy due to cross-talk and background noise.

"So, could you now, at the end of all depositions, go ask for the judge again, because I . . . ."

"I'm going to have to think about it," Petrocelli said.

"Is he an asshole, or does he just want me in his courtroom?" Trump asked, emphatically pronouncing the insult in two syllables, ass-hole, as if he were mouthing it to someone across the room.

"The latter, I think," Petrocelli said.

"You really think so?" Trump asked Petrocelli about Judge Curiel. "You know him a little bit?"

"He's an average judge. He's on the wrong side of the aisle, too, that's not helping," Petrocelli said, a reference to Judge Curiel's being nominated by President Barack Obama, Trump's gadfly.

Trump glanced around the room, as though he was making sure no one was nearby so they couldn't hear what he was about to say.

"What about the Spanish thing?" Trump asked. *The Spanish thing?!* Judge Curiel's parents grew up in Mexico, but Judge Curiel himself had been born in Indiana. Evidently, in Trump's mind, Judge Curiel was biased against him because of Trump's hardline anti-immigration and anti-Mexico stances.

He continued, discussing "the first judge," since-retired Judge Irma Gonzalez, who had ruled in his favor in 2010 by allowing the countersuit against Tarla Makaeff, a decision that was later overturned. It was fascinating seeing Trump speak so glowingly about Judge Gonzalez—who happened to be the first Mexican-American female federal judge—while at the same time trashing Judge Curiel because of *the Spanish thing.* As though a person's race or nation of origin only mattered if they seemed to be against him.

"Then I got this guy, NOTHING," Trump said of Judge Curiel.

50/50 SHOT

Trump wondered about his odds of winning the case.

Petrocelli interlocked his fingers as he responded, like an ER doctor trying to explain the right way to tell someone of their relative's precarious prognosis. "If we had to try this case, I think we would win this case," he said. "I think you're a big reason why, because the jurors like you."

"You think it's an easy win?" Trump asked.

"Not a slam dunk," Petrocelli said. "I've had easier cases. But I'd put it at about 50%."

Trump, gesturing with his hand as he spoke, highlighted Judge Curiel's ruling that the damages in the case would not be part of the class action.

"Doesn't that kill them? They got to bring separate cases for everybody to get damages?" Trump asked.

Not exactly . . . my counsel said it would have been nice to have damages included, but that each student's individual cases would have bled Trump dry and increased his legal costs.

"Yeah, that's just getting played out right now," Petrocelli said.

"But isn't that a great win for us?" Trump asked.

"It's a significant win," Petrocelli said. "The judge doesn't know what to do with this case."

Not exactly . . . .

BOOM

The conversation shifted to Judge Curiel's decision to certify the nationwide class, the centerpiece for the entire case.

"If we had it decertified, we'd essentially walk away," Trump said.

"Oh yeah, then it's over," Petrocelli responded.

"Didn't we almost have it decertified?"

"He had it half-decertified, exactly, because now everybody has to prove their own individual damages," the attorney said.

Trump, taking his hand away from his face, questioned what was taking my counsel so long to continue the deposition, as though he wanted to shoo away anyone within earshot.

"Hey Dan, want to get your colleagues?" Petrocelli asked Dan Pfefferbaum, a member of my legal team who was still in the room.

"We actually waited 10 minutes by the way," Trump said.

"Trump is one of the rare people who makes everyone around him worse. He makes somebody a worse person, both worldly and in terms of competence. There's no doubt because he's just a terrible manager, he's a terrible businessman, he's a terrible administrator, and he's a terrible human being."

-TRISTAN SNELL, NEW YORK STATE ASSISTANT AG, 2011-2014

"We were here a half hour at lunch," Pfefferbaum responded with notes of sarcasm, referencing Trump's late return from the early afternoon recess.

With Pfefferbaum away, Trump continued his conversation with his attorney, whispering so parts of the conversation were indecipherable. But what I heard was chilling.

"Go in there and say that thing, about him. Understand?" Trump asked. He appeared to be giving his attorney a directive to tell Judge Curiel something. Something that could potentially cause Judge Curiel to decertify the class or throw out the case.

"I'll give it a shot," Petrocelli said.

"You go ahead and give it a shot. Just do it."

"I'll see what I can do."

"And the other thing is . . . we'll wait."

"Let's wait. We'll talk separately."

"We give that a shot after this?" Trump asked. "You get a better shot after this . . . then boom . . . maybe you get lucky." As Trump said, "boom," he put his hands in the air, as though a mock explosion were going off, and for me, it might as well have been.

PHONE TAG

Moments later, Trump—speaking to his longtime bodyguard Keith Schiller, who was off-camera—asked Schiller to check and see if he had received any phone calls. Minutes later, Schiller reentered the room.

"Pete Bevacqua, he said he'd talk tomorrow, he just wanted to catch up," Schiller said, referencing the then-CEO of the PGA, the Professional Golf Association of America who was chummy with Trump.

The timing of Bevacqua's call was interesting. One day after the deposition, in the wake of Trump's anti-Muslim comments, the PGA Tour announced it would consider other sites for the WGC-Cadillac Championship, traditionally held at Trump National Doral, one of his Florida courses. "Mr. Trump's comments are inconsistent with our strong commitment to an inclusive and welcoming environment in the game of golf," the PGA Tour said in a statement.

WITH FRIENDS LIKE THESE . . .

As Trump wound his watch, he brought up his and Petrocelli's mutual friend, the investor Thomas Barrack, who had helped connect the attorney and client a month earlier.

"How's our Barrack man doing?" Trump asked.

"He's got a new bride, a couple new kids," Petrocelli said.

"What's that all about?" Trump asked, a look of surprise on his face. "When did he get married?"

"He got married about a year ago," said Petrocelli, who attended the wedding along with a range of celebs like actor Rob Lowe . . . maybe Trump's invitation got lost in the mail? Either way, he remained focused on superficiality.

"Is she beautiful?"

"Yeah, young. She's 38, 37."

"How old is he, 65?"

"I think he's like 67, 68."

"He gets a kick out of this whole thing."

Within a year of Trump's deposition, Rachelle Barrack would follow the lead of Trump's first two wives and file for divorce.

NEVER TELL ME THE ODDS!

Trump was getting tired of waiting for the deposition to resume. "Can you believe this, sitting here with this bullshit?" he asked Petrocelli.

"With everything on your mind, I don't know how you're doing this. I really feel bad for you," the attorney said.

Trump pressed Petrocelli once more about the odds of winning the case.

"You never go above 70 percent in a case," Petrocelli told him.

"Even if it's a lock?"

"Yeah, yeah. There's always an X-factor."

"You mean, even if you think you've got a lock, you're not going to tell the client 100 percent?" Trump asked.

Petrocelli said he has never gone above 75 percent.

Trump explained to his attorney how he discusses his odds in the presidential race. "If someone said, 'what's your chances of getting the nomination?' I said 50 even though I'm at 40. You understand? . . . I don't want to say I'm going to get it," Trump said.

Petrocelli rated their odds as "above average . . . I've had stronger cases but I've had weaker cases. I think the guys under you sort of let you down, (they were) a little sloppy."

FOR BETTER, OR WORSE

As Trump spoke to Petrocelli, he discussed another time he had his lawyers carry out a campaign of threats and intimidation, this one against the Better Business Bureau, which had given Trump University a D- grade.

"You know what that is? That's a kill for you," Trump said.

Trump recounted how he had a lawyer call the nonprofit and threaten to sue. "Got the D removed and gives it an A," Trump said.

"Did you know we were rated D? My guy . . . 'an Alan Garten type,' he's tough, gave them a call," Trump said, referring to Trump Organization's longtime general counsel.

Trump seemed giddy and proud as he discussed his plot to bully and pressure the BBB. The exchange was telling. His braggadocio was a textbook example of extortion that foreshadowed his similar actions throughout his presidency. He could have worked to fix the problems with Trump University and developed an educational experience that actually provided value. But he wasn't interested in student satisfaction, only in using his influence to get his way. He wanted people to bend to his will. He wanted affirmation for his failures. He wanted people to believe whatever HE wanted them to believe.

With that, Jason Forge returned to the meeting room, and after a conversation about the delay—and the free lunch provided earlier, which Forge didn't eat—the deposition continued for another 45 minutes or so, until Trump had to leave for his speech in New Hampshire.

TROUBLE AHEAD

I struggled to make sense of the 13-minute hot-mic conversation, but it troubled me deeply. The way I saw it, Trump was trying to wage a personal attack against Judge Curiel to make the Trump University cases go away.

The coded language, "talk to him about that thing, about him," the hushed tones, *the Spanish thing* . . . it made me want to shout and scream and warn everyone, especially Judge Curiel, but I thought the best approach would be to talk to my counsel, which I did a few days later. I couldn't get the conversation out of my head—I was worried that Trump had actual dirt on Judge Curiel, or that he was going to blackmail the judge, or . . . I don't really even know, but my mind wouldn't stop thinking the worst.

My counsel was adamant that they did not want to know the contents of what I'd witnessed over the video feed. They assured me that Judge Curiel was beyond reproach, that there was nothing about him that could be bribed or persuaded. They advised me to stay quiet about the situation as the case was ongoing. Any false move could undermine years of effort and keep Trump University victims from getting any sense of justice.

I didn't know what to do.

CHAPTER 11

THE CAMPAIGN TRAIL

I had a pit in my stomach each day.

What was Donald Trump going to do next? How was he going to undermine the Trump University cases? Would I face any personal blowback? How was he going to go after Judge Curiel?

I grappled internally with what to do. My counsel wanted me to stay silent—anything I said about what I'd witnessed during Trump's deposition could undermine our case—but the silence was tearing me up. I was apprehensive about Judge Curiel's safety and well-being, as well as the outlook for the case. I thought about somehow contacting the judge, but that would probably get back to my counsel, then I'd likely be out as lead plaintiff . . . no, that wouldn't work. I wanted to see this process through.

I also wanted the public to see what Trump, who was running for president, was all about. To see him for the person he was when he didn't think anyone was paying attention.

I considered leaking the video footage of Trump's deposition to the media . . . .

It was a compelling idea, but no, I couldn't do that either. Not at the time, anyway. There was too much at risk, too much to lose. The leaked footage would link back to me somehow, and I'd be in hot water, then I'd be out as lead plaintiff, and thousands of Trump University victims like me would potentially see their chance at justice thwarted. The case would be forever tainted.

And Donald Trump would escape accountability. Again.

Silence wasn't golden. Far from it. But I didn't have any other option. I couldn't even talk about what I'd seen to *anyone*. So the pit remained in my stomach as Trump took up more and more national attention.

THE WEIGHT OF IT ALL

Primary season began February 1, 2016 with Iowa. A chance for voters in each state to choose who they wished to see on the presidential ticket that November. The voters would see through Trump, right?!

But there was Trump, getting nearly a quarter of the votes, coming in second behind Ted Cruz. New Hampshire followed on February 9 . . . a landslide for Trump. He drew thirty-five percent of the vote among ten candidates. He followed by winning South Carolina, Nevada . . . he couldn't be stopped.

The better Trump performed in the primaries, the higher likelihood that Trump University would enter the national spotlight. Tarla Makaeff knew it, too. In early February 2016, my counsel requested to have Tarla withdrawn as lead plaintiff in her case—she'd been fighting this battle since 2010. Trump targeted her directly with the anti-SLAPP lawsuit, which was later overturned. She'd shown lots of resilience in facing down his unrelenting attacks.

But now that he was running for president, she decided it was time for her to bow out, and I couldn't blame her.

"Makaeff has endured health problems, family loss, and financial troubles in the years since this case began," our counsel wrote in a court filing. "Trump was a celebrity when the case was filed, but no one could have anticipated that he would become a viable presidential candidate and a 24/7 media obsession as this case neared trial. Makaeff has done her share, and the Class is better off as a result, but it would be in Makaeff's and the Class's best interests to let the remaining class representatives carry this ball over the goal line. Subjecting herself to the intense media attention and likely barbs from Trump and his agents and followers simply would not be healthy for her." Many of her fears—such as facing public insults from Trump—would sadly be realized in the weeks ahead.

DEBATE AND DECEIVE

As Trump became the leading Republican candidate, his challengers sharpened their swords and daggers.

During a debate on February 25, Marco Rubio, a senator from Florida, went on the attack, rattling off Trump's business failures and hypocrisies such as recruiting overseas workers or having his branded ties and suits made in other countries.

And then Rubio turned his attention to Trump University.

"I don't know anything about starting a university . . . a fake university! A fake university! There are people who borrowed $36,000 to go to Trump University and they're suing him now. $36,000 to go to a university that's a fake school!" he said.

"And you know what they got? They got to take a picture with a cardboard cutout of Donald Trump."

Trump tried to brush it all aside.

"And by the way, I've won most of the lawsuit. And they actually did a very good job. But I've won most of the lawsuit."

Rubio didn't skip a beat. "Most of the lawsuit? That means you've lost part of the lawsuit."

In fact, Trump hadn't won any of the lawsuits—plural. My case, the Makaeff case, or the New York state case. His only victory, the ruling over Tarla Makaeff in the anti-SLAPP ruling, was overturned, and she was awarded roughly $800,000. In my case and the Makaeff case, classes were certified, and Trump's motions to dismiss were rejected. Any "victories" he'd encountered thus far, such as bifurcating damages or limiting the class in the Makaeff case to student-victims from three states, were neither good nor bad. The impact of those decisions would become apparent as the cases reached trial.

PURE NONSENSE

Minutes after Rubio made his attack, Ted Cruz picked up the conversation.

"It's a fraud case. His lawyers have scheduled the trial for July," Cruz said. "I want you to think about if this man is the nominee, having the Republican nominee on the stand in court, being cross-examined about whether he committed fraud. You don't think the mainstream media will go crazy on that?"

It was a fair point. And Cruz's comments further aroused my concerns from what I heard during that hot-mic moment. Cruz instinctively targeted Trump's underbelly and was attempting to cut him open. Trump knew that weakness, and he had a plan that wasn't yet revealed. Trump wouldn't let the criticisms rest, trying to come back with the same tired talking points.

"Keep swinging for the fences, let me tell you," Trump said. "The Trump University case is a civil case. It's a case where people try to get . . . it's a case that is nonsense. It's something I could have settled many times; I could settle it right now, for very little money, but I don't want to do it out of principle. People who took the course, most signed—many—signed report cards saying it was fantastic, it was wonderful, it was beautiful. And believe me, I'll win that case. It's an easy case. A civil case."

Other than it being a civil matter that he could have settled many times, Trump's arguments were pure bunk. Fugazi. Especially when considering the things I listened to him say months earlier during the deposition and hot-mic moment.

1. It wasn't an easy case. His own attorney told him his chances of winning were 50/50—which isn't great odds when wanting to take a case to trial. And we had multiple bites at the apple, meaning if the Makaeff case failed, we could retool and take a different tack for the second trial.

2. Instead of being "nonsense," the cases involved more than 6,000 Class Members nationwide and were still intact after withstanding years of challenges.

3. A finding of guilt in the RICO case came with treble damages, meaning he potentially could be personally liable for more than $100 million, which wasn't "very little money," even for a self-proclaimed billionaire. With the RICO designation, our negotiation position was much stronger. A settlement would come with a substantial figure.

4. The "report cards" were surveys and questionnaires that were distributed to people who wanted to impress or befriend the speakers who promised access to Trump and his properties when they decided to sign up for Trump University packages. They were filled out at the event, not after the students tried to put their "education" into practice.

PACS POUNCE

The Trump University situation struck a nerve. And the American Future Fund—a conservative group with connections to the billionaire Koch Brothers—was ready to pounce. One day after the debate, the nonprofit announced a national ad buy involving videos featuring three Trump University victims: Bob Guillo, Sherri Simpson, and Kevin Scott. The videos showed the victims talking directly into the camera, discussing how Trump had duped them. Simpson, a single mom, said signing up for Trump University "ruined my credit and ruined my life."

A separate ad was also released by Our Principles PAC, an anti-Trump committee led by Katie Packer, a former Mitt Romney aide. The Republican establishment was pushing back against the possibility that Trump could wind up on the party's ticket. They saw Trump University as a means of sticking with voters far more than his other scandals: failed marriages, shady connections to Russia, bankruptcies, vindictiveness.

No one could credibly suggest that Trump was a *good guy*. Many of his supporters appreciated him because he wasn't a good guy or begrudgingly went along because of what he could do for them.

But Trump University spoke to darker truths about Trump—namely, that he wasn't a great business leader, after all, and appeared indifferent at the suffering he caused people. It captured his ill intent and mismanagement, two qualities unbecoming of an executive, let alone the potential leader of the free world. Trump University showed, depending on your view, that Trump was either a scam artist or a bad leader (or, I would argue, both), and he sat idly by as his name and reputation were used to rip people off.

On the same day the advertisements emerged, Trump's attorneys filed a response to Tarla Makaeff's motion to withdraw, bristling against her request, suggesting that they'd been preparing their legal strategy around her participation in the trial and that her withdrawal should mean the end of the case. This was the woman who started it all . . . and Trump wasn't going to let her walk away without her facing his cruelty.

"Litigation is hard. Witnesses are compelled all the time to testify in criminal and civil trials across the country, whether young or old, rich or poor, healthy or ill," Trump's attorney Daniel Petrocelli wrote in a response. "This duty to participate in the court process is necessary to assure the reliability and integrity of our justice system." I'm glad Donald Trump was so worried about the *integrity of our justice system.*

While Tarla was the lead plaintiff, Sonny Low, one of the other named plaintiffs, could slide in as lead plaintiff since he was already appointed as a class representative for all California residents, in addition to representing the California financial elder abuse subclass. So even without Tarla, my counsel had California covered. If she were out of the mix, he could serve as a representative for both subclasses. Tarla was one of the thousands of other Trump University victims who had a similar story. It wasn't typical seeing a lead plaintiff withdraw with a trial pending, but a fraud case against a vindictive presidential candidate wasn't typical, either.

122

ON THE ATTACK

On February 27—two days after Trump University was mentioned on the debate stage—the day I feared finally arrived.

During a speech at an airport in northwest Arkansas with his lapdog Chris Christie, the feckless former prosecutor and New Jersey governor, Trump affixed his public ire on Tarla Makaeff and Judge Curiel.

After stewing over *the Spanish thing* privately for months, he decided to bring his racist attack out in the open. In his rambling address to the crowd in Arkansas, Trump rattled off the same talking points before calling the Trump University legal saga "a simple civil case" again. And then he sniped at Tarla Makaeff, who was the subject of his lawyer's ire in the legal filing one day earlier. "The person who started the suit wrote a great statement saying it was fantastic and did a film clip, and they just asked that she be taken out of the case. She doesn't want to be in the case anymore. And the reason they want is that she's a terrible plaintiff because she said all these great things about Trump University, and she's on film saying how great it is. So, they put in a motion, and of course the papers don't write this . . . her name is 'Tarloff' or something. Take her out of the case. The reason they want her out of the case is she is a horrible, horrible witness. She's got in writing that she loves it."

He couldn't even get her name right. While it's true that Tarla had participated in a Trump University video that would have played at trial, and it was true that she conducted a handful of media interviews, those things didn't change any of the facts of the case. At trial, her experiences—not her credibility—would be under scrutiny. And her experiences, being drawn in by the hope of learning Trump's real estate secrets and signing up for a program that turned out to be worthless, were universal for each member of the class.

Trump also focused on New York Attorney General Eric Schneiderman, who'd been an ongoing thorn in his side, during the speech in Arkansas.

"The attorney general of New York meets with Barack Obama in Syracuse. The following day, he sues me. What they don't say is, I believe, $15,000, or a lot of money, was paid to the attorney general by the law firm in

California that's suing me." (In fact, two partners with Robbins Geller Rudman & Dowd LLP donated to Schneiderman's campaign in 2010, years before the law firm got involved in the case . . . on the other hand, Trump's own attorney donated to Hillary Clinton's campaign in January 2016, according to federal donor records, so there's that).

"Isn't this more interesting than talking about trade? Trade is easy for us. But this is sort of life. This is almost like a story on success. Because this is the way the world works," Trump said. *Shamelessly ripping off thousands of people was almost like a story on success? This is the way the world works?! Um . . . .*

Of the New York lawsuit, Trump erroneously told the crowd, "Much of that lawsuit has been won by me . . . they missed the statute of limitations, and most of that lawsuit is going away.

"But nobody writes that. Nobody wants to write that."

And that's when the conversation turned.

"The rest of it we're doing very well. We have a very hostile judge, because to be honest with you, the judge should have thrown the case out on summary judgment," Trump said.

"But because it was me, and because there's a hostility toward me by the judge, tremendous hostility, beyond belief. I believe he happens to be Spanish . . . which is fine . . . he's Hispanic . . . which is fine . . . and we haven't asked for recusal, which we may do, but we have a judge who's very hostile, should've been thrown out, wasn't thrown out, and I say, 'I'd rather go to court.' Because when you go to court, and you have witnesses go up there and . . . I just wanted to give you a little bit of the parameters because you keep hearing about Trump University. It's a civil case; it's a sleazebag law firm that does these class-action cases, they're very routine, and I will win the case in the end. I just didn't want to be forced to settle, and I could've settled it before I did this, and I knew somebody would try to use it for publicity, but I believe I can turn it around just to show you just how dishonest these people are. And that's the case."

The comments drew a smattering of cheers, the audience unaware of the ramifications of Trump's words—a clear and alarming attack on the rule of law. Trump's pauses as he highlighted Judge Curiel's heritage underscored the racial overtones. There was absolutely no other reason to discuss his heritage.

The same conclusion was reached by Schneiderman, whose lawsuit against Trump University was ongoing. "There is no place in this process for racial demagoguery directed at respected members of the judiciary," Schneiderman said in a statement.

One person who couldn't respond: Judge Curiel. He was barred from saying anything publicly on the matter due to the judicial code of conduct. His only responses would come in courtroom hearings and legal filings. Same with Tarla, who was staying silent out of growing concern about the attention surrounding the presidential race. I could relate to the difficulty that Judge Curiel and Tarla were going through.

Anyone encountering Trump's comments about Judge Curiel would think they were off-the-cuff, that the emotion of the moment got the best of him. He'd had these attacks on Judge Curiel ready for more than two months, maybe longer. With national attention focusing on Trump University, and seeing an opportunity with Tarla Makaeff hoping to withdraw as lead plaintiff, Trump decided it was time to bring up *the Spanish thing* and launch a racist attack against a federal judge, and hopefully, bring down the whole case.

CHAOS AGENT

Say something incendiary, then double down. It was a page out of Trump's playbook—not the Trump University Playbook, the booklet of scamming instructions distributed to TrumpU instructors, but his own personal mode of generating headlines.

Following his speech in Arkansas in which he discussed Judge Curiel's heritage, Trump appeared on "Fox News Sunday" and was interviewed by Christopher Wallace. Trump University was the main focus of the interview.

The bombastic bloviator tried to explain away the problem in glowing terms. "They ran a good school." In terms of the costs for student-victims, he said, "They didn't pay a huge amount of money."

"Wait a minute," Wallace said. "Some of them paid $35,000. That's a lot of money."

Trump was undeterred, discussing his chances in court.

"I'm gonna win the case in court. Because I do that. I win cases in court. I'm not a settler. I don't believe in settling cases. I believe in winning cases," Trump said.

Wallace asked Trump about his comments regarding Judge Curiel.

"I think the judge has been extremely hostile to me, I think it has to do perhaps with the fact that I'm very very strong on the border, very very strong on the border, and he has been extremely hostile to me," Trump said.

"This is a case, in our opinion, should have been won a long time ago, it's a case we should have won on summary judgment . . . we have a very hostile judge. Now, he is Hispanic, I believe, and he is a very hostile judge to me, and I've said it loud and clear."

"Why even bring up that he's Hispanic?" Wallace asked.

"Because you always bring it up, Chris; because you always say how the Hispanics don't like Donald Trump. You always bring it up in your poll numbers. You say the Hispanics don't like Donald Trump. You're the one who brings it up." *Pure projection.*

"I don't think I ever brought it up," Wallace said.

"This is a judge that in my opinion does not like Donald Trump."

Judge Curiel had been a consistent, practical jurist. Sure, he'd made some judgments against Trump, but some had gone in Trump's favor, too. And at the end of the day, *Trump's sham university was used to scam thousands of victims.* Additionally, if Trump hadn't focused so heavily on delaying the cases as long as possible, this all could have been resolved. The delays were mainly Trump's doing. We all wanted closure. We wanted to move on, not to serve as a sideshow act to the presidential race.

But he wanted to make a mockery of the judicial system. And here we were, along for the ride.

CRIME AND PUNISHMENT

Super Tuesday wasn't very super to me.

March 1, 2016. Eleven states held their primaries. Even with Trump University generating negative attention, Trump won seven states: Alabama, Arkansas, Georgia, Massachusetts, Tennessee, Vermont and Virginia, all but locking up the race for the Republican nomination.

It was horrifying to watch the results coming in. Here I was, fighting Trump in court on behalf of people whose lives he turned upside down, and neighbors and friends and relatives adored him.

You would think that Trump's success in the Republican primaries would shift his attention from speaking further about Trump University. Or at least from denigrating Tarla Makaeff as she attempted to withdraw as lead plaintiff.

But with Trump, cruelty is everything. A March 3 legal filing by my counsel—exhibits supporting Tarla Makaeff's wishes to withdraw from the case—made that point perfectly clear. My counsel had long decided not to respond to Trump's barbs in public. We were trying to win in the court of law, not the court of public opinion. But that didn't mean we couldn't be petty and passive-aggressive. When you're getting bombarded by vitriol from one of the most famous people in the world and can't speak up to defend yourself, what else can you do? The exhibits included sections from Trump's deposition transcripts where he admitted he couldn't name any of his so-called "hand-picked" Trump University instructors. Another deposition transcript excerpt reveals Trump, after being shown testimony of a Trump University mentor admitting his lack of experience, remarking, "He defrauded us" and "sue him."

Rachel Jensen skewered Trump in her declaration in support of Tarla's withdrawal:

Trump, who falsely represented he had hand-picked all of TU's "people," asserts he did not defraud those he influenced to enroll at TU. Rather, it is all somehow Makaeff's fault. Trump's big secret would have stayed secret if she had quietly accepted getting fleeced, so taking her money is not enough. Trump's opposition and recent stump speech, in which he denigrated her on national television, confirm that Trump wants to punish Makaeff. Because Makaeff had nothing to do with Trump's fraud, her withdrawal has nothing to do with any legitimate defense. "Prejudicing" Trump's desire to turn this trial into a circus of gratuitous personal attacks is not the type of prejudice the law protects against. For Makaeff's well-being and the dignity of these proceedings, the Court should grant her motion to withdraw.

Hours after those documents were filed, Trump participated in another Republican debate moderated by Fox personalities such as Megyn Kelly— and this time, the Better Business Bureau would play a key role.

Marco Rubio was again on the offensive, discussing how some of Trump University's "best people" turned out to be Buffalo Wild Wings employees and how the lessons taught to student-victims turned out to be "stuff you can pull off of Zillow."

When Trump used his misleading line about the A rating from the Better Business Bureau, Rubio didn't hesitate.

"That's false," he said.

"We have an A from the Better Business Bureau, and people like it," Trump responded. No, no Rubio said, TrumpU had a D-minus rating.

Kelly jumped in. "The rating from the Better Business Bureau was a D-, that's the last publicly available rating in 2010, and that was a result of the number of complaints they received . . . ," she said.

"Not correct," Trump said.

" . . . In 2010, and it was the result of a number of complaints," Kelly restated.

"It was elevated to an A," Trump said. "It was elevated."

"That's never been publicly released," Kelly said.

"I can give it to you. I will give it to you," Trump said.

Kelly rattled off a CliffsNotes version of the case as Trump stewed under the studio lighting. The classes are certified. His countersuit against Tarla Makaeff, the one that was later overturned. And then Kelly read that statement from the Court of Appeals ruling that alluded to Bernie Madoff's victims: "Victims of con artists often sing the praises of their victimizers until the moment they realize they have been fleeced."

Trump was not pleased. "You know what, let's see what happens in court. This is a civil case, very easy to have settled, I could settle it now . . . let's see what happens at the end of a couple of years when this case is settled."

"It's been going for five years," she said.

"Yeah, it's been going for a long time. We'll win the case."

But Marco Rubio still had something to say, a final parting shot, a message that captured why Trump University mattered—and how it connected to everything that lay ahead for Trump and America.

"This is why this is relevant to this discussion: He's trying to do to the American voter what he did to the people who signed up for this course. He's making promises he has no intention of keeping. And it won't be just $36,000 they lose; it's our country that's at stake here. The future of the United States and the most important election of our generation, and he is trying to con people into giving him their vote just like he conned these people into giving him their money." Rubio foreshadowed the importance of the election and the imminent threat that Trump presented to our country.

FOR BETTER AND WORSE

During a break in the debate, Trump produced a piece of paper.

"The Better Business Bureau just sent it," he told moderator Bret Baier. "This just came in, we just got it."

The paper showed a supposed BBB review for The Trump Entrepreneur Initiative, the subsequent name for Trump University before the program was suspended. It showed that the program had an A rating.

Trump also posted an image of a review on social media that was evidently from 2014.

In the days ahead, the BBB was forced to issue a press release to clarify the debacle, stating that it did not send a document to the debate site—and that the current rating for Trump University was "no rating" after dipping as low as D-minus. The only reason the rating improved, according to the bureau, was because old complaints rolled off the review site.

This was the most interesting aspect of the press release for me: "At no point did BBB change the rating of Trump University based upon a demand from anyone. BBB followed its standard evaluation process applicable to all businesses."

Which was in direct contradiction to the statements I heard him make during his hot-mic conversation with his attorney Daniel Petrocelli on the day of his deposition hearing the previous December. That day, he told Petrocelli the grade only changed because he'd threatened the BBB. While the Better Business Bureau claimed it never changed Trump University's rating because of the demand, it didn't deny in the statement that a demand had been made.

A NEW GENERATION OF GRIFT

Trump wouldn't stop talking about Trump University. "Meet the Press." Portland, Maine. "Morning Joe" on MSNBC. He tweeted about Tarla Makaeff on March 6: "The primary plaintiff in the phony Trump University suit wants to abandon the case. Disgraceful!"

> **"I had to deactivate my Facebook account because people were contacting me saying things that were not good. I'm strong enough to be able to say these people are losers, they don't have a better way of expressing themselves than to tear somebody else down. But I did get some backlash."**
>
> -JOHN BROWN
> NAMED PLAINTIFF IN MAKAEFF/LOW CLASS ACTION LAWSUIT

It was disgraceful, all right.

A YouTube video posted on his campaign website had the feel of an infomercial from a sleazy lawyer—a shallow, petty man sitting at a wooden desk next to a fern holding up copies of questionnaires filled out by two people who appeared in a commercial criticizing him.

Trump, speaking in Jupiter, Florida, on March 8, laid out his vision for the future of Trump University. "We're putting it on hold. If I become president, that means Ivanka, Don, Eric, and my family will start it up," he said.

SHE DIDN'T SIGN UP FOR THIS

A motion hearing was held in front of Judge Curiel on March 11 to discuss Tarla's hopes of withdrawing as lead plaintiff. If there were any questions about her fears that the case would push her into the middle of a national conversation, Trump's insults and attacks provided an easy answer.

"This case obviously involves humans and human conditions and human emotions, and I don't think anybody could have anticipated a year ago where we would find ourselves. And Miss Makaeff has not only suffered through a million-dollar counterclaim that was directed by Mr. Trump personally, but she's now been derided and called out by name on the campaign trail, on Twitter, and even on the GOP presidential stage. I don't think that Miss Makaeff signed up for that, and even if someone could have said, 'Oh, well, he has political aspirations,' I don't think even the most brilliant political mind could have anticipated we would be where we are, with the very real possibility if this case goes to trial during the election,

131

and Miss Makaeff simply has been put through too much," Rachel Jensen said.

Meanwhile, Petrocelli suggested that Tarla "started the publicity" because she criticized Trump University over the years—and then he tried to blame the briefs being filed in the case for sparking attention during the debates. Petrocelli also tried to argue that the attention to the case "has been fueled by opposing forces . . . there are very serious issues being raised about whether the defendants can ever get a fair trial if the atmosphere and the environment are being poisoned." He especially took offense to the transcript excerpts included in depositions.

"There are also allegations that the poison is a two-way street," Judge Curiel shot back.

"I don't think those allegations are fair," said the attorney representing the man holding the firewood, dry tinder, kerosene, and lighter.

BUTTERFLY EFFECT

Judge Curiel—who could understand on a personal level what it meant to face Trump's wrath—issued an order excusing Tarla Makaeff of her duties as a class representative. She would remain eligible to participate in the class for recovery purposes.

"Neither pundits, counsel, or the parties anticipated the media obsession that this case would create due to Defendant Trump becoming a candidate for President of the United States. It is also plain that with every additional candidate's debate and state primary, the case's attention has grown. While Makaeff's request to withdraw at the pre-trial stage is unusual, so is the unforeseen degree of attention this case has engendered at the present stage of the litigation," Judge Curiel wrote. "Nor, given the degree of public scrutiny to which Makaeff has been recently subjected, is her apprehension that experiencing further publicity as a named plaintiff would have a negative impact on her professional prospects unreasonable."

> "Tarla told me the horror stories. When she got the class action thing going, Trump sued her. I didn't even blink an eye when the law firm asked me if she dropped out, if I would be willing to replace her. I said I'd do it and I didn't give it any second thoughts. And if Trump tried to sue me, I felt that I would be well-represented."

-SONNY LOW
LEAD PLAINTIFF IN LOW V. TRUMP UNIVERSITY CLASS ACTION LAWSUIT

As the calendar turned to May, Judge Curiel faced an important decision regarding timing. When would Donald Trump face his day in court? I wanted to get the trials underway. I wanted to see Trump held accountable. I wanted Trump shamed with his fraud exposed. I wanted financial relief for people who'd waited so long for closure. I worried that all of those things would elude us.

As it turned out, I had good reason to have that pit in my stomach—the ramifications of Judge Curiel's decision would be massive. It wasn't clear at the time, but our country's democracy was at stake.

CHAPTER 12

DELAY

A big decision was looming, a decision that would impact everything.

On May 6, 2016, during a pre-trial conference in a San Diego courtroom, Judge Curiel would announce his decision to schedule the first of the Trump University cases.

Events from the preceding months weighed on the outcome.

Judge Curiel had the authority to do what dozens of Donald Trump's Republican presidential challengers couldn't—to take Trump off the campaign trail. If Judge Curiel scheduled the trial for August, which was the original plan, Trump would be forced to endure an embarrassing, painful fraud trial while running for president and required to tell the truth under the threat of perjury.

Wouldn't that be something . . . ?

MARKING THE CALENDAR

January 25, 1951.

Donald Trump was 4 years old when the oldest ongoing lawsuit on Judge Curiel's docket, *United States of America v. Fallbrook Public Utility District,* was filed. The riparian rights case involved using the water from the Santa Margarita River upstream from Camp Pendleton. The court ruled in the government's favor, but the court modified its ruling in the mid-1960s, and the sides continued settlement talks for a half-century.

By 2015, *Makaeff v. Trump* was the second-oldest case on Judge Curiel's docket, behind only the Fallbrook case. Judge Curiel brought up the Fallbrook case during a December 4, 2015, status hearing involving the Trump University saga.

"After that one, this is my oldest case, so I am anxious to move it forward," he said.

"Obviously, everyone knows this is a unique set of circumstances that we have here. There's not many cases where there's a presidential candidate who is one of the parties in the case, and I appreciate that Mr. Trump himself would like to have a trial date for any number of reasons, vindication or for purposes of finality. The plaintiffs would like a trial date for purposes of vindication, finality. Everyone would like some form of finality in the foreseeable future. And I expect that there's probably not a perfect date for a trial date in the next year or two, but it is my goal to set a trial next year, and hopefully the middle of next year."

At that December hearing, Trump's attorney Daniel Petrocelli discussed the upcoming conflicts posed by his client's busy schedule.

"As much as we would like finality and like to have these matters put to rest, given the primary season—March 1 is Super Tuesday," he said. "We will know a lot more by the spring. I think the convention on the Republican side is in July. We would certainly request that a trial not be set sooner than July so that Mr. Trump has the ability to complete that part of the campaign."

Judge Curiel suggested that an August trial "makes sense." And it did. It didn't impact Trump's ability to lock up the Republican nomination and avoided the Republican convention. It wasn't perfect, but it was the best option.

Trump, at his deposition hearing the following week, seemed agreeable to August. Or maybe he knew something we didn't.

'THIS WILL BE A ZOO'

But when the spring rolled around—after Trump had denigrated Judge Curiel and shot to the front of the pack among Republican candidates—Trump's team wanted to delay the trial. During the March 11, 2016 motion hearing, Petrocelli expressed concern about the media attention surrounding the case, the media attention *that his client had inflamed with his public statements.*

"This will be a zoo if it were to go to trial," Petrocelli told Judge Curiel.

In terms of scheduling for a trial after the July RNC convention, "I'm going to have a lot to say on that subject if Mr. Trump is the nominee," Trump's attorney said.

Judge Curiel asked Petrocelli about scheduling the trial for August if Trump became the Republican nominee.

"I am not, Your Honor, in all likelihood," he said, before discussing his concern about "the integrity of the proceedings," as though his client were worried about that.

"We should not be litigating this case on a public debate forum for President of the United States, and it's deeply prejudicing. Everybody that comes up to me now knows about this case, and based on what they read in the papers, they usually don't have something nice to say to me about it, and I think if it continues, it's only going to dig a deeper hole for us, Your Honor," he said. Petrocelli also tried to argue that Tarla Makaeff's withdrawal from the case merited a delay so Trump's legal squad could recalibrate its legal approach.

Jason Forge suggested, since Donald Trump had the Republican nomination all but wrapped up, that June could also work for a trial. "I would be foolish to even pretend to know how a case like this should be handled at this point because it really is an unprecedented level of publicity," Jason said.

"Scrutiny," Judge Curiel added.

"And unprecedented, different forms of that publicity. We've all seen high-profile cases, but nothing like this. Now, whether that impacts our ability to pick a fair jury, it would be foolish for me to say it wouldn't."

As Jason Forge continued talking about the possibility of moving forward with a trial in August, Judge Curiel struck a deeper truth. "To the extent that this scrutiny, this focus, this obsession with this case is what it is, how would it be possible to avoid all of that with any form of trial in this case?" Judge Curiel asked.

Judge Curiel was asking about the obsession with the case out of direct knowledge. I remember Jason Forge telling me during a phone conversation in the spring of 2016 that Judge Curiel had received death threats, which troubled me deeply. Judge Curiel was simply doing his job and trying to be fair, and people had threatened his life over it.

Settlement seemed like the logical option. But Donald Trump was no settler. Or so he said.

As the Makaeff/Low case approached its moment of truth, my case trudged along. A settlement conference was scheduled for January 27, 2016. I was initially hoping to attend the conference telephonically, but that was denied. But then Judge Gallo, who was handling the conference, had a death in the family and had to reschedule, so the conference got bumped to March 29. Alan Garten, a lawyer for The Trump Organization, was there on Trump's behalf. I crossed paths with Garten—he was exiting the courtroom as we entered. His square face and heavy-rimmed glasses were hard to miss as I attempted to avoid eye contact. I can only recall his name once mentioned related to my case, and that was during Trump's hot-mic moment. I remembered Trump's bragging about his attorney threatening the BBB with a lawsuit if they didn't change the Trump University grade. And then Trump's saying under his breath of the lawyer, "He's an Alan Garten type—tough."

I was concerned about what tactics this "tough" lawyer might attempt. I gathered with my counsel and the other plaintiffs in Judge Gallo's chambers, but any settlement talks didn't go very far. The sides were too far apart.

MOMENT OF TRUTH

And then came the May 6, 2016 hearing in the San Diego courtroom. The hearing was a chance to discuss the time needed to try the case and the difficulties finding impartial jurors. There was always the concern from my counsel that jurors could find Donald Trump not guilty simply because they supported him as a politician or if he turned on his charm on the witness stand. Or the reality that Trump could bring havoc upon jurors' lives, pushing private citizens performing their civic duty into the worst parts of the public sphere. If he had this little respect for a federal judge . . . where was his line?

My counsel suggested a trial in late July or early August. Trump's attorneys wanted "to defer setting it for trial until after the nation's presidential election in November." A punt. A delay. The same argument Trump made for waiting to fill the vacancy left by the death of Supreme Court Justice Antonin Scalia. Let the voters make their choice, then things can be sorted out later.

Petrocelli cited the "unprecedented circumstances" surrounding Trump's presidential run for the delay. How the case had become a "lightning rod."

And how Trump needed to devote his "full-time efforts and energies to running his campaign and running for office, and I don't believe that it would be fair to him—in fact, I think it would be a virtually impossible burden on him to have to defend himself at trial between now and November." Petrocelli suggested if Trump won the election in November, "we could pick a date after the election, sometime in the beginning of the year, and have our trial then. I don't believe there is any compelling reason, given that the case is already six years old, why it has to be tried now, particularly given the effects that it could have on the election process."

Fair. What was fair? We'd waited more than *half a decade* to get closure. I'd personally devoted years of my life to this effort. And now this guy was too busy running for president to deal with us.

Judge Curiel asked whether the case could be tried between the election and inauguration.

"I would think it would be more reasonable to wait until after the inauguration because that is an extremely hectic time, when a president is putting together a transition team, making all sorts of extremely important appointments, not to mention you have a couple of holidays in there, with Thanksgiving and Christmas and New Year's," Petrocelli said. "And I would think, for example—early February is what I would propose be a reasonable time."

February? Next year?

Judge Curiel suggested that a jury questionnaire—which is used to gather information about potential jurors—would aid in a fair jury being selected. The key for the judge was to have the jury decide the case "based on the evidence and the law and not outside circumstances, not outside publicity, media, not outside events."

Ultimately, Judge Curiel was worried about the jurors. And based on the hot-mic transcript and death threats, I believe he was also worried about himself and the court.

"I realize there's two aspects of holding a trial before the November election. One is in terms of Mr. Trump's availability to prepare, to participate in the trial. That's one thing. But then second is the—if not Pandora's box, the unleashing of forces that we can only speculate would occur in the event that we held a trial in this courthouse prior to the election date. We can look at the events of the last month or two to give us some indication of what might happen, and so to the extent that the past is prologue to what might happen, I am thinking of my jury. I am thinking of will they be able to stay clear of the media frenzy that will occur, that will arise? Will we be able to insulate them from events that may occur around this courthouse? So ultimately, that's my number one concern."

The media swarm would undoubtedly be a problem, but the more significant issue here was Trump. What would he do? How would he undermine the case?

The national glare from Trump's running for office and uncertainty surrounding his efforts to undermine the case made it damn near impossible to seat a jury. So Judge Curiel settled on starting the trial for the Monday after Thanksgiving, November 28, 2016.

Another pass.

I've always wondered if a sequestered jury would have been possible . . . curiously, it wasn't discussed during the May 6 hearing. Was some backroom consensus reached? I have no personal knowledge of one, but it's interesting how everyone galvanized around this idea of a November trial start date. Judge Curiel's concern for the jury was genuine. What the judge didn't know was that his decision to grant a delay represented a swing of a wrecking ball to the walls of democracy.

CALM BEFORE THE STORM

I'm sure Judge Curiel thought the delay might help to turn down the temperature—it was a strong sign that he wasn't treating Trump unfairly merely because of the politician's stances on immigration, or even because of all of Trump's statements about *the Spanish thing*.

Things were calmer for a few weeks.

Until May 27, to be exact, when Judge Curiel ordered that the Trump University playbooks, the documents outlining instructors' tactics to generate sales, be unsealed and released. In his order, the judge added a line that spoke to Trump's impact on the proceedings. "Defendant became the front-runner for the Republican nomination in the 2016 presidential race and has placed the integrity of these court proceedings at issue," Judge Curiel wrote. *The Washington Post* had requested the documents be released. The judge didn't believe they contained anything of value or any proprietary information.

That date coincided with Donald Trump speaking in San Diego—the place where the Trump University cases originated, the place where trials were slated to be held, the place from which prospective jurors would be selected.

LIES, LIES, AND MORE LIES

Twelve minutes.

That's how long Trump spent discussing Trump University during his hour-long speech, railing against Judge Curiel, Judge Gallo, Tarla Makaeff, the law firm representing us, and . . . me.

He called the way the federal court was treating him "a disgrace." He suggested, incorrectly, that everyone who took the course was located in San Diego, failing to acknowledge the nationwide class that had been certified, or the classes that had been certified for Florida or New York, or the separate lawsuit brought by New York AG Eric Schneiderman.

"The trial—they wanted it to start while I'm running for president. The trial is going to take place sometime in November. There should be no trial. This should have been dismissed on summary judgment easily," Trump said, disregarding the reality that summary judgment is only applied where there are no disputed issues of fact . . . which was not the case here.

He proceeded to call Judge Curiel "a hater of Donald Trump, a hater. He's a hater." Trump read from a sheet and held his hand in the air. These remarks and attacks were prepared. "His name is . . . *Gon-zal-o Cur-i-alllll*," he said, dragging out the syllables, making the judge's name sound more ethnic while frumpling his chin and shaking his head and pausing amid the chorus of boos. " . . . and he is not doing the right thing."

Trump went into his usual schtick about the school's quality before making an interesting statement—crediting staff for having students fill out questionnaires, that somehow these "report cards" were the key to his case.

"My people did a good job for a couple of reasons," he said. "One of the reasons was they had everybody that took the course sign like a report card. So we had, let's say, 10,000 people. Almost that many signed their report card. And the report cards are unbelievable."

"By the way, without that, it's their word versus these people or me. But I'm getting railroaded by a legal system that . . . frankly, they should be ashamed because this is a case that . . . I'll be here in November."

He continued trashing Judge Curiel, calling on the judge to recuse himself. "He's given us ruling after ruling after ruling, negative, negative, negative. I have a top lawyer who said he's never seen anything like this before.

"So, what happens is we get sued. We have a magistrate named William Gallo who truly hates us." Judge Gallo! Judge Gallo issued numerous rulings *favorable* for Trump.

Trump, as he did during the day of his deposition hearing in December 2015, remained confused about the jury pool of a federal civil trial.

"Now, the good news is it's a jury trial. But we can't even get a full jury. We're entitled to a jury. We want a jury of twelve people and you're going to watch. First of all, it should be dismissed before the trial, but if we have a trial, we'll go all the way," he said.

How was anyone buying this crap?

He also went after Robbins Geller Rudman & Dowd, one of the law firms representing the other plaintiffs and me, reading from his paper again as he mentioned in his muddy language how an early founding partner at the firm was among those who went to prison "for doing very bad things illegally" more than a decade earlier while he was a partner at a separate law firm, Milburg Weiss—another cheap shot.

And then he went back in on Judge Curiel.

"So what happens is the judge, who happens to be, we believe, Mexican, which is great. I think that's fine. You know what? I think the Mexicans are going to end up loving Donald Trump when I give all these jobs, OK? I think they're going to end up . . . I think they're going to love me . . . !"

The crowd applauded.

"So here's what happens. We get sued by a woman and she turns out to be a disaster for them. Her name is Tarla . . . *Mark-off.*" *If you're going to keep dragging this woman through the mud, the least you could do is say her name correctly!* Speaking in a nationally broadcast speech, Trump argued that Tarla was removed from the case because she was "such a disaster . . . it was her against us." And that Judge Curiel screwed up by allowing her to leave the case, as though Trump's team hadn't tried to previously have her removed, as though the case hinged on her and her alone, as though there wasn't another plaintiff certified to represent all California victims, as though other class representatives weren't also certified in Florida and New York for the Makaeff/Low case, and across the country for my case.

HE'S TALKING ABOUT ME

Trump blustered, rattling off those who had wronged him. " . . . And then we have a guy named Art Cohen."

Here we go.

" . . . and he was late to file. So, he signed a survey in which he rated the program either a four or a five. I will tell you this, how smart was it to ask everybody that took the course to sign a report card?" he asked the crowd. "So, he signed all fives and fours, out of a possible—the highest marks. And indicated that his only complaint was the lack of nice lunch sandwiches. OK? Think of it."

"So he was late. So they went to the judge and the judge said, 'He's late; why don't you file under RICO, organized crime?' Now, we've all been sued in business for RICO, even Papa John probably . . . . So I get sued. Here's a guy gives me all good marks. He's late. So they're starting a new lawsuit."

How many lies or mistruths could he cram into 30 seconds of a speech?

1. I wasn't late to file.

2. He declined to mention my answer to the sixth question on the survey, "How could Trump University help you meet your goals?" "Mentoring key to success," I wrote.

3. The RICO angle only became possible through the discovery that Donald Trump personally owned 93 percent of Trump University and

that New York state officials warned of using the "university" title in 2005.

4. Jason Forge guided the RICO angle of our lawsuit; the judge did not suggest it. In fact, the judge had to be convinced that it was adequate.

5. But here was the most watched, most talked-about, most visible person in the news, speaking my name to a TV audience of millions. Didn't he have anything better to focus on than the guy who just wanted his $35,000 back?

Trump dropping my name on the campaign trail forced me to withdraw further, tighten up my social media presence, and be more careful and guarded. I felt like I had to watch my back. Someone might be following me.

SEE YOU IN NOVEMBER

As Trump wound down his TED Talk on running a for-profit education scam, he threw out some heavy-handed signals that he would torpedo any chance at a fair trial in November.

"So I'll be seeing you . . . in November . . . either as president . . .

"I look forward to going before a jury, not this judge, a jury, and we will win that trial. We will win that trial. Check it out. Check it out, folks.

"And you know, I tell this to people—November 28th, I think it's scheduled for, shouldn't be a trial; should be a summary judgment dismissal.

"By the way, friends of mine that are great lawyers, in fact, one of them represents you, said, 'How the hell do you get sued under RICO for a guy that took a course, loved the course, said great things about the course, and then you get sued under RICO?'

"This court system, the judges in this court system, federal court. They ought to look into that Judge Curiel because what Judge Curiel is doing is a total disgrace. OK?

"But we'll come back in November. Wouldn't that be wild if I'm president and I come back to do a civil case?"

Wouldn't that be wild.

WINNING AT ANY COST

Everyone else wanted Trump to let this thing go, to pivot his campaign. Hillary Clinton had emerged as the leading Democratic candidate . . . it was going to be a bitter race to the White House. His energy needed to be on his political opponent, not on racist attacks against a federal judge in a civil matter.

But Trump needed to be *right*. He had to *win*. He was vindictive and petty and mean, and this judge made Trump feel small, so Trump was going to make the judge feel small, too.

And in the days to come, Trump continued his attack on the judiciary.

"I have a judge in the Trump University civil case, Gonzalo Curiel (San Diego), who is very unfair. An Obama pick. Totally biased-hates Trump," Trump tweeted.

Trump's rhetoric was given new life on May 31 when Judge Curiel ordered that some of the exhibits unsealed days earlier needed to be resealed with redactions added before they could be released—that some of the unredacted documents were "mistakenly" unsealed.

Trump kept blabbing about TrumpU to *The Wall Street Journal*, calling Judge Curiel's association with the case "an inherent conflict of interest," especially since the judge worked as a federal prosecutor a decade earlier with Jason Forge. Of course, Judge Curiel wasn't saying anything. He couldn't say anything.

But lots of other people were saying something. Hillary Clinton. Paul Ryan. Bob Corker. Mitch McConnell. "I couldn't disagree more with a statement like that," McConnell said, with all the intensity of a crumpled paper bag. Newt Gingrich—a man who knows a thing or two about mistakes—suggested Trump's comments about Judge Curiel represented "one of the worst mistakes Trump has made." OK, it wasn't a repudiation. But it was . . . something.

TV pundits continued asking Trump about his comments, and he only made things worse. He tried to argue to CNN's Jake Tapper that an earlier judge—who happened to be retired Judge Irma Gonzalez, also Mexican-American—was much fairer to him than Judge Curiel. "This judge is of Mexican heritage. I'm building a wall, OK? I'm going to do very well with the Hispanics, the Mexicans," Trump said.

"So no Mexican judge could ever be involved in a case that involves you?" Tapper asked.

"Well, he's a member of a society that's very pro-Mexico, and that's *fine* . . . it's all fine. But I think he should recuse himself." Ah, yes, Judge Curiel was a member of the Hispanic National Bar Association, which a year earlier put out a statement denouncing Trump's comments that Mexico was sending rapists and criminals into the country.

Tapper stood firm amid the bluster. "But you're invoking his race when talking about whether or not he can do his job," the TV journalist said.

"Jake . . . I'm building a wall, OK? I'm building a wall." *Trump's mouth hung open as he spoke, as though he was trying to breathe on Tapper.* "I'm trying to keep business out of Mexico."

"But he's an American."

"He's of Mexican heritage. And he's very proud of it."

Tapper tried to keep Trump on point.

"If you invoke his race as a reason why he can't do his job . . . ?"

"I think that's why he's doing it."

In a separate interview on CBS *Face the Nation*, Trump was asked if he believed a Muslim judge might also be biased against him because he'd proposed a temporary ban on Muslims entering the country. "It's possible, yes. Yeah. That would be possible, absolutely," he said.

LATE-NIGHT LAUGHS

Late-night TV hosts and comedians pounced at Trump University. Even if it wasn't a joke to me, the rip-off was ripe with humor. Of my "mentor for life," high-pressure salesman James Harris, NBC's Seth Meyers said, "It's never a good sign when your teacher looks like he's wearing a Guy Fieri Halloween costume." Meyers also compared mealy-mouthed Republicans who backed Trump to party hosts who let their friend bring a dog, even though they were worried that the dog would soil their rug, "and long story short, Paul Ryan is in a West Elm right now buying a new rug." *Ellen* ran a clip of "Trump University" graduates falling while walking in their graduation robes. *The Daily Show* worked on something, too, that never surfaced.

The most scathing takedown came from John Oliver, a liberal-leaning Brit satirist and host of HBO's *Last Week Tonight* who'd been a consistent critic of Trump. Oliver cut through BS, and Trump's entire body of work was BS. Oliver devoted a segment on a 2016 episode of his show to Trump University, focusing on Trump's introductory seminar video promising "success."

"The world of success," Oliver said. "It sounds like what Donald Trump calls his bedroom. 'Welcome to the world of success. Please enjoy your mint and a non-disclosure agreement.'" Oliver also broke down TrumpU to the name itself. "Trump University wasn't even a university, which is enough to make you wonder what there was in Trump Steaks? Oh God, it was possum, you monsters!"

In Trump University, Oliver recognized the false mythos surrounding Donald Trump—and how the scam spoke for something larger.

Perhaps the most valuable lesson to come out of Trump University is the one that it's currently giving all of us in what's behind Trump's campaign strategy, because the Playbook tells his salespeople, "You don't sell products, benefits, or solutions—you sell feelings." And that is what is happening now. Crowds at a Trump rally might not be able to point to a concrete benefit or solution he offers, but they know how he makes them feel. And that is jacked up and ready to boo any name that sounds vaguely

Latino. So if you are planning to vote for Trump in November, I'd like to direct you to a quote from the top of Trump University's old homepage: "Take the risk, but before you do, learn what you're getting yourself into."

ATTACKING THE RULE OF LAW

Trump's campaign wanted to distance from the scandal since it was doing real damage. Some Republican heavyweights were calling on the party to choose another nominee at the Republican National Convention.

On a June 6 conference call, Trump could have reinforced a new tone. He could have pivoted. He could have shifted gears to focus on Hillary Clinton. Instead, he called on his surrogates to *continue* attacking Judge Curiel in the media. To do his bidding.

"We will overcome," Trump said on the call, according to *Bloomberg*. "The people asking the questions (the media), those are the racists," he added. "I would go at 'em." He walked back his campaign staff's messaging not to talk about Trump University.

His impulse was to go against sound guidance, Republican leadership, common decency, and his campaign team to attack the rule of law.

Because that's all this was.

Retired law professor David Post, interviewed by the *New York Times* in June 2016, said Trump's comments crossed a significant line. "This is how authoritarianism starts, with a president who does not respect the judiciary," Post said. "You can criticize the judicial system; you can criticize individual cases; you can criticize individual judges. But the president has to be clear that the law is the law and that he enforces the law. That is his constitutional obligation.

"If he is signaling that that is not his position, that's a very serious constitutional problem."

A CURIOUS SILENCE

One day after Trump's conference call, on June 7, he vowed to stop talking about Trump University and Judge Curiel. The highlights (or lowlights):

"It is unfortunate that my comments have been misconstrued as a categorical attack against people of Mexican heritage," he said in the statement, no doubt heavily guided by lawyers or campaign staff. "I am friends with and employ thousands of people of Mexican and Hispanic descent. The American justice system relies on fair and impartial judges. All judges should be held to that standard. I do not feel that one's heritage makes them incapable of being impartial, but, based on the rulings that I have received in the Trump University civil case, I feel justified in questioning whether I am receiving a fair trial.

"Normally, legal issues in a civil case would be heard in a neutral environment. However, given my unique circumstances as nominee of the Republican Party and the core issues of my campaign that focus on illegal immigration, jobs and unfair trade, I have concerns as to my ability to receive a fair trial.

"Due to what I believe are unfair and mistaken rulings in this case and the Judge's reported associations with certain professional organizations, questions were raised regarding the Obama appointed Judge's impartiality. It is a fair question. I hope it is not the case.

"Fortunately, Judge Curiel is a very thoughtful and well-reasoned judge, and I don't think any of Trump's statements or his presidential race otherwise impacted the litigation, but it definitely gave it a circus element."

-AMBER ECK
HAEGGQUIST & ECK, LLP PARTNER AND TRIAL ATTORNEY

"While this lawsuit should have been dismissed, it is now scheduled for trial in November. I do not intend to comment on this matter any further. With all of the thousands of people who have given the courses such high marks and accolades, we will win this case!"

He also appeared on Bill O'Reilly's show on Fox News, *The O'Reilly Factor,* that night, his final chance to talk about TrumpU before his forced silence—another chance to discuss how Tarla Makaeff was an "absolute disaster," how the judge treated him unfairly, the "report cards" filled out by students.

And then, after he couldn't stop talking about Trump University, he somehow stuck to his word and never spoke about it again on the campaign trail. He'd accomplished his outcome of bringing up *the Spanish thing* by shifting the conversation from fraud to racism. Racism was something he could more easily brush away.

It all felt like a giant stunt—subterfuge for something else.

It's curious to consider the date that Trump decided he was done talking about Trump University. June 7, 2016. That day, his oldest son Donald Trump Jr. confirmed a meeting, held two days later, at Trump Tower that also involved Trump's campaign manager Paul Manafort, his son-in-law Jared Kushner, and a Russian lawyer, Natalia Veselnitskaya, who had supposed "dirt" on Hillary Clinton

CHAPTER 13

RUNAWAY TRAIN

Words and truth still mattered.

By the spring of 2016, Donald Trump's counsel was arguing—not convincingly—in a motion for summary judgment that the facts of my case were straightforward and that it should be dismissed.

Most notably, they suggested that references to "secrets," "hand-picked" instructors, and "university" represented "classic examples of sales puffery common to advertising everywhere."

Just matters of mere exaggerations.

For "secrets," Trump's counsel tried to argue that his secrets to success, "focus, hard work, and tenacity," were "central to TU's teachings." Those weren't secrets, simply ideas. It's not clear where loans and bailouts from a rich father were reflected in any of these "secrets."

Trump's counsel also suggested that the word "hand-picked" is "another catchy and popular word in advertising." To prove that point, they linked to a newsletter for Michigan Mittens, a company that sells mittens with maps of Michigan's Upper Peninsula on one mitten and the Lower Peninsula on the other "to represent the 'Mitten State.'"

"You've been 'hand' picked—to receive free shipping thru May 1st!" the newsletter reads.

A play on words by a company making mittens with maps printed on them, in which the "hand-picked" reference connects to the service being offered, has nothing in common with a business scion fleecing the public by falsely claiming that seminars featuring his name and brand and likeness were taught by people that he personally selected.

And then there was *university*.... The examples they cited included FedEx University, which offers personal development courses online; the Clinton Global Initiative's CGI University, a yearly meeting for a "network of global young leaders"; Farmers Insurance ads featuring actor J.K. Simmons as Professor Nathaniel Burke at the University of Farmers; and employee training programs in FedEx University, Disney University, Motorola University, and McDonalds' Hamburger University.

The big difference: Hamburger University was a legitimate program established in 1961 that has offered McDonald's employees the chance to improve their leadership and business talents while also earning college credits that can be applied toward an associate or bachelor's degree.

Hamburger University beefed up attendees' outlook and opportunities.

Trump University was a load of bull.

FILE AWAY

After Trump's legal team filed its motion for summary judgment (which was eventually denied), my counsel filed its opposition on June 3, 2016. Jason Forge tried to include video clips from Trump's deposition hearings in the electronic filing, but the files were too large.

The files could not be electronically filed, therefore my counsel had to obtain leave of Court before submitting them. If he had only embedded the videos in the PDFs, instead of attempting to upload the video files separately. It would have been an interesting workaround to get his deposition videos on the record and out to the public.

But alas, now the defense had a chance to object to the video being included in the court filings, and of course, they did, arguing that the video was "duplicative of the deposition transcripts" and that the release of the footage "serves only to harass and unfairly prejudice Mr. Trump."

Mr. Trump happened to be running for the most visible job in the world, which is why the media got involved, too. All the big names stumbled over themselves to get a hold of the video I watched from my home on December 10, 2015, as well as footage of Trump's second deposition hearing in January 2016 in Las Vegas—CNN, CBS, ABC, NBC, *The New York Times*, *The Washington Post*, as well as Tribune Publishing, a decaying newspaper chain that would soon adopt the ridiculous moniker "Tronc."

The media mavens suggested that Trump University had become a "prominent electoral issue," something that cut through Trump's murky statements about his business career. "Defendant has cited TU as an example of his business success and made this litigation itself a campaign issue," the media organizations cited in a June 10, 2016 filing. "Given the undeniable and substantial public interest in these proceedings, the need for transparency could not be greater."

Transcripts alone couldn't capture Trump's mannerisms and tone. They couldn't show him unable to remember a single Trump University instructor or admitting that he had no real clue what was taught in the seminars. They couldn't show him getting madder and madder as he was forced to answer questions about people losing their life savings.

ONE LONG CON

In a June 15 filing, Trump's legal team expressed concern about preventing the "sensationalism" surrounding the case.

They also suggested that "Dissemination of the deposition videos in this litigation would not only prejudice Defendants' rights but would undermine the function of discovery by deterring others from appearing for videotaped depositions."

Wait . . . a key argument was that making Trump's deposition videos public would convince witnesses—who are generally compelled to testify—hesitant to participate in depositions? As someone who participated in my own deposition hearings in this specific case, I can honestly say that Trump's deposition videos' potential release didn't make me think twice about appearing.

That's because, unlike Trump, who was driving a manure spreader across the campaign trail, I didn't have anything to hide.

Trump's deposition videos showed him forced to face his lies.

The truth was the scariest thing to him. Because beneath the bluster and aura and deceit, there was a petty man trying to convince himself of the myth of his greatness.

The truth told a different story—a trail of devastation and failure, a life of undeserved bailouts and limitless privilege. People and groups ignored their gut instinct and bent the rules for Trump because of the potential benefits. His whole life was one long con. He just had to maintain the con for a few more months.

He had to keep the truth about Trump University hidden because he was selling a new group of people on his latest scheme, and this time he was going to share his secrets and bring you unprecedented wealth, and all you had to do was show your support by pressing a button or writing his name on Election Day.

SUMMER OF UNREST

Trump University generated tons of headlines and attention as Donald Trump secured the Republican nomination, but a series of tragic stories pushed TrumpU off newspaper front pages and into the background.

A June 12 shooting at Pulse nightclub in Orlando, Florida left 49 people dead and 53 injured. The following month, police shootings of two black men, Alton Sterling in New Orleans and Philando Castile in Minnesota, sparked national outrage. At the same time, a sniper in Dallas opened fire on police, killing five officers.

Amid a summer of unrest, the State Department decided it would reopen its review of Hillary Clinton's use of a private email server while Secretary of State, giving legs to a controversy that, in hindsight, paled in comparison to numerous Trump scandals such as Trump University.

'A CONSUMMATE LIAR'

Like Trump, there was one other witness in the case who tried their damnedest to shake off a deposition—James Harris, my "instructor" at my 2009 live event, the one who called himself my "mentor for life" and who reminded me of a can of Red Bull personified.

The power salesman's manipulative tactics drove me to sign on the dotted line. And then he disappeared, slipping out of sitting for a deposition despite being served with seven subpoenas.

Even if the deposition didn't happen, Harris' presence would loom large as the trials neared—he and other instructors were using the dream of fame and riches, and the name and image of Donald Trump, to sell air.

Through discovery and due diligence, my counsel found that Harris didn't have the squeaky record he projected. In fact, he was a convicted felon, having pleaded guilty to aggravated assault in Georgia in 2001.

His estranged wife, in a court filing a decade later, alleged long-term physical and emotional abuse. "James is the consummate salesman, but also a consummate liar," she wrote in a statement. "He is extremely convincing and persuasive, and if that doesn't work, he will tell you what he thinks you want to hear, or manipulate, threaten or coerce you to get his way."

I saw a glimpse of that side from my time in his TrumpU seminar. He told me what I wanted to hear, and I was sold. Oh, how wrong I was to trust him . . . his wife's allegations were gut-wrenching. She wrote that she feared for her life and that after she told Harris she wanted a divorce, he showed up at their children's school and attempted to pull them out of class.

By the summer of 2016, I was doing my best to brush the memory of James Harris out of my life until he showed up on CNN being interviewed by investigative reporter Drew Griffin. Here was this worm, with his bleached hair and blindingly white teeth, the one who couldn't be bothered to sit for a deposition, going on TV to talk about Trump University?

Luckily Griffin wasn't giving him a free pass. The reporter had studied my counsel's court filings, which included a transcript of a 2009 presentation by Harris in San Bernardino, California a few months before I attended my seminar with him.

"Do you remember when you said this? 'I'm a former licensed agent broker. At 29, I became the top 1 percent broker in the country. I build homes in Atlanta, Georgia, and I used to live in Beverly Hills,'" Griffin said, reading directly from the transcript.

"Yes," Harris said, nodding. "If I said those things, they are true. I did live in Beverly Hills and I—"

"We have no record of you ever living in Beverly Hills."

"OK, well . . . ."

"We can't find your broker's license anywhere," Griffin continued.

"OK," Harris said.

"And I have no idea what homes you built in Atlanta, Georgia. Did you build homes in Georgia?"

"I'm not prepared to answer those questions today," Harris said.

"This is part of your pitch. Is any of that true?" Griffin asked.

"Again, I'm not going to answer those questions because I haven't seen that."

"Well, you certainly know what you've done in your life." Griffin, peering over his glasses, continued to hammer Harris. "Well, what do you know about real estate?"

"Again, I'm not prepared to answer those questions today. This is about Trump University," Harris said.

If we couldn't get Harris to sit on the hot seat for a deposition, getting shamed on national TV was the next best thing. Harris described the Trump University sales formula as "a little upsell... if you pay this amount, we're going to teach you this much. If you pay (more), we're going to go further with you."

Griffin fired back by highlighting an email Harris wrote to a colleague. "I just spoke to Austin and Irene, the older retired couple who had to pull the $30,000 balance for the gold and she said it's done and should be in Monday, so that will be another $35K. We will have another $100K hit by Friday. Yahoo."

The associate, Brian, responded to Harris. "We've always been a dangerous team, brother man. These peeps don't have a chance against us."

I guess we really didn't.

"That's called sales," Harris told the reporter.

"Is that called ripping off an old couple?" Griffin asked.

"Absolutely not," said my mentor for life. He tried to explain it away by passing the buck. "I was doing my job. We did our job."[3]

---

[3] By 2021, Harris was living in Mexico, calling himself "James Paradise" and posting shirtless videos of himself to YouTube and TikTok in which he explained how people could make money through real estate investing, bitcoin, affiliate links, and other streams. In a video from December 2020 titled "2021 REAL ESTATE CRASH How to buy Foreclosures & Bank Owned properties," "James Paradise" alluded to his previous Trump University experiences while warning of a crash that didn't happen. "Back in 2008, 2009, I was traveling around the USA and Canada doing live real estate seminars called 'fast track to foreclosures.' And I'm telling you right now, in the next 4, 5, 6, 7, 8, 9, 10 months from December—today's December 11th, 2020—into next year, I'm talking into about March, April, May, you are going to see more foreclosures and bank owned properties starting to pop up than we've seen in the last 12 years." Sure, James Paradise. Sure.

THE REPUBLICAN NOMINEE

Ivanka Trump smiled and glowed as she discussed her father, trying to soften his edges for a national audience.

Cleveland's Quicken Loans Arena, July 21, 2016.

Donald John Trump was there to accept the Republican nomination for president. He came to the stage and clapped and pointed at the crowd, soaking in the adoration. American flags drooped behind him. Giant letters hung above the stage. T-R-U-M-P.

The fire and brimstone speech was classic Trump: fear of the other, attacks on his rivals, empty promises. "My sole and exclusive mission is to go to work for our country, to go to work for you. It is time to deliver a victory for the American people. We don't win anymore, but we are going to start winning again," he said.

Hoo-boy. You could have fit in some lines from his introductory video played at Trump University events—*success, it's going to happen to you*—and it would have matched perfectly. But this wasn't some promotional video, it was the presidency. Trump proved to be inept or corrupt, or both, overseeing a real estate seminar program, and that was supposed to be his area of expertise. What damage could he do overseeing a real problem, heaven forbid, like a terror attack or a pandemic?

It was easy to dismiss Trump's campaign as a joke early on, but you couldn't write it off by the summer of 2016. I spoke to Jason Forge a number of times about Trump's presidential chances. Initially Jason didn't think Trump would secure the Republican nomination, but after he did, Jason was convinced that Trump would win the election. I hoped he was wrong—I was all in on Hillary Clinton—but Jason Forge's instincts were rarely wrong.

As Trump's chances of winning intensified, I felt like I was carrying a heavy weight with me everywhere I went. I was holding something big—a video stored on my phone from Trump's deposition. It was important. People needed to see it. And even if I couldn't do anything at the time, I looked forward to the day when I could share the video with someone, to let them see the side of Donald Trump that I'd seen.

GETTING POLITICAL

Before getting connected with Trump University, I didn't see myself as a very political person. I leaned liberal on social causes, and I stayed informed on key issues, but politics wasn't a main identifier for me. But by the summer of 2016—fueled by Trump's political rise and getting more involved with organizations in the Bay Area—I ended up serving as an alternate delegate from California for Hillary Clinton. Running for a delegate seat was an eye-opening experience on how caucuses operate. One Sunday I had to gather as many of my supporters as possible to arrive at a specified location to vote for me during the hours between 1 and 2 p.m. With thirteen men vying for the one or two slots designated for men, I wasn't confident I'd win. But it turned out that my community service activities helped me gather enough support to squeak by a second-place showing and at the time, based on current percentages between Hillary Clinton and Bernie Sanders, I was assigned a delegate seat. By the time I reached Philadelphia, the numbers shifted in favor to Sanders and my district lost a seat, so my new position was alternate delegate. Same access and responsibilities, but now I'd only deliver the actual delegate vote for Clinton if the first-place delegate were not attending for the vote.

California's delegate process is confusing. Candidates need to reach 15 percent in any congressional districts, or statewide, to receive pledged delegates. Based on the outcome of California's primary, Hillary Clinton wound up receiving 320 of the state's 551 delegates on her way to securing the Democratic nomination.

Serving as a delegate meant I got the chance to attend the Democratic National Convention in my hometown of Philadelphia, which was special. The energy, and excitement and momentum to defeat Trump warmed my heart. But while there, I had such a tough time staying quiet about my role as lead plaintiff in the Trump University lawsuit. I had a secret. I wanted to tell *everyone* about it.

At one point, I was at a bar and recognized David Corn, the respected author and sharp *Mother Jones* journalist. *Hey, have I got a scoop for you . . .* I thought about telling him and asked Corn to take a photo together, but he had to run. Maybe I'd talk to him another time.

The experience motivated me to get more deeply involved with the Silicon Valley Democratic Club, which helped me connect with state and national politicians—real politicians, not aggrieved reality TV stars masquerading as politicians.

RISKS AND REWARDS

Two weeks after Donald Trump accepted the Republican nomination for president, Judge Curiel—the impartial federal judge he'd spent months trying to destroy—issued his ruling on whether to release the embarrassing, inflammatory videos of Trump's depositions from late 2015 and early 2016.

What payback that could be if Judge Curiel were a vindictive person.

But he wasn't a vindictive person. Judge Curiel was a judge who consistently stuck to Ninth District precedent in his decisions, as he did with the August 2, 2016 order.

"There is a greater potential for harm to result from the release of the deposition videos because of the high likelihood that media scrutiny in this case will be ongoing," Judge Curiel wrote. "Although here, trial is three months away . . . there is no reason to believe that 'memories will fade' before the beginning of trial. Rather, there is every reason to believe that release of the deposition videos would contribute to an ongoing 'media frenzy' that would increase the difficulty of seating an impartial jury."

Judge Curiel considered the public's need to view the video and the blowback that could come from their release and weighed the risks and rewards.

"The core question is whether the public's interest in viewing the demeanor of Defendant in the deposition videos outweighs the impairment to judicial efficiency likely to result. The Court concludes that it does not. While there is a degree of legitimate public interest in the demeanor of the Defendant in the deposition videos, it is not a substantial interest."

Donald Trump was avoiding accountability. Again.

And now Americans would have to vote without the ability to see what I'd seen, without recognizing the depth of Trump's rotten core. I thought for a moment about leaking the video from the December 2015 deposition . . . no, I couldn't jeopardize the case like that.

It was going to be up to Hillary Clinton and the American public to stop a runaway train.

CHAPTER 14

DECISION

The fall of 2016 sprinted past like a thief.

Which was fitting, because all the talk was on a crook who was trying to steal the presidential election.

The Trump University situation was still unresolved, but Donald Trump was aiming for the White House. Democrat Hillary Clinton had a steady lead over Trump in polling. Five points, six points, 10 points.

Clinton's lead looked more and more secure on October 7, when *The Washington Post* published a hot-mic recording from 2005 featuring Trump talking with TV entertainment reporter Billy Bush about forcing himself on women.

"I moved on her like a bitch," he said of Bush's then-*Access Hollywood* co-host Nancy O'Dell, who reportedly rebuffed his advances after he took her furniture shopping.

The hot-mic moment came before Trump and Bush met soap opera actress Arianne Zucker.

"I better use some Tic Tacs just in case I start kissing her," he said. "You know, I'm automatically attracted to beautiful . . . I just start kissing them. It's like a magnet. Just kiss. I don't even wait. And when you're a star, they let you do it. You can do anything. Grab 'em by the pussy. You can do anything."

It wasn't the hot-mic conversation I'd witnessed from Trump's deposition, but this new explosive hot-mic video carried a lot of similar themes, namely that if you're Donald John Trump, *you can do anything* without consequences . . . .

And he really loved those Tic Tacs. I was still bothered that the public hadn't been able to witness Trump's December 2015 deposition. But at least people were getting a chance to see glimpses of his true behavior.

'TALKING DOWN OUR DEMOCRACY'

Trump's awfulness hung over the presidential race just like it had the Trump University legal battle. He was relentless and cruel, declining to follow expected norms or maintain a shred of decency.

As Clinton shared the debate stage with Trump, she warned America of the doom that would come if he were elected. During their third 2016 debate, Trump did not say whether he would accept the election outcome if he lost.

"He is denigrating, and he is talking down our democracy," Clinton said. "And I, for one, am appalled that somebody who is the nominee of one of our two major parties would take that kind of a position."

NIGHTMARE

Election Day.

November 8, 2016.

So much was at stake. The future of the country. The state of our democracy.

The Trump University cases had been largely pushed out of the public consciousness, but they were hanging in the balance, too. In a few weeks, I could be forced to take the stand in court against the *President-elect of the United States.*

The national media glare was bad enough during the campaign.

If Trump won, it would be unbearable.

If Trump won . . . how would the cases proceed? Would a Trump supporter wind up on the jury and vote to acquit him merely because of their political slant?

I proudly voted for Clinton on Election Day. This vote was personal. Hillary Clinton was a respectable candidate. She was smart and sharp. And she hadn't ripped me off for $35,000 and waged a years-long legal battle against other victims and me.

I wanted to be optimistic . . . but a feeling of dread knotted in my stomach. Trump would say and do anything. And instead of recognizing the danger he represented, instead of realizing that his word meant nothing, people loved him for it.

Clinton's election results weren't as strong as I'd hoped. She wasn't performing as strongly as Barack Obama in key battleground states.

Florida and Michigan, and Pennsylvania became crucial for her path to election. As the hours passed, the math continued to elude Clinton.

Her path to the presidency narrowed. Until it closed.

Donald Trump—who I'd sued for overseeing a criminal enterprise—was inexplicably the United States president-elect after more than 62 million Americans voted for him, earning him 305 Electoral College votes.

How did this happen?! I couldn't believe it . . . or maybe I could. Trump had fooled me into signing up for a fake university, and now he had fooled America into electing a fraudulent president.

GOOD NEWS / BAD NEWS

Two days after Election Day, November 10, my lawyers and Trump's were in a San Diego courtroom with Judge Curiel for a hearing.

The inauguration was two months away. And even though Trump was preparing to enter the White House, he'd still have to deal with that little Trump University thing.

The first trial was set to begin on November 28 . . . or was it?

"Donald Trump's election benefited Trump University students around the country. For everyone else, all I could say was 'I'm sorry.'"

-RACHEL JENSEN, LEAD COUNSEL IN TRUMP UNIVERSITY CLASS
ACTION LAWSUITS, TO THE WASHINGTON POST

Early into the November 10 hearing, Daniel Petrocelli, Trump's lawyer, made his next request to delay the trial. He'd already gotten the trial bumped from the summer because Trump was running for president, and now that his client won, he was too busy.

"He ought not to have to proceed to trial at this moment in time given that he only has 70 days, now that he's been elected president, to perform the extraordinary task of going through the transition process and picking cabinet members," Petrocelli said. "There are over 3,000 appointees. All of that is not going to get done before the inauguration. But they are following a long and exhausting and hard-fought campaign. The good news is that he was elected; the bad news is that he has even more work to do now."

Petrocelli continued: "And we feel like there is a compelling justification to ask that the Court put this trial off until after the inauguration, particularly given, Your Honor, that we have a second trial, the Cohen case, in which Mr. Trump is the sole defendant. And the idea that we would have two of these trials . . . ."

"Certainly, that's not going to go to trial before he is president, and so I don't think we have to worry about that," Judge Curiel said.

Imagine that: me against the sitting president, the leader of the free world, in court. Petrocelli suggested, as he had months earlier, that the first case be put off until early 2017. He also wondered about Trump appearing in court, whether accommodations could be given to allow him to testify by video. "There has never been a case in the history of our country where a sitting president has been required to come into a courtroom or to my knowledge . . . ," Petrocelli said.

"That's right. And that's what we are trying to avoid," Judge Curiel said.

A LAST GASP TO SETTLE

During the hearing, Judge Curiel mentioned another possibility: work with longtime District Court Judge Jeffrey Miller and hammer out a settlement. Judge Miller, a Bill Clinton appointee who assumed senior status in 2010, represented the last gasp to settle.

Trump, despite his many public statements, never really wanted the cases to go to trial. Not with the reality that he'd face difficult questions and the threat of perjury and potentially forced to pay treble damages out of his own pocket.

"I think it might have been possible to hold the trial while he was running for president, while he was just a candidate, but once he was elected president, I don't think it would have been. It would have been impossible to pick an unbiased jury when the defendant was the newly elected president."

-AMBER ECK
HAEGGQUIST & ECK, LLP PARTNER AND TRIAL ATTORNEY

If he wanted to fight us in court, he wouldn't have spent half a decade littering the path to trial with roadblocks. Otherwise, this all would go on and on and on and on and on, and Trump would try to drag this out as long as that riparian rights case on the docket since 1951.

"I think it would be wise because there's no certainty in these proceedings," Judge Curiel said in support of mediation. "There's no certainty that a jury will be able to render a unanimous verdict. There's no certainty that, even if there is a verdict, that the Court of Appeals will uphold that. So we are talking about the possibility of millions and millions of dollars, hours being spent on these matters. It would be wise for the plaintiffs, for the defendants, to look closely at the prospect of trying to resolve this case, given all else that's involved."

PREPARING FOR BATTLE

My counsel was hopeful that a settlement could be hammered out.

But if this trial was happening, my counsel was going to be ready. They'd been preparing for this moment since Tarla Makaeff called Amber Eck's law firm in 2010 seeking representation because she'd been ripped off.

With the settlement talks ongoing, my legal team participated in trial prep in November 2016—a chance to simulate the elements of the trial ahead of time and fine-tune the weak spots. J. R. Everett, John Brown, and Sonny Low, the named plaintiffs of the original Makaeff case, attended the trial prep. I participated remotely via phone. I was peppered with questions as if on the stand. The instructions were different now as a witness compared to the rules of a deposition. It was an opportunity to tell my story. If opposing counsel asked open-ended questions, I was instructed to take advantage of it and tell my story's details of how I was conned. How much time I spent trying to make it work and learning that much of the advice they gave was found to be not legal. Speak to the jury. Make eye contact. Make a connection to what you experienced. These instructions were contrary to that of my deposition. It was our turn to explain how we were promised a bill of goods and taken advantage.

We were ready for anything.

US AGAINST GOLIATH

Settlement talks began in earnest on November 16.

The sides met in Judge Miller's chambers, "Then he split us up for the rest of the day," Jason Forge said later. "The strange thing about this one, no numbers were disclosed to either side until we had a deal. We would explain the range we were looking for, they would do the same thing, but then not disclose to us."

The settlement talks centered on a number: $25,000,000, not counting legal fees. The settlement would wash away the upcoming trials, for which there were no guarantees that we would receive anything.

I had to agree on that amount because I wanted Trump's victims to be able to get at least half of their money back. That was the minimum I told Jason Forge I would accept. They'd be able to do that with a $25 million settlement. That was a lot more substantial than the hotel vouchers they'd proposed years earlier.

It wasn't everything. If I had my wish, the American public would have recognized the threat of a Donald Trump presidency before it was too late.

I couldn't begin to quantify the amount of time, effort, and energy I'd devoted to the case. I couldn't fix the marriages that dissolved or bring back the victims who'd died during the years we were fighting these cases.

And this was a fight—me and Tarla Makaeff and Sonny Low and J. R. Everett and John Brown—against Goliath, our counsel there every step of the way.

"I think we lucked out when he decided he was just going to settle because he could scam more as the president of the United States."

-SONNY LOW
LEAD PLAINTIFF IN LOW V. TRUMP UNIVERSITY CLASS ACTION LAWSUIT

We stood firm against one of the most powerful people on the planet. And for all of Trump's talk about winning, about never settling, he'd finally have to pay. It was the largest public settlement against Trump—EVER.

Yes.

Please.

Yes, let's get this thing settled.

I recall exactly where and when I received the call from Jason Forge that there was a $25 million settlement offer on the table. I was at my boys' school attending a parent-teacher conference. I saw Jason's name come up on the iPhone screen and told my wife I had to take the call and promptly walked out of the conference. It was a short but impactful conversation. Jason said he thought we had a settlement offer we could accept. Jason asked me if I would take a $25 million offer on behalf of the class. I wondered if the net amount after legal expenses would amount to at least 50 cents on the dollar. Jason reassured me it would, because his firm was going to waive all the fees and costs.

"We should get at least 70 or 80 cents on the dollar, depending on how many students filed for legitimate claims," he said. He said that this settlement would cover Sonny Low's case and mine, along with the lawsuit in New York.

Wow.

"Yes I will accept this settlement on behalf of all the thousands of students," I said.

I felt such a range of emotions to see a settlement being hammered, but more than anything, a weight had been lifted. I could get my life back again.

My optimism lasted for one day, until Jason Forge sent an email to the named plaintiffs.

"We are sorry to ramp up everyone's stress levels, but the settlement discussions have hit a significant snag," he wrote.

FLY IN THE OINTMENT

The snag was New York Attorney General Eric Schneiderman, who filed the state lawsuit against Trump University in 2013.

Schneiderman—who did not have a rep present at the November 16 settlement talks guided by Judge Miller—wanted injunctive relief in addition to the money to bar Trump and his ilk from ever running an educational program again.

My lawyers, and Trump's, were aligned in making the settlement financial only. That wasn't good enough for Schneiderman. The New York AG was, as Forge later told *The Wall Street Journal*, "a fly in the ointment."

And Schneiderman wouldn't budge. He wasn't listening to reason. For Schneiderman, it was still all about politics.

But my counsel wasn't going to let Schneiderman derail the settlement.

Trump's team felt the same way.

"Most of his companies are actually chartered not in Delaware or Florida, or someplace else, but in New York. In my view, what should have happened after that case is that all of his business licenses should have been revoked. That would have been justice because his record of fraud in that case was so egregious."

-TRISTAN SNELL, NEW YORK STATE ASSISTANT AG, 2011-2014

Daniel Petrocelli ended up calling Schneiderman and telling him that the lawyers from both sides were aligned on settling the two cases, Jason Forge told me. Schneiderman could waive his demand for injunctive relief and join in on the settlement, or the two sides would move on without him—and Schneiderman would be vilified for holding up a settlement for TrumpU's New York victims.

Fine. Schneiderman begrudgingly agreed to join in on the settlement he contributed to in no way other than slow it down.

And pretty much as soon as he did, his office put out a press release trumpeting the settlement:

In 2013, my office sued Donald Trump for swindling thousands of innocent Americans out of millions of dollars through a scheme known as

Trump University. Donald Trump fought us every step of the way, filing baseless charges and fruitless appeals and refusing to settle for even modest amounts of compensation for the victims of his phony university. Today, that all changes. Today's $25 million settlement agreement is a stunning reversal by Donald Trump and a major victory for the over 6,000 victims of his fraudulent university.

I am pleased that under the terms of this settlement, every victim will receive restitution and that Donald Trump will pay up to $1 million in penalties to the State of New York for violating state education laws. The victims of Trump University have waited years for today's result and I am pleased that their patience—and persistence—will be rewarded by this $25 million settlement.

The nerve . . . It wasn't easy finding common ground between Trump's team and Trump University victims, but the sides were aligned in their disdain for Schneiderman's antics.

SO MUCH WINNING

Trump—who previously vowed never to settle, guaranteed victory at trial, and called the lawsuits "nonsense"—tried to explain away his decision to settle the cases and fork over a bunch of money.

"I settled the Trump University lawsuit for a small fraction of the potential award because as President I have to focus on our country," he wrote on Twitter.

"The ONLY bad thing about winning the Presidency is that I did not have the time to go through a long but winning trial on Trump U. Too bad!"

Too bad.

> **"I wish that we had gotten not $25 million but $100 million from him. Yes, I got the money back for the class that I paid for, but I was paying $450 a month just in interest on three credit cards. And that was for how many years? Seven years? Eight years?"**
>
> -JOHN BROWN
> NAMED PLAINTIFF IN MAKAEFF/LOW CLASS ACTION LAWSUIT

As it stood, $21 million of the settlement was to be earmarked for the classes in my case and the Makaeff/Low case, and $4 million would go to New York victims and administrative fees. We had 30 days to hammer out the details of the settlement agreement and sign off.

My counsel also waived their legal fees to allow the victims to receive the maximum amount of money—a generous gesture. With legal fees included, Trump and The Trump Organization was on the hook for about $40 million.

Judge Curiel, who'd faced death threats because of Donald Trump's racist attacks, was relieved that a settlement was reached. "This does represent an important development, stage, day with respect to not just this litigation, but hopefully with respect to this country and beginning a healing process that this country very sorely needs," he said during a November 18 hearing. Hindsight being 20-20, Judge Curiel could have never been so wrong concerning the "healing process." But at the time, it was a sweet sentiment.

THANK YOU

I wrote my lawyers an email after the settlement was reached, trying to capture our years of effort in a few hundred words.

"My sincere thanks for all of your services the past 3+ years for me and over 6+ years on the cases themselves. Your firms deserve special accolades for agreeing to waive your attorney's fees in order to ensure a reasonable recovery for the thousands of students that were ripped off by Trump. No one could have foreseen when the suits were filed that we would be up against a President-elect and likely in court with a President! As you all know, I have had numerous experiences in various legal matters and have never experienced law firms willing to waive all its fees. Your press releases will shine favorable light on attorneys in general and certainly for both your firms," I wrote.

"I'm so happy that we were able to get such a fantastic result for so many people."

-AMBER ECK
HAEGGQUIST & ECK, LLP PARTNER AND TRIAL ATTORNEY

"The experience for me has been one of learning, albeit stressful at times," I continued, noting my family's relief that we could finally put this all behind us. "My grandkids might someday enjoy the story of how we sued and settled against a President Trump (hard to express how difficult that is to type, especially given my role as a California congressional delegate at the Democratic Convention in Philadelphia)."

I also noted the efforts of my fellow plaintiffs.

"I want to also thank Sonny, John and JR. Although we only met and spoke a few times, we all had a common goal and we achieved it on behalf of ourselves and the entire class of students we represented.

"I hope we someday get an opportunity to share a drink together to celebrate this victory. It was a long and hard-fought battle and the good guys won!"

THE FINE PRINT

The sides had 30 days to finalize the settlement, and the plaintiffs needed to sign off. The final settlement was due on December 19, and we were still kicking back and forth edits one day before the deadline.

A lot of the settlement was legalese, the who, what, when, where, and why of the settlement. I tried to read it as closely as I could. My years connected with the case gave me a better understanding of deciphering legal writing.

Under the terms of the settlement, Donald J. Trump needed to pay the settlement money by January 18, two days before he'd be inaugurated as the 45th U.S. president. The money would be placed in escrow until it was cleared to be distributed to Class Members. The sides were also barred from suing each other in the future. The agreement was public, which precluded any confidentiality terms.

Ironically, the Better Business Bureau of Metropolitan New York, the very organization that Trump had his lawyer bully years earlier in order to change Trump University's grade, was chosen to oversee the payouts.

I suggested adding explicit language barring Trump from suing any of the plaintiffs' "spouses, ex-spouses and related family members" in the future—I wanted to make sure Trump couldn't turn the legal system against our families or us as retribution.

I also wanted to ensure that Trump didn't have an escape hatch to avoid paying the money. What if he didn't have legal control over his assets? Between the lead plaintiffs, we worried if Trump would try to delay or defer payment or try to renege by transferring his business interests to his children.

But all in all, with some minor adjustments, the settlement looked fair.

So on December 19, 2016—7 years, 7 months, and 9 days after I attended a seminar because I wanted to make some money in real estate—maybe I could finally start to put this all behind me.

As 2016 came to a close, I exchanged text messages with Jason Forge wishing him a happy new year and thanking him for his efforts to bring justice. "It's been a long road," he wrote. "Your commitment and strength as a witness made a huge difference. I actually don't think the Low case would've settled without your case looming on the horizon."

CHAPTER 15

HOLDOUT

Donald Trump finally paid up.

No, it wasn't the day in court that I wished he would have endured.

No, it didn't disqualify him from getting elected.

But on January 17, 2017, three days before he placed his hand on a bible and swore to preserve, protect, and defend the Constitution of the United States as the 45th President of the United States, Donald Trump, and his Trump Entrepreneur Initiative made the $25 million Trump University settlement payment.

It felt like a weight was lifted off my shoulders.

However, the timing didn't give me a chance to celebrate, since the end of my personal battle against Trump coincided with the start of his presidency. During Trump's inaugural address, he presented a dark vision of America, warning of "the crime, and the gangs, and the drugs that have stolen too many lives and robbed our country of so much unrealized potential. This American carnage stops right here and stops right now."

ONE PERSON AGAINST THE REST

Thousands of people submitted claim forms seeking retribution.

While most of the claims were valid, some people submitted multiple claims, and other submissions were rejected because they involved seminars that weren't part of the class—for example, webinars or phone coaching, or events that happened outside of the country.

The deadline for objections to the settlement was March 6, 2017. Everything seemed to be headed toward a quick resolution.

As the big day approached, it all felt like a formality—like a wedding ceremony when the officiant asks the audience if anyone objects.

And you wait, and wait . . . .

At the last possible moment, someone spoke up and filed an objection, a fellow Trump University victim who'd tried to warn America of Trump's deceit: Sherri Simpson, who appeared in Political Action Committee ads during the 2016 presidential campaign.

Simpson—a Florida attorney who signed up for a Gold Elite Program in 2010, spending about $19,000—wanted to opt out of the settlement so she could sue Trump personally and face him in court.

As the plaintiff who *sued Donald Trump personally,* I understood her desire to hold Trump accountable, as well as the challenges. I'd spent years battling Trump, sat for two depositions, endured indescribable stress and anguish, and was called out by name by the eventual President of the United States, all to be able to secure a settlement for my fellow victims.

Given the uncertainty that comes with bringing a case to trial, as well as Trump's underhanded tactics and massive platform, the settlement was our best possible outcome. It represented the best possible outcome for Trump, too. He didn't want the Trump University saga hanging over his head anymore. He had a country to run.

It's fascinating when you fight like hell against someone in court then have to find common ground to reach a settlement—for that small window of time, you're aligned in this arrangement of convenience.

And that's where we were, in the spring of 2017, with Donald Trump's camp. We all wanted this situation to go away.

If the judge allowed Simpson's motion to proceed, it could dissolve the settlement agreement—wasting years of effort and denying Trump University's thousands of other student-victims the refund they were set to receive.

Her ploy was pure selfishness. And it worried the hell out of me.

REAL MONEY AT STAKE

Sherri Simpson was among the only Class Members who objected to the settlement on or before the March 6 deadline. Another, Harold Doe, wanted a better settlement (Doe's objection wasn't deemed procedurally valid).

A Texas activist, Leeland White, also filed paperwork hoping for the Department of Justice to investigate Trump, order the United States to hold a new election, "deny the settlement agreement and conduct a jury trial, unless the amount offered in settlement awards treble damages to the class action plaintiffs, totaling at least $120 million; and delay the presidential inauguration." Which was amusing to me but didn't go very far.

Simpson and Doe represented two out of a pool of thousands—3,730 Class Members, Attorneys General in states nationwide, even Donald Trump's attorneys were satisfied with the settlement.

The settlement wasn't perfect. But it was fair. In class action lawsuits, you'll often get a check in the mail for some ungodly low amount. Maybe it's $3.25 or $45 or $150, representing a fraction of the losses you hoped to recoup. There are too many members of the class and the damages are capped, and that's that.

With Trump University, everyone was slated to get about 90 percent of their money back. This was real money. Car money or house money or credit card bill money or retirement fund money. And she was OK depriving people of getting their money because she wanted to make a point.

Simpson had been in touch with my counsel dozens of times—she was one of the more involved Class Members.

She wished to sue Trump herself in 2010 or 2011, but she declined to do so after learning about Tarla Makaeff's class action lawsuit. She decided to become a class member and was satisfied with my counsel's efforts.

"I had a lot of communications with Sherri Simpson. I probably spoke with her dozens of times over the six or seven years since she first contacted us at the beginning of the case. Sherri was well-spoken, she was an attorney, and was very bright. She also had a really compelling story. We even talked at times about her serving as a plaintiff or trial witness in the case. So, we were extremely surprised when she filed an Objection to the settlement, asking to opt out. I believe that she, and many other people, felt strongly about not settling the case, and trying to force Donald Trump to stand trial. It was just very frustrating here, because we had negotiated such a great settlement for the class, and these Objections were delaying every class member from receiving their share of the settlement."

-AMBER ECK
HAEGGQUIST & ECK, LLP PARTNER AND TRIAL ATTORNEY

In November 2016, Simpson emailed our legal team and was informed that a settlement was in store. She did not respond further to the email exchange. She did not raise any objections or issues at that time. She did not voice displeasure in the settlement terms. She did not ask to be removed from the class.

In early 2017, she filed a claim to settlement proceeds without expressing any reservations.

An outside law firm was soliciting Trump University victims in February 2017, weeks ahead of the deadline for objections. Bob Guillo, who appeared with Simpson in anti-Trump advertisements, claimed that he received a phone call seeking to represent him but declined.

Seemingly out of nowhere, as the deadline approached, Sherri Simpson decided to object to the settlement.

TEN WORDS THAT CHANGED EVERYTHING

Simpson's objection dealt with the fine print in a notice sent to Class Members in 2015. That notice highlighted that Class Members had to "decide whether to stay in the classes or ask to be excluded before the trial, and you have to decide this now." By remaining a member of the class in 2015—which Simpson had—she seemingly agreed to waive her right to personally sue Donald Trump over Trump University in a separate lawsuit.

But in her objection, she focused on a paragraph that described what would happen if Class Members did nothing, and a settlement was reached:

*You don't have to do anything now if you want to keep the possibility of getting money or benefits from these lawsuits. By doing nothing, you are staying in one or both of the Classes. If you stay in and the Plaintiffs obtain money or benefits, either as a result of the trial or a settlement, you will be notified about how to obtain a share (**or how to ask to be excluded from any settlement**).*

Simpson expressed the belief, based on the wording in the 2015 class notice, that she would receive an additional opt-out notice after the settlement was reached allowing her to either stay in the class and receive a settlement, or withdraw from the class and sue Donald Trump herself.

The settlement agreement contained a different sentiment: "Because all individuals who did not opt out are deemed to be Class Members for all purposes, the Parties agree that no new opportunity to opt out will be provided as a part of this Settlement."

Ten words.

Ten words in a years-old class notice threatened to torpedo the settlement we'd spent half a decade trying to secure.

IN COURT WITH A CONSUMMATE PRO

A final approval hearing was held on March 30, 2017. I was in court that day, along with Sonny Low and a small army of our attorneys, including Jason Forge, Rachel Jensen, Amber Eck, Patrick Coughlin, Daniel Pfefferbaum, and Robert Prine. Daniel Petrocelli, Jill Martin and David Kirman were there on behalf of Trump. Also in attendance was Simpson's counsel, Gary Friedman and Ilann Maazel—the latter had represented Green Party candidate Jill Stein's recount efforts following the 2016 election. As if we had any doubt that this was all a political stunt.

The hearing was actually my first time face-to-face with Judge Curiel, since Judge Gallo usually handled the mandatory settlement conferences I attended.

I was struck by Judge Curiel's professionalism. He was commanding and smooth, tough but fair. After everything he'd been through, he still didn't tip his hand one way or another. Judges sometimes have this habit of talking down to people in their courtroom and admonishing them. Judge Curiel didn't need to do that. You wanted to give Judge Curiel your best. It made Trump's attacks against him all the more egregious. He wasn't the ogre Trump had made him out to be. Judge Curiel was simply very good at his job of upholding the law. And because of that, Trump tried to make his life a living hell.

WAITING TOO LONG

At the hearing, Judge Curiel outlined our journey so far—the battles waged, the clashes, the amount of work done on both sides.

"We know exactly what the other side is aiming to offer at trial, and we know what the Court was prepared to do with respect to admitting or excluding evidence," Judge Curiel said. "So to that extent, it is extraordinary in terms of the amount of work, the amount of institutional knowledge, that all of us would have about this case."

He called the settlement "fair" and "reasonable."

He shifted to Sherri Simpson's objection, going back and forth with Friedman, her attorney. Friedman explained Simpson's issues with the settlement. "She was unhappy that there was not a right to opt out. She had expected that she would have the right to opt out of any settlement," he said.

He also addressed the solicitations he'd made to Simpson and other Trump University student-victims. "In terms of me calling her, the idea that that violated some ethical rule is absolutely false," he said. Ethical violation or no, his legal ploy was threatening to unravel the settlement.

Patrick Coughlin, the attorney Jason Forge called "honey badger," was a welcome addition at the hearing as he addressed Simpson's desire to have it both ways. "What she is looking for is an apology, and you can't get that in litigation," Coughlin said.

The hearing represented a victory lap for my team—the outcome was all but certain. Jason Forge and Rachel Jensen looked effervescent as they faced the firing squad of TV cameras outside the courtroom. All of the attorneys were there, along with fellow plaintiff Sonny Low, who I had deep admiration for—I wanted this for Sonny. He was 75 years old and had $8,000 debt from Trump University that he was still paying off. Sonny and I stood to the side as the attorneys were peppered with questions. Jason, Rachel, and Patrick happily took the questions explaining to the press the importance of this win. We had reason to celebrate. We went to a local restaurant and enjoyed a few drinks, with toasting flying high. There was reason to be joyful.

I wanted the settlement in honor of Trump University victims like Boyce Chait, a longtime New Jersey business owner who served in the Navy and maintained quality affordable housing and spent 57 years married to the same woman and who died on January 28, 2017, before he could see a settlement.

There were too many Boyce Chaits. Too many people who'd waited too long.

One day after the hearing, Judge Curiel made official what we had anticipated: the settlement was granted. As for Simpson, he wrote, "That only one procedurally valid objection was filed, after 8,253 potential Class Members received notice of the Settlement and the opportunity to object, is indicative of the fairness, adequacy, and reasonableness of the Settlement."

MONEY FOR MY TROUBLE

Along with the settlement approval, the named plaintiffs, including myself, were granted class representative awards of $15,000, within the range of typical awards for class representatives on notable cases.

"As a gay man, I had been bullied for years . . . (this experience) reminded me of the bullying that takes place and the fears that surround that. It made me even stronger when it comes to supporting what I believe is right.

"If I was the only one left, I was going to face this guy in court and live my truth and let him know he's a liar and a conman.

"This helped me recognize how much stronger I've become as an adult. Now I can face people and not be afraid."

-JOHN BROWN
NAMED PLAINTIFF IN MAKAEFF/LOW CLASS ACTION LAWSUIT

During my deposition years earlier, I had gotten into hot water with my counsel for suggesting that I should be rewarded for my time—but now, the court was doing precisely that.

I was proud of my efforts. And my counsel's tireless commitment to the cause. And my fellow named plaintiffs.

We stood up to the most powerful man in America, and we didn't back down.

All we needed now was a final approval order.

And then . . . our joyful moment was crushed.

THE FINAL OBSTACLE

Sherri Simpson filed a notice of appeal to the 9th Circuit on May 1, 2017. Meaning the payouts would have to wait. Again.

Rachel Jensen didn't hold back in her criticisms of Simpson in a court filing weeks later.

"After enduring six-and-a-half years of hard-fought litigation, and a decade since some Class Members used their credit cards to purchase a Trump University Live Event, the only obstacle remaining in the way of Eligible Class Members recovering 90 cents on the dollar is Sherri Simpson's meritless appeal of this Court's order approving the Settlement," Jensen wrote. "Simpson's appeal is delaying Settlement payments to Class Members that they may need to get out of debt, replenish retirement funds, or confidently enter retirement. As the appeal may well take years to resolve, payments will be delayed too long for many Class Members who may declare bankruptcy, lose homes, a decline in health to the point where they cannot enjoy the money, or die before it is over."

My team pleaded with the Court of Appeals to speed up the matter. They also suggested that Simpson be required to post $220,000 bond to pursue her appeal (that request was denied).

We would have to wait until November—NOVEMBER!—for Sherri Simpson's appeal hearing.

In the months ahead of the hearing, Simpson brought on a new attorney: Deepak Gupta, a rising legal star who'd argued cases in front of the Supreme Court. Gupta represented a handful of anti-Trump clients. Now he was getting involved with the Trump University legal saga.

MANEUVERING THROUGH A MINEFIELD

I attended the Ninth Circuit Court of Appeals hearing on November 15, 2017, in Pasadena, which is in southern California, a short flight from San Jose. I've never been to an appeals hearing. I arrived early at the courthouse and got a chance to walk through the halls, noticing the elaborate court library and many photos of prior judges throughout the courthouse.

I felt a deep sense of importance and gravity as I walked into the courtroom where the hearing would be held.

The hearing involved three judges, not one. Hearings are tightly scheduled, and questions come in succession from any of the judges, an animated and free-flowing conversation that involves rapid-fire questions and cross-talk. The judges are liable to talk over answers and ask a question as you're answering what another judge asked—meaning Deepak Gupta would have to swivel as he maneuvered through the minefield of questions he'd face.

Early into the hearing, Judge Andrew Hurwitz, a purple bow tie peeking over the collar on his robe, highlighted the final line from Simpson's declaration filed on March 29: "If given the opportunity, I will opt out of the class actions and pursue individual litigation."

"Even when she filed those two documents with the court, neither of them said, 'and I opt out,'" Judge Hurwitz said.

"Let's be clear. What she's objecting to is a settlement that does something very unusual that the class action professors say they've never seen before," Gupta responded.

Judge Hurwitz took the early lead in trying to get to the heart of Simpson's wishes. "Let's assume you win. And we say the relief is your client may sue individually, is that what you're seeking?" he asked, gesturing with his hands.

"Yes," Gupta responded.

"Seeking to file one lawsuit on behalf of one person? Because nobody else asked to be excluded," Judge Hurwitz continued.

"We are objecting to the provision in the settlement."

"That's why I'm asking the question . . . do you want us to disapprove the settlement and put this back into litigation, even though you can see that the settlement is fair? Or do you want us simply to say . . . your client may bring an individual lawsuit against Trump University?"

The sides went back and forth trying to pinpoint Simpson's ultimate wishes.

"We are seeking the only thing we can seek, which is the reversal of the district court's order approving the settlement," Gupta said, unflappable as he answered question after question.

"So if we were simply to today say the settlement offer, the settlement order was approved, but we're excluding your client from it, that's not what you're seeking?" Judge Hurwitz asked.

"That is what we're seeking. I'm not sure you can—"

Judge Jacqueline Nguyen, sitting in the middle, jumped in. "Those are two separate remedies here, and I don't understand your answer to an important question," she said. "Let me clarify. Are you saying that if we were to say, 'settlement stays, your client is the only one who's out, she can go off and do whatever she wants with it,' that that's fine?"

"I think the problem with that is you would have to blue pencil the agreement. I mean, you'd have to cross out—"

"So that's not what you're asking."

"No, I mean, I wish we could ask for that . . . ."

"You're asking for us to send it back, unravel the settlement and send it back, right?"

"Yes. I mean, you have to disapprove the settlement because it has this provision."

There it was. Sherri Simpson wanted the settlement tossed so she could sue Donald Trump herself.

As Gupta's time wore down, Judge Hurwitz offered his perspective.

"Let me give you my big world problem with your position here," the judge said. "We have a settlement that you can see is fair, or at least don't argue is unfair. It looks like a heck of a good settlement, right? You got one person in the class of how many?"

"Uh, about 4,000, but we don't know how many people . . . ," Gupta said.

"No, we know nobody else. Nobody else spoke up later and said, 'gee, I thought I had the right to opt out again.' Nobody else objected to the settlement timely. There's one other objection, but it's not timely. And what you're asking us to do is to unravel a settlement that's fair for thousands of people because your client thinks she could have opted out of it again.

"Now, maybe we should do that. Maybe. But I have to tell you, when I think about this case in real-world terms, that's what troubles me."

'A LITTLE POLITICAL ASPECT'

Steven Hubachek from Robbins Geller Rudman & Dowd spoke next, representing me and my fellow victims. Attorney David Kirman followed on behalf of the defendant, the President of the United States. Mine and Trump's attorneys were aligned in our desire to end this charade.

A central focus for Trump settling the lawsuit was that Class Members would be barred from suing him again for Trump University matters. Judge Hurwitz wondered what might happen if Simpson were allowed to opt out of the settlement, like a handful of others previously had, knowing that she intended to sue Trump personally.

"Your Honor, this is a material term of the settlement. I don't think that we have a settlement if we add one more name to that list," Hubachek said.

"I'm just really asking if the two of you could sit down together, but I suppose they want more really in this case than just her right to sue," Judge Hurwitz said as a grin crept across his face.

"That's correct, Your Honor. There's a little political aspect, I believe," Hubachek said.

TEXTBOOK EXAMPLE

Kirman followed on behalf of Trump, calling Judge Curiel's efforts a "textbook example of a district court properly administering a settlement."

"So your client's view of Judge Curiel has changed," Judge Hurwitz said. *Wow.* You couldn't help but choke on your coffee when you heard that. The judge's response was full of so much venom, so much lingering bitterness and frustration for the way Donald Trump had attacked his fellow judge. I was glad Judge Hurwitz wasn't letting off Trump's camp easily.

Kirman let out a nervous giggle as he responded. "Your Honor, uh . . . yes, it's our position that Judge Curiel administered this settlement in a textbook fashion. In this court, there's three requirements in administering the settlement and the class. Number one, class notice with one opportunity to opt out; number two, an opportunity for the Class Members to object; and number three, a fairness hearing and approval by the court, and the district court complied with all three here."

Kirman was posed the same question about the possibility of letting Simpson opt out of the settlement—if the settlement could be preserved if Simpson were allowed to opt out.

"The answer to that, Your Honor, is no," Kirman said. "The only issue before the district court was whether or not to approve or deny the settlement. The district court did not have authority to rewrite the settlement. And I believe that same jurisdiction runs to this court and the opt-out provision was a material term to the settlement. And the defendant would not have proceeded with the settlement without those terms."

THE WAIT IS OVER

With the hearing complete, we waited for the appeals court to announce its decision.

Days turned to weeks.

Weeks turned to months.

The decision finally came on February 6, 2018. The Ninth Circuit rejected Simpson's objection and affirmed Judge Curiel's final approval order, clearing the way for the settlement money to FINALLY be dispersed. No more appeals or roadblocks.

> "I think Sherri Simpson and some other people just wanted to see Donald Trump go to trial and face these claims. But number one, I don't think that was going to happen with him as president-elect, and number two, it doesn't make sense to have him face trial with the risk that you may not prevail, and then instead of thousands of people recovering 90% of their losses, you have everyone getting nothing. That's a real risk. We were very glad when that ended and the proceeds could be distributed."
>
> AMBER ECK
> HAEGGQUIST & ECK, LLP PARTNER AND TRIAL ATTORNEY

In the end, Sherri Simpson's selfishness delayed Trump University's victims getting paid by about a year.

Half a decade after filing my lawsuit, I was happy for myself and other Trump University victims to finally start getting our money back. But I was still unsettled. I had something else I still had to do. I needed to get something off my chest. Or off my phone.

With Governor Gavin
Newsom @ DNC Convention in
Philadelphia, 2016

David Corn at Democratic
Convention, 2016

I met with San Francisco Mayor Ed
Lee @ Philadelphia's DNC
convention, 2016

With Philadelphia Mayor, Jim Kenney,
@DNC Convention, 2016

With Senator Boxer at DNC Convention
in Philadelphia, 2016

With Governor and former
presidential candidate, Howard
Dean, 2016

On the floor at DNC, 2016

Need to Impeach sticker attached to my wallet, 2017

With Congressmen Ro
Khanna @ Silicon Valley Democratic
Club Picnic event, 2019

With Congresswoman
Zoe Lofgren @ her offices in
Washington D.C., 2018

With Congressman Adam Schiff in
Milpitas, CA, 2019

With Congresswoman
Anna Eshoo, 2019

With 2020 Democratic Party candidate, Andrew Yang—first Asian American in a major political party running for President, 2019

With Senator Cory Booker in San Francisco, 2019

With Senator Elizabeth Warren in San Francisco, 2019

With CA Lieutenant Governor Eleni Kounalakis @ Silicon Valley Democratic Club Holiday Party, 2018

At the 9th Circuit Court of Appeals in
Pasadena, CA, 2017

Court room where appeal arguments
took place, 2017

Hallway to Courtroom 3 where appeals
hearing took place, 2017

9th Circuit Court of Appeals
in Pasadena, CA, 2017

Trump looks at photo of myself and Kerry Lucas. Doesn't recognize Lucas as a "mentor or professor of Trump University" during the deposition, 2015

During Trump's deposition, he puts on his reading glasses — rarely seen in public — to review documents my lawyer, Jason Forge, referenced. It explains why most of the time, he uses a Sharpie with giant written notes on the campaign trail — can't read without glasses, 2015

Trump continues talking with Petrocelli about Judge Curiel and complaining why he is personally sued — while bragging about how he had one of his attorneys threaten the BBB to change the Trump University rating from a D to an A, 2015

Attorneys Jason Forge, Rachel Jensen
and Patrick Coughlin (nicknamed
"Honeybadger"), 2017

Attorney Jason Forge talks with press
outside federal court building about
hearing to approve Trump University
Settlement, 2017

With core legal team, including Jason
Forge, Rachel Jensen, and Amber Eck, 2017

Attorney Patrick Coughlin talks
with press about hearing to
approve Trump University
Settlement, 2017

With core legal team and lead plaintiff, Sonny Low, 2017

With attorneys Rachel Jensen and Jason Forge following our
court hearing, 2017

CHAPTER 16

ILLEGITIMATE PRESIDENT

The waiting was tearing me apart inside.

I wanted to share my story and video about Donald Trump with the proper officials or authorities—maybe they could determine whether Trump broke the law (again) during his secret conversation. If that didn't go anywhere, I could always take my story to the media and try the matter in the court of public opinion, a familiar tactic of Trump's.

I needed to share what I'd seen with *someone.*

In the wake of the final approval order being affirmed in 2018, the first chunk of money was distributed to Trump University victims. But a second allocation needed to be made for the remaining funds.

Meaning more waiting . . . .

As I grew more and more impatient, so much happened. SO MUCH. Some of the details emerged in real-time. And some of it remained hidden for months or years, drips and drabs of deceit that, for me, all shared parallels with the Trump University legal saga and secret conversation.

I had hoped against hope that Trump would learn a lesson from Trump University, that he could find it within himself to be better or rise to the challenge of his new role. But after being elected, he only got more brazen. His blueprint had helped get him into the White House, and he was going to do everything he could to stay in power.

'THE BEST PEOPLE'

During his campaign, Trump often boasted that he'd hire "the best people" if elected—an empty promise that paralleled his suggestion that Trump University's instructors were "hand-picked experts" (when in fact, they turned out to be haphazardly selected amateurs).

Trump stocked his cabinet and administration with questionable figures who were generally unqualified for their significant responsibilities.

His son-in-law Jared Kushner, who wasn't good enough to get into Harvard without a hefty donation from his felonious father, was somehow tasked with solving all of the world's problems: addiction, criminal justice reform, Mideast peace, overhauling Veterans Affairs, trade negotiations . . . .

Kellyanne Conway, a longtime pollster who guided Trump's campaign, coined the term "alternative facts" days into Trump's presidency—Trump and his administration wasn't interested in sharing the truth, it was interested in sharing *the truth as Trump saw it, w*hich represented two very different things.

Neurosurgeon Ben Carson became head of Housing and Urban Development despite having no experience with housing or urban development. His office planned to spend $31,000 in taxpayer money for a new dining set (the expenditure was later canceled, and Carson was cleared of wrongdoing in a watchdog probe).

Betsy Devos—a Republican donor whose family is one of the richest in America—was put in charge of the Department of Education, despite having no demonstrable qualifications or experience for such a complex and important role.

The most dangerous choice—at least from a security standpoint—was retired Army Lieutenant General Michael Flynn as national security advisor. Flynn spent decades in the military but was pushed out by the Obama administration and started making inroads with foreign entities, specifically Turkey and Russia. In late 2015, he sat at Russian President Vladimir Putin's table and was paid $45,000 to deliver a speech at a banquet honoring state-run network RT.

Barack Obama specifically warned Trump about Flynn—he was compromised by foreign entities. But the warnings didn't deter Trump from making him one of the highest-ranking government officials. Flynn had given Trump credibility during the campaign, and Trump was going to repay the favor.

HALLS OF DECEPTION

On December 29, 2016, weeks before Trump was inaugurated, the outgoing Obama administration sanctioned Russia for its efforts to meddle in the election. The United States awaited a retaliatory response from Russian President Vladimir Putin.

But Putin was eerily quiet.

As it turned out, Flynn—who was not yet in his role as national security advisor—shared multiple phone conversations urging Russian diplomat Sergey Kislyak to get the Kremlin to avoid escalating the situation.

The phone calls themselves were not illegal. But when Flynn was asked by the FBI about the calls, he lied. And the FBI knew he lied.

I found it unlikely, given what I knew about Trump, that someone in his orbit would go rogue in making the overture to Russia. Flynn was working on behalf of *someone,* and all signs pointed to the possibility that Flynn made the calls, made the ask, and lied, on behalf of Trump.

People usually don't lie to the FBI if they have nothing to hide.

Flynn resigned from his position weeks into Trump's presidency on February 13, 2017. In the wake of the resignation, Trump said Flynn was "a wonderful man" who "was just doing his job."

PUTTING THE PUZZLE PIECES TOGETHER

As he entered office and early into his presidency, Trump spoke privately with FBI director James Comey, whose agency was investigating any possible ties between Russia and Trump's team. The FBI had also received an unconfirmed tip suggesting there may have been a recording involving Trump and prostitutes during a visit by Trump to Russia years earlier.

On a January 27, 2017 dinner with Trump, Comey wrote that it was "chaotic, with topics touched, left, then returned to later, making it very difficult to recount in a linear fashion"—the same thing I noticed with his hot-mic conversation in 2015.

"It really was conversation-as-jigsaw-puzzle in a way, with pieces picked up, then discarded, then returned to," Comey wrote.

During the conversation, Trump asked Comey about his future ambitions and told the FBI director that he needed loyalty. Comey responded that he'd always be honest with Trump.

Trump said he wanted "honest loyalty."

"You will get that from me," Comey said.

That need for "honest loyalty" came through one day after Flynn's resignation, when Trump found a way to meet again with Comey, clearing the room during an Oval Office gathering. "I hope you can see your way clear to letting this go, to letting Flynn go. He is a good guy. I hope you can let this go," Trump told Comey.

There was the ask—the request to make the investigation into Flynn go away. But Comey didn't follow through on that request.

During a congressional hearing about Russia in March 2017, Comey publicly confirmed an investigation into connections between the Trump campaign and Russia.

'THAT THING' . . . AGAIN

Trump grew increasingly perturbed, asking Comey during a March 30 phone call to "lift the cloud" of the Russia probe and tell the public that he wasn't being investigated.

On April 11, 2017, with the investigation intensifying, Trump called Comey a final time, asking again for Comey to "get out" that he wasn't being investigated—a request Comey had passed to Deputy Attorney General Rod Rosenstein (Trump's AG, Jeff Sessions, had been forced to recuse himself from all things Russia due to his own meetings in 2016 with the diplomat Sergey Kislyak).

"I have been very loyal to you, very loyal; we had that thing, you know," Trump told Comey.

There were those two words again: *that thing.* During his 2015 hot-mic conversation, "that thing" referred to whatever he wanted his attorney Daniel Petrocelli to confront Judge Curiel about, "Go in there and say that thing, about him."

The pattern was so obvious.

The wording was clear to Comey, too, who didn't feel the need to follow up with Trump to understand the meaning of "that thing." He knew Trump was referring to the loyalty pledge during their dinner months earlier.

"It didn't seem to me to be important for the conversation we were having to understand ('that thing')," Comey said during a June 8, 2017 Senate hearing. "I took it to be some . . . an effort to communicate to me that there is a relationship between us where I've been good to you, you should be good to me."

A NEW PROBLEM FOR TRUMP

Comey didn't follow through on *that thing* for Trump, and he was fired on May 8, 2017. Trump was legally allowed to remove Comey—Bill Clinton had done just the same to his FBI director in 1993—but the dismissal needed to be tied to poor performance, not to quash an investigation into Trump and his close colleagues. With Trump, it was always tricky to pin down his actual intent, primarily because of his use of coded language.

A few days after Comey's dismissal, in an interview with NBC's Lester Holt, Trump explained the real reasons why he sacked the FBI director.

"In fact, when I decided to just do it, I said to myself, I said, 'You know, this Russia thing with Trump and Russia is a made-up story, it's an excuse by the Democrats for having lost an election that they should've won,'" Trump told Holt.

Amid increasing pressure in the wake of Comey's firing, Rosenstein appointed lifelong lawman Robert Mueller, a former FBI director, as special counsel to oversee the Russia/Trump FBI investigation.

Maybe now—finally—Trump might be held accountable for something.

But I wasn't holding my breath.

For a while, Trump and his team didn't say much publicly about the Mueller investigation, and Trump refrained from making any personal statements about Mueller.

But that restraint would only last so long.

'THIS IS THE END OF MY PRESIDENCY'

Behind the scenes, Trump was unraveling like a spool of thread.

"Oh my God. This is terrible. This is the end of my presidency. I'm fucked," he said after his AG Jeff Sessions warned him that a special counsel had been appointed. He urged Sessions to "un-recuse" himself to steer the investigation away from Mueller.

Trump tried to undermine Mueller in his usual petty ways, claiming that the lawman had a conflict of interest due to an issue involving membership fees at a Trump golf course in Virginia—a counterbalance to his accusations that Judge Curiel was biased due to his Mexican heritage. There was always a reason why someone was "biased" against him whenever they were seeking the truth. For Trump, the truth getting out was the worst possible thing.

By June 2017, reports emerged that Trump was being investigated by Mueller for obstruction of justice for his attempts to bury the Russia investigation—the same type of charge that I felt could be applicable to his attacks against the court and Judge Curiel over the Trump University cases.

Trump took to Twitter on June 15, 2017 to criticize the investigation.

"They made-up a phony collusion with the Russians story, found zero proof, so now they go for obstruction of justice on the phony story. Nice," he wrote, perpetually casting himself as the victim.

MESSAGES SENT BUT NOT CARRIED OUT

But words didn't mean much without actions behind them.

As Mueller's investigation intensified, Trump asked White House counsel Don McGahn to contact Rod Rosenstein and have Rosenstein remove Mueller. "Mueller has to go," Trump told McGahn.

McGahn did not follow the command—he was worried it would spark a constitutional crisis.

Days later, Trump asked his former campaign manager Corey Lewandowski to share a message with Jeff Sessions. He wanted Sessions to disregard his recusal and come out with a statement undermining Mueller's investigation, suggesting that Trump was "being treated very unfairly" and that "he shouldn't have a special prosecutor/counsel" because "he hasn't done anything wrong." And he wanted Sessions to meet with Mueller to narrow the scope of the investigation.

Lewandowski never followed through on sharing that message with Sessions.

His requests to McGahn and Lewandowski mirrored his request to Daniel Petrocelli on December 10, 2015—he wanted them all to share a message on his behalf with the intent of ending investigations centered on him.

It didn't matter if McGahn, Lewandowski, or Petrocelli declined to carry out the ask on Trump's behalf. The crime of conspiracy to obstruct justice is centered on the request that clarifies one's intent or state of mind, not the successful implementation of the request itself.

CROOKED NUMBERS

Trump's rottenness didn't only apply to the Mueller investigation.

It also emerged after Hurricane Maria slammed Puerto Rico on September 20, 2017. The Category 4 storm made landfall with 155 mph winds.

The U.S. territory wasn't equipped to handle such a powerful storm, especially since it was still recovering from Hurricane Irma weeks earlier. Its power grid and water systems were already struggling before the storm struck . . . . Maria devastated towns, toppled buildings, and brought massive flooding, causing an estimated tens of billions of dollars' worth of damage and destroyed the island's power grid.

"I still feel a twinge of anger whenever I see him on the TV screen. (My anger) is still there. I don't know if it will ever be completely gone. He did some damage to me. I think he did damage to all of us. He lied to us, he took our money under false pretenses, he would not give it back, he bullied us or tried to bully us. He did all of the awful things that a terrible person would do to somebody else without any remorse."

-JOHN BROWN
NAMED PLAINTIFF IN MAKAEFF/LOW CLASS ACTION LAWSUIT

Despite reports and accounts of high death tolls, officials had confirmed sixteen deaths by the time Trump visited Puerto Rico on October 3, 2017, allowing him to take an unearned victory lap as he compared the premature death toll data to Hurricane Katrina, which had killed thousands of people after making landfall on Louisiana in 2005. "Sixteen versus literally thousands of people," he said during his trip to storm-ravaged Puerto Rico. "You can be very proud. Everybody around this table and everybody watching can really be very proud of what's taken place in Puerto Rico."

During the visit to the hurricane-devastated island, he threw rolls of paper towels to a crowd of survivors, shooting them with his fingers as though they were basketballs. To me, the paper towels were symbolic of the free rooms he had floated as a potential settlement to Trump University student-victims. They would serve little purpose amid a deluge of suffering.

The official death toll was increased to 34 the day after Trump's trip, but after it reached 64 by December, it wasn't updated. That number didn't take into account deaths that were indirectly connected to Maria, such as residents who died because they couldn't get access to medical care.

Even if unconfirmed data suggested the death toll was hundreds or thousands higher than the official count, the government's announced death toll allowed Trump to freeze and frame the tragedy in a way that was advantageous to him; the same way he paraded out stats about the 97% or 98% of TrumpU students who filled out surveys expressing their enthusiasm at the time they signed up for packages and never accounting for those students soon realizing they'd been ripped off.

He didn't care about actual devastation. He only wanted numbers that made him look good.

When the Hurricane Maria death toll in Puerto Rico was updated to 2,975 in August 2018, Trump was incredulous.

"3000 people did not die in the two hurricanes that hit Puerto Rico," he wrote on Twitter, suggesting the revised number was an effort by Democrats to make him look bad. Thousands of people were dead, and it was still all about him. It was always about him.

THE INVESTIGATION CIRCLES AROUND TRUMP

The first charges brought against Trump's aides due to Mueller's investigation had little or nothing to do directly with Trump.

George Papadopoulos, a foreign policy advisor on Trump's campaign, and Michael Flynn both pleaded guilty to lying to the FBI.

Campaign manager Paul Manafort pleaded guilty to foreign lobbying, bank fraud, and tax fraud charges. Deputy campaign manager Rick Gates,

Manafort's right-hand man, pleaded guilty to conspiracy and false statements charges.

By early 2018, nearly a year into Mueller's investigation, it all felt like a big letdown. Mueller's team hadn't uncovered direct ties between Russia's hacking of Hillary Clinton's emails, and the charges had loose connections at best to Trump.

But after a *New York Times* report that the probe was circling around Trump and his family, Trump went on a more direct attack against Mueller—a line he'd been urged not to cross.

"The Mueller probe should never have been started in that there was no collusion and there was no crime," Trump wrote on Twitter. He suggested Mueller's team consisted of "13 hardened Democrats, some big Crooked Hillary supporters, and Zero Republicans."

Things were finally heating up.

A RAID AND A RAT

April 9, 2018.

That's the day the investigation changed.

That's the day that FBI agents raided properties connected to Michael Cohen, Trump's longtime personal lawyer, seizing more than 4 million files.

Michael Cohen—again, no relation!—had dirt on Trump. He'd been his lawyer for more than a decade.

Initially, Trump was supportive of his longtime lawyer following the raid. But as it became increasingly clear that Cohen wasn't going to fall on his sword to save his longtime client, Cohen was suddenly a *rat* in Trump's eyes, someone who shouldn't be trusted.

ONE GANGSTER AND ANOTHER

Ahead of Paul Manafort's sentencing in August 2018, Trump made a series of overtures to jurors in the case to go easy on his friend.

He claimed Manafort was being treated worse than gangster Al Capone.

"Paul Manafort worked for Ronald Reagan, Bob Dole and many other highly prominent and respected political leaders. He worked for me for a very short time. Why didn't government tell me that he was under investigation. These old charges have nothing to do with Collusion—a Hoax!" he wrote on Twitter.

I was used to seeing him trying to taint a jury pool—let's not forget "the unleashing of forces" that made Judge Curiel admit he was "thinking about my jury" when he decided to delay the Trump University cases until after the election—but this was so shameless and blatant.

The President of the United States should not have been suggesting to jurors that his former campaign manager, convicted of hiding taxes from the U.S. government and failing to register as a foreign agent, should be treated kindly.

It later emerged that Trump had also been telegraphing messages to Manafort's attorney that Trump would protect Manafort if he stayed quiet.

THE CRIMES OF INDIVIDUAL-1

In August 2018, Trump's longtime fixer, Michael Cohen—who years earlier had paid off TrumpU victims and shaken down vendors—pleaded guilty to a range of charges, two of which related to the 2016 election.

Documents and audio recordings seized in the raids of Cohen's properties revealed that he'd orchestrated hush-money payouts with two women, Karen McDougal and Stephanie Clifford, the adult film star known as Stormy Daniels, after both were poised to come forward with allegations that they'd had sexual encounters with Trump.

The payments—$150,000 to McDougal, $130,000 to Clifford—were deemed violations of campaign finance laws because they were used to benefit Trump's campaign to keep the stories from being made public. Stories from McDougal and Clifford, much like Trump's fear of holding the Trump University trials before the election, centered on the reality that the truth could damage Trump's election chances.

In a December 2018 sentencing memo, Trump was referenced as "Individual-1." It was pretty easy who the Southern District of New York prosecutors were referring to when they wrote that Individual-1 "began an ultimately successful campaign for President of the United States."

For both payments, Cohen "acted in coordination with and at the direction of Individual-1," the prosecutors wrote. They also highlighted their concerns that Cohen—and by default, Trump—had undermined a core tenet of our democracy with "brazen violations of the election laws."

Cohen's commission of two campaign finance crimes on the eve of the 2016 election for President of the United States struck a blow to one of the core goals of the federal campaign finance laws: transparency. While many Americans who desired a particular outcome to the election knocked on doors, toiled at phone banks, or found any number of other legal ways to make their voices heard, Cohen sought to influence the election from the shadows. He did so by orchestrating secret and illegal payments to silence two women who otherwise would have made public their alleged extramarital affairs with Individual-1. In the process, Cohen deceived the voting public by hiding alleged facts that he believed would have had a substantial effect on the election.

The sentencing memo reflected the irrefutable truth that the now-president had committed crimes to enter office, something I believe also occurred in Trump's actions with Trump University.

His election win was tainted. Donald John Trump was an illegitimate president.

But did anybody care?

'HE SPEAKS IN CODE'

Before Michael Cohen reported to federal prison to begin serving a three-year sentence, he appeared before Congress on February 27, 2019 to discuss his former client.

"He doesn't give you questions, he doesn't give you orders. He speaks in code," Cohen said. "And I understand the code because I've been around him for decades."

I understood the code, too.

It was sad for me to see Trump's corruption coming to light. I wished I could have done more to stop this, stop him, expose the danger he represented . . . even as the final Trump University money was distributed in early 2019, I felt like there was more I could do.

TRUMP SKATES, AGAIN

Robert Mueller had the power to fix everything. Or so we thought.

Like Judge Curiel, he had the authority to take Trump to task.

Mueller's team uncovered numerous crimes connected to Trump's campaign team. But instead of charging Trump, Mueller punted, declining to make a "traditional prosecutorial judgment" because of a Department of Justice policy around charging a sitting president with a federal crime.

"If we had confidence after a thorough investigation of the facts that the President clearly did not commit obstruction of justice, we would so state," Mueller wrote in his report, released April 18, 2019. "Based on the facts and the applicable legal standards, however, we are unable to reach that judgment. Accordingly, while this report does not conclude that the President committed a crime, it also does not *exonerate* him."

Trump skated again.

There was always something. He couldn't be held accountable because he was too busy, because he was running for president, because he was elected president, because he had become president . . . .

He was now insulated from prosecution because he was President of the United States. Which was absurd, especially when you consider that the crimes required to get into the White House made him an illegitimate president.

To summarize: you could commit crimes to win the election; then as president, you could avoid prosecution because you're effectively above the law. Got it.

I was beyond disappointed, but with the final Trump University settlement money distributed, nothing was holding me back from telling *my* story, nothing the court could undo, nothing that was keeping me silent.

I couldn't fully hold Trump accountable by suing him—and as president he had managed to effectively become above the law. But maybe I could take action in a different capacity.

CHAPTER 17

THE WHISTLEBLOWER

I felt like a spy, a spook.

I was sitting on top-secret evidence that I believed showed the President of the United States attempting to obstruct justice and undermine the rule of law.

I'd been holding onto the video clips from Donald Trump's 2015 deposition silently for more than three years out of deference to Trump University's thousands of victims. But within weeks of the final settlement funds being released in January 2019, I was ready to share my secrets.

I didn't reach that decision lightly. I worried that I'd be putting my family and me in danger, or that I'd face a wave of death threats like Judge Curiel had for coming forward. I worried that the President of the United States would weaponize the legal and criminal justice systems against me.

But I couldn't stay silent any longer and still look at myself in the mirror. I feared our country's future was at stake. There was a danger lurking in the White House.

Exposing my information could come through political, legal, or media channels, and due to my emerging political connections, I decided to pursue that channel first. I'd end up crossing paths with some of the country's most influential Democrats—many who had their interest in holding Trump accountable or taking him down. One of those connections, Congressman Ro Khanna, endorsed me for a leadership role.

HAIL TO THE CHIEF

I was president now—the president of the Silicon Valley Democratic Club, that is. I wound up getting more deeply involved in the San Jose-area political scene through my business connections and *unexpected* role in national politics, and I was elected to serve as club president for 2019.

The role presented a curious duality for me. Various representatives and local leaders would speak at our general meetings, and the position allowed me access to a *Who's Who* of prominent Democrats. Throughout 2018 and 2019, I attended a speech by former Senator and Vice President Joe Biden and posed for selfies with Cory Booker and Elizabeth Warren, Andrew Yang and Tulsi Gabbard—all presidential hopefuls—and California Gov. Gavin Newsom.

I also snapped a photo with U.S. Rep. Adam Schiff at a California Democratic Party Conference held in San Francisco. He was sharp and affable and would soon become a significant figure in the fight against Donald Trump.

Since I hadn't tried to attract extra attention during my long legal battle with Trump, and since my name was relatively common, the reputation hadn't fully followed me. Did they know they were standing next to the guy who sued Trump?

The guy who had secret video footage of Trump!

I made a point not to use my platform with the club for my interests, but I also didn't hold back when opportunities to open up presented themselves. And they did.

A FAMILIAR FACE

I connected with the office of Ro Khanna—a U.S. Rep for California, representing the 17th congressional district in the San Jose Bay area—on February 4, 2019, a few weeks before Khanna would be named a national co-chair of Bernie Sanders's 2020 presidential campaign.

I was proud Khanna was getting national recognition. I first met Khanna at a lunch arranged by one of his campaign managers in 2014, when he was interested in advertising at my theater and getting my support as a local businessman.

At the time, Ro was running against longtime incumbent Mike Honda. During my first meeting with Khanna, I was impressed with his progressive ideas, and was especially interested in education. He was also from my old stomping grounds of Philadelphia and had a background in IP law, so our conversation was effortless. While he lost in 2014, he won the second time around in 2016 and hasn't looked back.

Khanna's office connected me with Tom Steyer, a California billionaire who had launched the Need to Impeach campaign—his own effort to bring down Trump that, as it turned out, could have been called Need to Impeach Twice.

I met with two Need to Impeach reps in a conference room. I signed an NDA regarding the matter we discussed, so I'll only state that the conversation related to the existence of potential impeachable material. They gave me a sticker that ended up getting stuck to my wallet, and there it stayed for years.

I was later informed by Need to Impeach personnel that they didn't think my material was useful for their purposes. Steyer was gearing up for a presidential run, anyway—preparing to enter an overcrowded Democratic field.

Without any progress from Need to Impeach, I wound up meeting with U.S. Rep. Zoe Lofgren, who represents California District 19, where I currently reside.

Lofgren is razor-sharp—she's had a hand in every impeachment proceeding of the modern era (she was a staffer to a House Judiciary Committee member when articles of impeachment were prepared against Richard Nixon in 1974 before later becoming a House member herself).

I met with Rep. Lofgren on April 15, 2019, and told her my story about Donald Trump. Lofgren listened intently, then directed me to Daniel

Noble, Senior Investigative Counsel of the House Permanent Select Committee on Intelligence, chaired by Schiff.

Noble got in touch with me. He was interested in seeing the video. But I still grappled with the best way to share the footage. I didn't trust sending it through the mail—what if the package was intercepted?

Maybe Mr. Cohen could go to Washington?

A FIELD FULL OF CRICKETS

Kamala Harris encountered glass ceilings, and she didn't smash through them—breaking glass is messy and dangerous, sending glass shards raining down. Instead, she showed off her resourcefulness by using glass-cutting tools.

The Oakland native spent her life cutting and climbing through glass ceilings. The daughter of an Indian biologist mother and Jamaican professor father, Harris rose to become District Attorney of San Francisco, then California's attorney general, before getting elected to the U.S. Senate in 2016.

Given her criminal justice background, I thought Harris might be interested in learning about Trump's hot-mic moment.

I reached out to her office in San Francisco. On July 16, 2019, I met with two members of her team, field representative Obi Rambo and district director Adam Mehis, who thought the matter was important and attempted to reach out to the regional director for California.

"These kinds of things don't come to our office very often," Mehis told me.

But Harris was prepping her tools to cut through another glass ceiling—by 2019, she was running for president. And unfortunately, after multiple calls and follow-up efforts, I wasn't able to secure a meeting with the woman who would become our country's first female vice president.

At the same time I was scheduling a meeting with Harris's staff, I also reached out to Rep. Anna Eshoo, an influential congresswoman who represented a fair number of members of the Silicon Valley Democratic Club living and working in her California District 18. She also happened to be a personal friend of House Speaker Nancy Pelosi.

My request to meet was greeted with enthusiasm and scheduled for July 17, 2019, one day after my conference with Harris's district director. My meeting with Eshoo included her chief of staff, Karen Chapman, who took copious notes. I explained what information I had and how it might help the House Judiciary Committee headed by Rep. Jerrold Nadler of New York. At this time, the committee was focused on the recently completed Mueller Report that detailed various examples of Trump's obstruction of justice. I believed that Trump's statements during the 2015 hot-mic conversation, paired with the Mueller findings, would be helpful in establishing a pattern of his legal intent. Trump's default was to undermine the rule of law, whether the matter involved a scam institution or Russia's election meddling.

Eshoo—who was incredibly busy, and only going to get busier—along with her chief of staff gave me a full hour, which was incredibly gracious. She genuinely cared about what I discussed and recognized its urgency and brought my information to Nadler's office.

Those efforts were consistent with the actions she took one year earlier after meeting with Palo Alto University professor Chrstine Blasey Ford, who alleged that she was sexually assaulted during the early 1980s by Supreme Court nominee Brett Kavanaugh (Kavanaugh denied the accusations). Eshoo told the professor she believed her and delivered a letter from Blasey Ford to Sen. Dianne Feinstein, the Senate Judiciary Committee's ranking Democrat.

But after Eshoo tried to connect me with Nadler's office . . . crickets.

The field of crickets was making my skin crawl.

So, I decided to try a different approach.

'FOR THE SAKE OF OUR COUNTRY'

I sent a message to the California Department of Justice on July 29, 2019, alerting authorities to my belief that Trump's hot-mic moment—when he suggested his attorney approach Judge Curiel and discuss "that thing about him"—amounted to a crime.

"Trump's actions demonstrated his intent to persuade the court by plotting to threaten a federal judge to remove or delay the trial: an act that led to obstructing justice," I wrote. "Trump's corrupt intent was manifested during the conversation because of his body language and speech. His overt act of threatening the judge in May 2016 at a public event in San Diego, CA precipitated death threats to the judge."

I remained worried about the blowback.

"I do have serious concerns discussing and disclosing this matter with you because of potential legal, financial and physical security to myself and my family," I wrote. "Trump's history shows that when attacked he initiates lawsuits and hate speech that many of his followers react in a violent and malicious manner.

"I now recognize that I must publicly expose this information for the sake of our country and its history, however, I would like to do it in a manner that has the support of the legal authorities that are not directly influenced by the Department of Justice headed by William Barr because of AG Barr's demonstrated bias to protect Trump," I wrote, in the first of what would become many episodes of correspondence with the California DOJ. My report was forwarded to the office's Fraud and Special Prosecutions Section, which investigates complex criminal cases related to financial, securities, and environmental fraud, as well as public corruption, tax fraud, and other crimes. I felt my concerns were with the right department. The report was assigned a Public Inquiry Unit, or PIU, number, 8-4-6-4-9-4.

Evidently, my concerns about *the sake of our country* were prescient. Four days before I reported Trump to the California DOJ for speaking in code and attempting to influence an investigation, he was on the phone with Ukraine's president . . . speaking in code and trying to influence an

222

investigation, dangling continued aid and a White House visit if Volodymyr Zelensky announced a criminal probe into Biden and his son Hunter, who served on the board of the natural gas company Burisma Holdings. As the leaders discussed United States aid to Ukraine, Trump shifted the conversation. "I would like you to do us a favor though . . . ," he said.

An Army lieutenant colonel named Alexander Vindman was listening to the conversation. Similar to my dread years earlier while watching Trump's hot-mic moment, Vindman immediately knew something wasn't right.

The Purple Heart recipient felt the need to notify the National Security Council's lead counsel that the call was "improper." In reporting what he'd witnessed and later testifying about it, Vindman put everything on the line—his career, his reputation, his safety.

Silence wasn't an option. Silence was complicity.

RAY OF HOPE

I crossed paths again with Adam Schiff at a conference held in Milpitas, California on August 28, 2019. By that point, the I-word—impeachment—was becoming a lot more prevalent involving Trump. Schiff urged patience that any articles of impeachment against Trump could be delayed before sending them to the Senate.

"Trump has no ideology apart from himself. It's why he vacillates on things five times a day. It doesn't matter what's good for the country. It doesn't matter what's good for the Republican party. What matters is what's good for Donald Trump," Schiff told the audience.

I had a few brief one-on-one moments with Schiff—first to take a quick photo together—then I followed him as he was departing the conference walking out to his car. It gave me a chance to ask a few questions without others crowding around us. During that brief walk from the conference room to the parking lot, I asked him if the impeachment's timing was considered. I expressed how the impeachment could impact Trump's re-election if it happened closer to the election date. He responded that they were researching when impeachment articles had to be delivered to the Senate.

When he said this, it was as if a light bulb flickered brightly. Impeachment could happen earlier or later, but the timing of articles being delivered to the Senate was being considered for ultimate impact. Brilliant strategy, I thought at the time. He had not mentioned this during his public talk that day, nor did the questions to him allow him to address this critical subject matter. While my moments with Rep. Schiff were brief, I also let him know of my role as lead plaintiff in the Trump University litigation, and he directed me to contact his office. I ended up sharing my report that I had sent to the California DOJ. The report, which mentioned the existence of the hot-mic video, was promptly forwarded to Daniel Noble with the House Intelligence Committee in Washington, DC.

"I've reviewed, and as we discussed, we would be interested in reviewing the audio and video of the deposition," Noble wrote. "If you'd like to send a copy to the Committee, the best way would be a thumb drive. I can give you our mailing address if that's doable."

We ended up having a phone conversation. Noble was interested in learning more about my hot-mic video.

"Was this a video within a video?" he asked.

I explained how I acquired the video footage, and we discussed how I might get the video in his hands, including my traveling to Washington. Still, Noble preferred an electronic transfer, if possible. I worried that it might not be the most secure method.

"I don't know if there is a way we can set up an electronic link so we can just view it? We could commit that we wouldn't take it, keep it or use it without your permission," he said.

Noble also worried that the video might not be the right fit for the House Intelligence Committee, which was focusing more and more on Trump's handling of Ukraine.

"We don't know if this deposition excerpt is up our alley," he said. "The Judiciary Committee might be more interested."

Luckily, I had already been trying to connect with the House Judiciary Committee through Rep. Anna Eshoo's office. I hoped to set up a meeting in Washington with both the intelligence and judiciary committees to review the video.

"I think that makes sense . . . we could probably coordinate that," Noble told me.

For the first time in a while, I felt a sense of hope that I may have finally found an outlet to get this information into the right hands.

Noble suggested I could bring a laptop featuring the footage and simply press "play."

All I had to do was wait for that all-important email from the Judiciary Committee.

I was assured from Eshoo's staff that it was forthcoming . . . .

THE SYSTEM FAILS, AGAIN

But that communication never came.

The House Judiciary Committee was busy conducting an impeachment inquiry into Trump. The inquiry started earlier in the year following the end of special counsel Robert Mueller's investigation and subsequent report into the 2016 election meddling, and the inquiry widened to include the July 25 call with Ukraine's president.

Basically a catch-all of Trump's worst acts.

Since Mueller's team uncovered clear evidence that Trump had obstructed justice in office—a pattern that overlapped with his hot-mic conversation that I witnessed—I hoped obstruction would represent one of the articles of impeachment.

If they pursued that avenue, my video could be helpful to them in helping to showcase the pattern.

But without the Judiciary Committee responding to me, I was stuck in a holding pattern.

I reached back out to Noble in an email on December 12, 2019, to underscore my desire to get him the video in the most confidential manner possible—I believed that to be in person. He wrote me back suggesting I make a submission in writing and mail a thumb drive or DVD of the video.

Welp. I still didn't feel comfortable sending this footage through the mail, but what other option did I have? I moved copies of the video files onto a thumb drive, put the thumb drive into a FedEx package, and tracked its journey to Washington. The package arrived at the Capitol on Dec. 17, 2019.

I called Noble and left him a message with a passcode to the thumb drive so his team could access the video files. The following day, the House voted to impeach the president for only the third time in United States history.

On Jan. 10, 2020, as the impeachment proceedings were set to begin, I reached back out to Noble, hoping to hear an update. "Mr. Cohen, I've been tied up with impeachment-related matters. I'll be in touch when I free up," he wrote.

My video had been pushed aside, again.

It was a recurring theme for Trump—people focused on the last, worst thing he did and tended to forget all of the other stuff before it. But he was running the same scams and schemes, the same plays and ploys, over and over and over and over.

The Republican-led Senate didn't take the impeachment hearings seriously and voted against his removal, another missed opportunity to hold Trump accountable.

Another example of the system failing.

Despite the outcome, Schiff and Lofgren were masterful as House managers. Schiff outlined the latest case against Trump in a chilling opening address, warning of Trump's "attempt to use the powers of the presidency to cheat in an election.

"For precisely this reason, the President's misconduct cannot be decided at the ballot box—for we cannot be assured that the vote will be fairly won," he said. "In corruptly using his office to gain a political advantage, in abusing the powers of that office in such a way as to jeopardize our national security and the integrity of our elections, in obstructing the investigation into his own wrongdoing, the President has shown that he believes that he is above the law and scornful of constraint."

Schiff ended his address by quoting a line from John F. Kennedy's inaugural address in 1961: "a good conscience our only sure reward." By 2020, I still hadn't been rewarded with a clear conscience because my efforts to expose Trump's hot-mic conversation had failed. Politicians kept punting. I had no idea if the California DOJ was taking my report seriously. Even with the obstacles and hang-ups, I had to get my video released ahead of the 2020 election. Voters had to see the version of Trump that I saw.

I had to share my footage somehow.

During one of my conversations, someone—I think it was Noble— suggested a more direct route to releasing the video since the political and legal channels I tried weren't panning out.

"Maybe this is something you talk to the press about," he said.

CHAPTER 18

ON THE RECORD

For a long time, I was guided by three words: Off the record.

I wasn't comfortable talking to the media while the Trump University case was ongoing. And after the case was resolved, I still didn't feel comfortable speaking to the press, either.

Having a direct view of how Trump-related publicity impacted Judge Curiel and Tarla Makaeff only strengthened those feelings. Coming forward would open me up to criticism and attacks, maybe even death threats. I also had a family to protect. I didn't want Trump to destroy my life. He was the president now, not just a shambolic real estate developer.

I fielded interview requests from time to time, but I kept my communications O-T-R. Which meant as long as I maintained my public silence, anything I said couldn't be quoted or reported directly. Off the record represented a cloak of invisibility, a safe step into getting comfortable with the idea of someday coming forward. It's similar, in a way, to opening up to a therapist or speaking to a priest in confession. Your secrets are supposed to be safe.

Off the record.

That's how I framed my emails in June 2019 with Kimberly Arp-Babbit, a CNN producer who was working on a piece about Donald Trump and Trump University. We shared some messages and scheduled time to talk, but she was busy, and life got in the way for me.

I still had hope that the complaint I filed with the California DOJ might turn into something, but any time I called or emailed about it, I'd get a blanket response that offered me no clues into the status of the matter.

But somehow, someway, I was going to take my story public ahead of the 2020 election. The ramifications of coming forward paled compared to the lifelong guilt I would harbor at not doing anything to inform others of the danger in the White House. My father fought against Nazi Germany in World War II. My staying silent would mean I was complicit in enabling a wannabe autocrat to run the United States.

By staying silent, I would be taking the freedoms that my father and so many others fought for and allowing them to lapse due to personal concerns. And that wasn't an option.

THE WRITE MOVES

Maybe I could write a book?

I had so much to tell, so much to say. A 60,000-word book would allow me to document everything. To tell my whole story to a depth that couldn't be found in a 3:00 TV package or 900-word newspaper article.

I started chipping away at writing a manuscript . . . which is a lot of work! And time-consuming. A wave of Trump-themed books kept popping up from his former aides, former employees, and relatives. One bestseller was even written by an unidentified government official who went by Anonymous. At the time, I thought I might call my book *Trumpbuster*. Or maybe *Cheater-in-Chief*.

As the Cheater-in-Chief's third year in office was coming to a close, I began shopping a book proposal—a document outlining the book's aims and structure, as well as my background and platform—to different literary agents, hoping they'd be interested to sign me as a client and connect the project with a publisher. In the mainstream publishing world, agents pitch book proposals to publishers, who then take on the project and guide it to publication.

It's a strange process.

All I needed was someone to say yes. But while I got some nibbles, the overriding response was: no thanks. Some of the responses I received:

- "Thank you, but this doesn't sound right for me."

- "We appreciate the fact that all Trump material is attractive, however, the amount of material currently is very large and growing larger."

- "Honestly, I think this material is more suited to an article than to a book. These events have been widely covered."

- "While I realize that you have a unique perspective, I am not sure that sufficient readers would pay $30 to read your perspective. Also, by the time the book is sold, finalized, edit, printed, and distributed, these events will be some years old, and Trump may be a thing of the past. I am sorry not to be more optimistic, but I want to be honest with you. Hope you understand."

I was also informed that similar projects "got multiple passes from top NY editors who: 1) didn't want to touch a Trump book; 2) passed for lack of a well-established national platform to reach a broad audience; 3) Trump exhaustion; 4) market saturation, etc., I still worry that we would have similar results, and, for these reasons, I will VERY respectfully step aside."

The rejections and indifference were demoralizing. Did my ordeal, and the president's possible crimes, not matter?

As the rejections piled up and days turned to weeks and months without an agent signing me, the opportunity to get a book out before Election Day grew dim.

Which meant to share my story, I'd need to pursue the option I'd been avoiding. I'd need to go from "off the record" to "on the record."

A DEAD END

My story needed to wind up in the right hands.

I thought Rachel Maddow—the sharp, witty, cerebral MSNBC host—would do an excellent job explaining the winding Trump University saga, so I emailed her team on January 20, 2020.

"I have witnessed Donald Trump boasting extortion of the BBB and obstructing justice by plotting to threaten the judge in the Trump University trial. And I have evidence. I would like you to report it. This is evidence of Trump's corrupt intent to extort a federal judge to get what he wants.

"As the 2020 election approaches, voters deserve to know the true story about the case that could have derailed Donald Trump's candidacy and exposed details of his long-hidden financial information," I wrote.

"There is little doubt to Trump's corrupt intentions. Its consequential impact to U.S. history should be reported."

I thought my email was powerful, but I didn't get a response.

TRUMP'S AMERICA

A big part of my problem—again—was Donald Trump.

As I struggled to bring my Trump University story forward, Trump was doing his best to entangle himself in new scandals. It was challenging to look back when fires were still raging.

After the Republican-led Senate failed to remove Trump in his impeachment trial in early 2020, Trump pretty much had carte blanche to do as he wished—the one body with authority to hold him accountable decided to give him a free pass.

Trump was effectively above the law. Our system of checks and balances had buckled.

Which was so scary for me. I recognized Donald Trump's impulses and corrupt intent. He wasn't going to play nice or use his power to push through needed reforms. He was going to do everything to consolidate his power, no matter the cost.

Our country's democracy, and its future, were at stake.

A reflection of that truth came in February 2020, when Trump's henchman Roger Stone—a dirty trickster whose ties to Trump date to the early 1980s—was getting sentenced after being found guilty of perjury and obstructing the investigation *into Trump's campaign.* Stone had a direct line to Trump and was known to call Trump personally.

Had Stone told the truth to investigators and Congress, he wouldn't have been in any personal trouble. But he repeatedly lied, as though he were trying to protect someone. Like with Michael Flynn, it's not too hard to imagine who Stone was lying for.

Stone was being sentenced by Judge Amy Berman Jackson of the U.S. District Court for the District of Columbia. Like Judge Curiel, who presided over the Trump University cases, Judge Jackson was an Obama appointee who'd garnered widespread support from both sides of the aisle. She was approved by a 97-0 count. A fair, seasoned, impartial jurist.

And *for some reason,* just like with Judge Curiel, Trump couldn't stop publicly criticizing Judge Jackson or suggesting that the jury forewoman was politically biased.

In sentencing Stone to 40 months in prison, Judge Jackson declined to bow to public pressure or meddling from Trump and his toady AG, Bill Barr. "He was not prosecuted, as some have claimed, for standing up for the president," she said of Stone. "He was prosecuted for covering up for the president."

This was Trump's America. Crime for his benefit was encouraged, loyalty was demanded, and he ultimately didn't care what happened to you as long as it helped him.

TRAGIC INACTION

News of a mysterious illness started emerging out of China in late 2019, right around the time Congress should have been holding Trump accountable.

An airborne virus that spread invisibly, person to person, was making it hard for people to breathe. Some people got it and didn't even realize their symptoms were so mild. Others were dead within days.

It crossed from one country to another. Italy and the United Kingdom were hit hard. New Zealand and South Korea kept it in check.

It was inevitably going to reach the United States.

But under Donald Trump, the federal government failed to take any real action to combat the COVID-19 pandemic. Testing lagged. People started to die, and hospitals became overwhelmed, and states were struggling— sometimes against each other—to secure resources.

Instead of addressing the issue, Trump worried about putting a spin on the numbers, the same way he'd focused on Trump University approval questionnaires or the death toll for Hurricane Maria soon after the storm slammed Puerto Rico.

The virus would magically go away, he suggested numerous times.

But it didn't go away.

SHUTDOWNS AND SADNESS

Against the backdrop of COVID-19, I was trying to get someone— anyone—to take my story seriously.

I connected with Jesse Wegman, a *New York Times* editorial board member and the author of the book *Let the People Pick the President,* which outlines the case for abolishing the Electoral College (the system that allowed Trump to become president after losing the popular vote to Hillary Clinton in 2016). Jesse was scheduled to attend a book signing in Menlo Park, California, on March 27, 2020, and we exchanged a few emails. I was excited to meet Jesse. I was hoping he could connect me with someone. Maybe he knew an agent or publisher who might be interested in my book.

But the week before Jesse's scheduled appearance, the country shut down. Everything was canceled. Life as we knew it wouldn't be the same.

SUNLIGHT, BLEACH, AND INDIFFERENCE

The pandemic made me angry and sad and scared.

The death toll in the United States kept climbing, higher and higher and higher, surpassing the losses from major wars. Under Trump's watch, by April 2020 during my first pandemic birthday, we were losing more than 2,000 Americans to COVID-19 every *day*. By the end of May, the U.S. death toll totaled more than 100,000—that's roughly the population of Temecula, California, or the crowd at a major college football game.

We were experiencing the death toll of the Sept. 11, 2001 attacks every few days. And many of the victims were dying alone, their relatives unable to visit the hospital and say a proper goodbye out of fear that COVID-19 would spread further.

It's one thing for a president to make a mistake, but at a basic level, you want them to *care*. I didn't agree with many of George W. Bush's policies and decisions in office, and the wars in the Middle East have had so many lingering consequences, but I never doubted that he carried an emotional burden for sending American troops to their deaths.

I worried about my health. Given my Type 1 Diabetes—considered a "pre-existing condition"—I was at a heightened risk of facing severe side effects from COVID-19. So whenever I went outside, I wore a mask over my mouth and nose, and I washed my hands as soon as I got home.

Those measures amounted to simple but essential steps to ensuring my health and the health of those I came in contact with.

A national mask mandate or support from the president could have saved many lives. But Trump failed to endorse masks and declined to wear one in public. Instead, he spouted fantastical cures that turned out to be pure bunk, such as the anti-malaria drug hydroxychloroquine, or wondered if sunlight and injecting disinfectants could help.

Breathing through a mask whenever I went out in public, feeling disconnected from the people in my life, seeing my routines and social constructs uprooted, I blamed Trump for all of it. And it cemented my need to come forward. **Now.** Lives were hanging in the balance especially if he won again in November.

SENDING A SIGNAL

I was introduced to the encrypted messaging app Signal while working on some IP matters.

It was a lot more secure than regular emails or text messages, which could be intercepted. Most notably, you could set a timer for messages to disappear after a certain amount of time had passed.

So when I started pursuing different media outlets to tell my story in June 2020, I decided to give Rachel Maddow another chance. I had no idea if the email I sent months earlier had been read. I assumed their general submission inbox was flooded with news tips like mine.

This time around, I decided I'd send a news tip through Signal. I felt like there was a higher likelihood it would be seen, and that I'd get a response. I also sharpened my message to focus on the most important details. If they only responded to a handful of messages each day, I wanted to make sure that mine was one of them.

SUBJECT: TRUMP DEPOSITION HOT-MIC VIDEO

Hello,

I have the video from Donald Trump's Dec. 10, 2015, deposition in the Trump University case—it's never been released to the public—and it contains a startling surprise: a never-reported <u>14-minute hot-mic conversation between Trump and his attorney, Daniel Petrocelli that was not included in the court transcript.</u> During that conversation, Trump:

- *Discussed supposed dirt about the judge and urged his attorney to confront the judge about it in hopes that Judge Curiel would reconsider the RICO class certification—paralleling his later obstructive efforts as president*

- *Highlighted the judge's heritage months before making similar statements publicly*

- *Talked about pressuring the BBB*

I sent the message on my phone and waited.

. . .

Just like I had before receiving the wave of rejections about my book.

. . .

I didn't think I could take another outright rejection; another tastemaker telling me my story wasn't viable for them.

. . .

And then I received a response. It was Rachel Maddow's producer Matthew Alexander. He was interested in talking to me. *He was interested in talking to me!* I knew there was a long road ahead before my story was airing on MSNBC. But the fact that Rachel Maddow's team thought it was worthwhile responding to me told me that I had something valuable to share.

We spoke, and I wound up FedExing Matthew a copy of my Trump deposition video on a flash drive.

"Trump unguarded is rare and therefore great," he wrote after viewing the video.

But Matthew struggled—understandably so—to figure out precisely what the story might become before pitching it to Rachel. The BBB thing? "That thing" with the judge? The *Spanish thing?* It was a complex, coded story. Moreover, the audio quality and Trump's hushed speaking tone made it difficult to discern elements of the conversation.

"I see what you mean about a lip reader," he wrote in an email.

Matthew gave the story a shot and pitched it to Rachel Maddow—according to Matthew, she watched the video and was interested in the BBB angle, but things ended up fizzling . . . so it goes. But his effort gave me hope that this story was going to get picked up. I just had to find the proper outlet. So I made a spreadsheet of prospective media targets and contacts.

I considered progressive news sites that had handled similar stories—fearless coverage of Donald Trump's corruption. I moved a handful of names near the top of the list:

- Jason Leopold and Anthony Cormier, investigative reporters at Buzzfeed

- *The Daily Beast*, and politics editor Sam Stein

- David Corn with *Mother Jones*, who I'd crossed paths with at the 2016 Democratic National Convention

- And CNN

Someone on that list would likely break open my story. But who?

BELLE OF THE BALL

I sent out my new batch of inquiries simultaneously to my media targets, as I'd done with Rachel Maddow's team and Jason Leopold with Buzzfeed—the popular news website that balanced hard news with irreverent quizzes of *Friends* TV-show trivia and cat meme listicles—was the first to respond.

I hopped on a video call and talked with Leopold and his colleague Anthony Cormier, and the Buzzfeed reporters were very, very interested in telling my story. I sent them a flash drive with the hot-mic video footage from Trump's deposition, and Buzzfeed's video team processed the footage while Leopold and Cormier drafted an article that they hoped to run.

Things were moving *fast*. They asked for exclusive rights to tell the story, which meant I couldn't move forward with any other outlets in the meantime. YES!!

As Buzzfeed was pulling together its coverage, I heard back from the other outlets I'd reached out to—Curt Devine, a producer at CNN, Sam Stein from *The Daily Beast*, and David Corn with *Mother Jones*, who I had a deep respect for. So, of course, I finally decided to go to the dance, and numerous suitors lined up to escort me. I had to tell the others, begrudgingly, that someone else had expressed interest, and I promised them an exclusive, but that I would stay in touch if anything changed.

Buzzfeed was planning to run the story by mid-July.

The story was ready.

They'd written more than 1,500 words, and read back the quotes of mine they planned to use to make sure they were accurate (a common practice on such stories).

The reporters needed sign-off from Buzzfeed's legal team. Through that process, Leopold and Cormier reached out to O'Melveny & Myers LLP, the law firm of Daniel Petrocelli, the lawyer who spoke with Trump during the hot-mic conversation, for comment.

And that's when everything fell apart.

The law firm threatened to sue Buzzfeed into oblivion if the news site published the story. And Buzzfeed blinked.

The story was dead.

PATIENCE PAYS OFF

Luckily, I still had interest from the other outlets.

CNN would have been a great landing spot, but there was so much maneuvering. The timing needed to be right. The Republican National Convention was taking up a lot of attention in the political world. My story was considered with access in mind. Would CNN get blowback for publishing my story and video footage? There were bigger stories for CNN to follow, and the bosses needed to sign off (and maybe even the boss's bosses). Producer Curt Devine gave it his best, but there wasn't a clear path forward for CNN to publish the story, so I turned back to David Corn, who had been waiting patiently since Buzzfeed jumped first at my story.

David *wanted* this story.

But he didn't push too hard. I could tell he genuinely cared. He had a fine touch on the phone, a softness that stood apart from his take-no-prisoners Twitter persona. During the Trump presidency, David famously tweeted, day after day, "Today would be a good day for @realDonaldTrump to release his tax returns."

I did for David Corn as I did the others—sent a flash drive to him via FedEx, spoke on the phone, emailed, waited.

The veteran journalist responded with enthusiasm. He recognized the news value in the video. "Watching it reminds me of mobsters and the way they talk," Corn told me of Trump's coded conversation.

After the *Mother Jones* lawyer signed off on using the video, Corn reached out to the White House and Daniel Petrocelli's law firm, just as Buzzfeed had, and got a harshly worded statement from the law firm "on behalf of Trump University and President Donald J. Trump" threatening to sue and demanding that *Mother Jones* "not publish the video or any article relating to it and immediately destroy the video."[4]

But where Buzzfeed stopped pursuing the story, David and *Mother Jones* were ready to proceed—the publication's lawyer reviewed further and made a few additional comments due to the legal threats.

---

[4] The authors intended to reach out to Petrocelli and the law firm for further comment for this book but declined out of fear that the project would be blocked or delayed from publication. Instead we've republished direct quotations from the firm's earlier statement to Mother Jones about the hot-mic video.

"A key thing for us legally is that I did not cause you to do this, you brought this to me," Corn told me of the video. Yes, I brought the video to Corn.

David asked me if I was willing to reveal that I'd shared the video with him. "Yes, I can be named that I obtained the video that I forwarded to you," I wrote.

There was no hiding now.

EXTRA! EXTRA! READ ALL ABOUT IT!

David Corn's story was published on *Mother Jones'* website on August 27, 2020.

The top of the story featured screengrabs of four images from Trump's hot-mic footage. The footage that I'd been holding onto since watching it nearly five years earlier in my home.

NEW HOT-MIC VIDEO: WHAT TRUMP TOLD HIS LAWYER WHEN HE DIDN'T KNOW A CAMERA WAS ROLLING

On December 10, 2015, Donald Trump took time off from campaigning for the Republican presidential nomination to spend hours sitting for a videotaped deposition in a lawsuit alleging that he and Trump University had defrauded people who had plunked down thousands of dollars to learn the secrets of his financial success as a developer. During a break in the proceedings, the camera continued to roll. And Trump and his attorney, Daniel Petrocelli, apparently unaware they were being recorded, were captured discussing the case.

In this 13-minute hot-mic video—a copy of which was provided to *Mother Jones*—Trump boasted about how his company threatened the Better Business Bureau to change the D rating it had assigned Trump University to an A. He complained about the federal judge overseeing the suit, Gonzalo Curiel, elliptically talking about how to challenge him and referring to "the Spanish thing." Trump also griped that he had been sued personally in this case, and Petrocelli had to explain to Trump that he, not just Trump University itself, was in the legal crosshairs because Trump had been accused of making false statements to promote the venture. And

Petrocelli pointed out that the case was not a lock for Trump because some of Trump's "guys" had been "sloppy."

My name was mentioned in the sixth paragraph.

Art Cohen, the lead plaintiff in one of two Trump University class-action lawsuits, gave a copy of this recording to *Mother Jones*. "I wanted to get this out before the election so people better understand how Trump behaves behind the scenes," Cohen says. "Staying quiet all this time has been frustrating for me, and I wish everybody had gotten the chance to see Trump's behavior as I did before the 2016 election. With 20/20 vision, we now have the opportunity to better understand his true nature and the gangster persona he shows in this video." Cohen maintains that Trump's ability to avoid a trial during the campaign cleared a major political obstacle for him, and he adds, "The Trump University legal saga is a footnote to history, but it helped Trump hone his blueprint for attacking the judiciary by publicly berating judges he deems adversarial."

Finally.

The article featured embedded videos showing the hot mic with commentary and analysis by Corn—thorough, authoritative coverage that made me proud. It took a long time, and there were lots of dead ends, but I was proud that the right journalist ended up telling this story. Corn's videos were viewed *millions* of times.

Maybe there was some interest in this story, after all.

FOLLOW-UP STORY

There was something else that David Corn was interested in obtaining. After he reported on the Trump hot-mic conversation, I was happy to provide to him the full video of Trump's deposition, the footage that was barred from release in 2016.

I sent him one more flash drive.

This time, I declined to take credit for sending Corn the video. Instead, I only was credited for confirming that the video footage he'd obtained was the video of Trump's actual deposition (the footage also aligned with the transcript that had been released).

David did a bang-up job on the story—it featured video of Trump in his glasses, forgetting his claim that he had the world's best memory and growing frustration over his previous praise of Hillary Clinton. The story's publication on September 18, 2020 was timed to coincide with his planned appearance on MSNBC's *The ReidOut,* hosted by Joy Reid.

David texted me the day before to alert me that he was invited to appear on Reid's show.

"Excellent. Will set my DVR," I wrote.

"Before you do that, just keep your fingers crossed that there are no news developments tomorrow that blow things up," he responded.

Those were ominous words. I crossed my fingers and toes, just in case. But I was excited and encouraged. What news could break that would blow things up?

SHOWTIME

Joy Reid promoted the segment on Trump's deposition video early in the September 18 show following a segment on the coronavirus pandemic.

"Also tonight, a *ReidOut* exclusive, David Corn from *Mother Jones* with the never-before-seen Trump University deposition tapes. The fraud, the settlement and the glasses that Trump doesn't want you to see him wearing," she said, as an image of Trump in his glasses was shown.

After B-block stories about Joe Biden's chances against Trump, Latino voters, and aid to Puerto Rico, it was finally time for the segment—my segment—to air on national TV.

The show returned with a clip of Donald Trump, the introductory Trump University video I watched at my seminar more than a decade earlier: "At Trump University, we teach success. That's what it's all about, success. It's going to happen to you. If you're going to achieve anything, you have to take action. And action is what Trump University is all about."

Joy Reid began a voice-over introducing the segment. Here it was! I was so excited I could barely breathe.

"Long before he succeeded at conning his way into the presidency, Trump conned people to enroll in his fake Trump University, luring people in with promises that they could make a fortune just like his, even though we now know that he was nowhere near as rich as he said he was and that the money he did have, he either inherited or glommed by licensing his name to buildings he didn't own and to skeevy products like Trump University, which offered programs that cost thousands of dollars, which one of his own employees described in an affidavit as misleading, fraudulent and dishonest," she said.

"The employee told the court that, while Trump University claimed it wanted to help consumers make money, in fact, Trump University was only interested in selling every person the most expensive seminars they possibly could.

"One student said that they wasted their entire life savings on Trump."

Trump University affidavits were showing on the screen. The story was happening! Reid was going to come back on camera, introduce the segment, bring on David Corn, and then a segment of my video was going to air nationwide on live TV.

But before any of that happened, the tone of Reid's voice changed.

"Um . . . ," Reid started. *Um.*

"... cause we have some breaking news that we, uh, have to report to you ..."

Breaking news.

"... so I'm gonna hold it right there in talking about Trump University ..."

Hold it. Right. There.

Reid was back on camera now, getting ready to say something. Something that she was struggling to put into words.

"... and unfortunately, that news is that ...." Reid exhaled before she continued, the kind of heavy exhale that comes before something horrible.

"... Ruth Bader Ginsburg, Associate Justice of the United States Supreme Court, has died, apparently. That is the news that we are getting right now."

Oh.

No.

My mind splintered in a million directions. First, my long wait to get my story told. Suppose they had only aired my segment five minutes earlier! If only they'd put it in B-block instead of C-block. Any other time, any other day, any other moment . . . with such a massive story emerging, my deposition video wasn't going to get another look from national media outlets.

Just as David Corn had warned, here was the news development that blew things up.

But this was so much bigger than me. Ruth Bader Ginsburg was a supreme talent and one of the most important women in the country's history. A leading critic of Trump. A pioneer. An icon. A national treasure. And if that wasn't bad enough, it also happened to be Jewish New Year.

Trump was escaping accountability again. And a Supreme Court spot was now open, and he was going to try to fill it immediately, and he was going to try to weaponize the high court to allow him to steal the election ....

Oh.

No.

David Corn—standing by to discuss Trump's long-hidden deposition footage—was instead forced to pivot and discuss Ginsberg's impact and legacy. He did admirably.

I felt bad for him. He felt bad for me. I felt horrible for the country all over again.

CHAPTER 19

PARALLELS TO THE PAST

As time marched ahead to November 2020, a familiar sense of dread crept over me.

Election Day, again.

The stakes in 2020 were even higher than in 2016. After enduring four years of grift and toxicity and cruelty and indifference, America had its only genuine chance to issue a referendum on Donald Trump. If Donald Trump won again . . . I tried not to entertain that thought, but it was still possible. This was *Trump,* after all. He would do anything to get his way, even if that meant destroying the country from the inside.

The tactics he deployed in the lead-up and aftermath of the election were many of the same tactics he used while fighting the Trump University lawsuits—Trump's six D's: Deceive, Defraud, Deny, Deflect, Dodge, and Delay. But this time, instead of securing a trial delay, Trump was using his strategies to undermine the sanctity of our elections and spark bloodshed in the halls of the U.S. Capitol.

BLAME A 'RIGGED' SYSTEM

More than three months ahead of the election, Trump already settled on a culprit for the outcome. "I think mail-in voting is going to rig the election," he told Fox News' Chris Wallace. As Trump saw it, mail-in voting would lead to the "most corrupt election in our nation's history" (in fact, mail-in ballots are less likely to be tampered with than voting machines, and Trump himself has voted through the mail).

The COVID-19 pandemic meant added health risks around in-person voting. As a result, it was safer to vote through mail-in ballots, and many states opened up their absentee voting procedures to accommodate voters. This was problematic for Trump because a widespread mail-in voting system would mean more voters, and Trump's chances at re-election improved with lower turnout since his base wasn't growing.

Before a single vote was cast in the 2020 presidential election, and without any proof, he was already calling foul.

Trump University parallel: Donald Trump's statements attacking Judge Curiel and the 9th U.S. Circuit Court of Appeals during a May 27, 2016 speech half a year ahead of a potential trial for a case that hadn't been decided. "It is a disgrace. It is a rigged system. This court system, the judges in this court system, federal court. They ought to look into Judge Curiel because what Judge Curiel is doing is a total disgrace, OK?"

THE RULE OF LAW VS. THE RULE OF TRUMP

The weeks after Ruth Bader Ginsberg's extremely untimely death on September 18 were a blur of activity. Republicans salivated at the chance to fill the open spot. Replacing Ginsberg's position with a Republican would shift the court to a 6-3 Republican majority. But they needed to act *now* with the balance of the Senate potentially up for grabs in November.

Trump's forcing through a nominee—conservative jurist Amy Coney Barrett—was done with an eye toward the election in case the high court had to weigh in. "I think this will end up in the Supreme Court, and I think it's very important that we have nine Justices," Trump said in September of the upcoming election.

Trump University parallel: Judge Curiel was the third jurist assigned to the Trump University litigation. Trump praised Judge Irma Gonzalez because of motion rulings in his favor and criticized Judge Curiel for ruling against him, arguing that Judge Curiel's Mexican heritage made him biased, when in fact Judge Gonzalez was also Mexican-American. For Trump, those who ruled against him were *Obama appointees* or politically biased, or in the case of Judge Curiel, supposedly prejudiced due to their heritage or some other reason. There was the rule of law and the rule of Trump, and only one mattered to him.

SIDELINED AND SILENCED

Donald Trump spent 2020 downplaying the COVID-19 pandemic, suggesting miracle cures and claiming the virus would "go away." It didn't. And in September, in the wake of Amy Coney Barrett's nomination, Trump himself contracted the coronavirus, sidelining him from the campaign trail for 10 days. Being hospitalized elevated the single issue Trump was trying to downplay, quieted him during a key stretch of the campaign, and fueled speculation about his fitness for office and health.

Trump University parallel: Being sidelined in 2016 to endure one or both Trump University trials during the lead-up to the election was a major fear of Trump's—it would have revealed the reality that he's a conman and failed businessman while removing him from the campaign trail and making him unable to contain the message. Trump's legal team spent months trying to get the trial delayed until after the election, a request that Judge Curiel granted in May 2016.

RIP OFF YOUR SUPPORTERS

Donald Trump's campaign had a money problem, lagging far behind Joe Biden's fundraising totals. The campaign needed a sustained boost ahead of Election Day.

That boost came through a recurring payment system where anyone who made an online donation to Trump's re-election efforts starting in September was automatically enrolled (unless they opted out) to make *weekly* donations in the same amount. The scam victims included cancer patients and elderly people struggling to scrape by, and the campaign ended up refunding more than $122 million to donors.

Trump University parallel: Much like with TrumpU, many of the victims of the campaign's recurring payment scheme happened to be vulnerable people who believed in Donald Trump. and got ripped off after failing to read the fine print—they were both get-rich-quick schemes that propped up Trump at tenuous times.

PREMATURE VICTORY LAP

Election Day came and went without a clear winner.

The counting of the mail-in ballots took longer, and some states had laws restricting ballot tabulation prior to Election Day. Meaning it was expected to take days for the election's outcome to emerge.

The Republican-leaning in-person votes could be tallied much more quickly than the mostly Democratic mail-in ballots and it appeared that Trump had taken massive leads in battleground states like Pennsylvania, Michigan, Wisconsin, and Arizona. In actuality, millions of correctly submitted ballots had not yet been counted.

Biden gave a brief and optimistic speech as the vote count continued.

"We believe we're on track to win this election," he said. "We knew because of the unprecedented early vote and the mail-in vote it was going to take a while. We're going to have to be patient until the hard work of tallying the votes is finished. And it ain't over until every vote is counted, every ballot is counted.

"As I've said all along, it's not my place or Donald Trump's place to declare who's won this election. That's the decision of the American people. But I'm optimistic about this outcome."

Trump waited until after 2 a.m. Eastern Time before walking to the stage and giving a horrifying address that portended the troubling times ahead.

"They can't catch us," Trump said. "We will win this, and as far as I'm concerned, we already have won." The outcome was undecided, but Trump was digging in and declaring himself the winner.

Trump University parallel: Trump, on many occasions, prematurely claimed he "won" or was "winning" the Trump University lawsuits when they were still ongoing—long before he ended up settling the cases for $25 million.

KEEP CLAIMING VICTORY AFTER DEFEAT

It took four agonizing days. But after the counting of the mail-in ballots, Biden secured narrow victories in key states that went to Trump four years earlier, including mine and Biden's home state of Pennsylvania.

"Congrats to us all!" I wrote in a Nov. 7, 2020 text message to David Corn after Biden emerged as the election winner.

"Indeed. I will never forget your courage and your part in this. It was great to be partners," Corn wrote.

The final Electoral College count, 306-232, was the same margin by which Trump won in 2016 (a margin he called "a landslide"). Biden also won the popular vote by 7 million votes and garnered the most votes of any candidate (81 million) in U.S. history. But despite a resounding defeat, Trump wasn't ready to concede. "I WON THIS ELECTION, BY A LOT!" he wrote on Twitter without any supporting evidence after Biden was declared the election winner. With Trump, winning is whatever he thinks it is.

Trump University parallel: Trump's thoughts on winning and losing came out during his December 10, 2015 deposition hearing, when he was asked about a defamation lawsuit he filed against journalist Timothy O'Brien (the lawsuit was dismissed, and an appeals court upheld that ruling). "I did very well in that lawsuit," Trump told my attorney Jason Forge. Forge followed up attempting to get Trump to explain how he did "very well" in an unsuccessful lawsuit. "I lost the lawsuit, but I made a very good point with that lawsuit," Trump said. "So you lost the lawsuit," Forge said. "Yes," Trump responded, "but I'm glad I brought that lawsuit. I made a very good point with that lawsuit."

SUE, SUE, SUE

Following the election, Donald Trump was well within his rights to legally challenge the results. But he took that right to the nth degree. A rogue collective of Trump-associated lawyers—including former New York City Mayor Rudy Giuliani and conspiracy theorist-promoting Sidney Powell— filed dozens of lawsuits in battleground states alleging fraud. The lawsuits were almost universally rejected, including by Trump-appointed judges.

Trump University parallel: Trump was prodigiously litigious throughout the Trump University saga, filing motion after motion after motion. Tarla Makaeff faced the worst of his ire, enduring a defamation countersuit that was stricken down on appeal that left Trump on the hook for nearly $800,000 in legal fees. At one point, his legal team argued (unsuccessfully) that Makaeff wasn't fit to serve as a lead plaintiff, then when she requested years later to withdraw as lead plaintiff due to the heavy toll she'd endured and Trump's presidential run, they filed an opposition calling her "*the critical witness in this case.*"

CORRUPT ASKS

Trump wasn't afraid to make a corrupt ask, especially in the waning days of his presidency. He placed calls with various Georgia officials in an attempt to get them to overturn the state's election results.

"All I want to do is this. I just want to find 11,780 votes, which is one more than we have. Because we won the state," he told Secretary of State Brad Raffensperger in a recorded phone conversation.

Trump thought his lawyers or fellow Republicans should do his bidding, and he didn't show restraint in telling them what he needed them to do.

Trump University parallel: The hot-mic moment during a break in Trump's December 10, 2015 deposition, when he told his attorney to confront Judge Curiel in an effort to get the cases tossed. "Go in there and say that thing, about him. Understand?"

FAIL TO CONCEDE

Even after a decisive election result and so many legal losses, Trump wasn't ready to concede defeat. And high-ranking officials such as Mark Milley, Chairman of the Joint Chiefs, worried that Trump and his allies could be planning a coup—especially as Trump loyalists were installed at the Pentagon.

Milley saw Trump as "the classic authoritarian leader with nothing to lose," according to Carol Leonnig and Philip Rucker's book *I Alone Can Fix It*.

Trump's rhetoric intensified into the new year. At a January 4, 2021, rally in Georgia, he said he was "fighting like hell" to remain in the White House. He reiterated that point on January 6 to a crowd of his ravenous supporters at a "Save America" rally in Washington.

"We will never give up; we will never concede. It doesn't happen. You don't concede when there's theft involved," he told them.

Trump University parallel: His suggestion to "never concede" the election parallels his oft-repeated claims that he would "never" settle the TrumpU cases out of principle (which he ended up settling following the 2016 election).

INFLAMING HIS BASE

Trump used lots of coded language during late 2020 and early 2021 to inflame his base, specifically targeting the most extreme of his supporters.

During the first presidential debate, when Joe Biden asked Trump if he would denounce the alt-right group the Proud Boys, Trump urged the group to "stand back and stand by."

The rhetoric intensified after his election defeat. He called on Republican lawmakers to support his efforts, and he spent weeks promoting the "Save

America" rally on January 6, 2021, the date members of Congress would certify the Electoral College results. "Big protest in D.C. on January 6th. Be there, will be wild!" Trump wrote to his Twitter followers.

At the rally, he called on his followers to walk to the Capitol, repeating the unfounded lie that the election was stolen. "We're going to walk down to the Capitol, and we're going to cheer on our brave senators, and congressmen and women. We're probably not going to be cheering so much for some of them, because you'll never take back our country with weakness. You have to show strength, and you have to be strong," he said.

While Trump did not walk to the Capitol, thousands of his followers did, and many breached the Capitol doors. A mob fueled by lies and hatred overwhelmed Metropolitan Police and stormed the building seeking to disrupt the transition of power. Violence broke out in the Capitol corridors as members of Congress hid in fear, terrified that they would be hunted down because they failed to help Trump throw the election.

Trump University parallel: During the fateful May 6, 2016 hearing, Judge Curiel expressed fear that holding a trial during Trump's presidential run could result in "the unleashing of forces" surrounding the case and jurors—a mixture of media exposure, public attention, and Trump's bombast making a trial all but impossible. It was difficult for Judge Curiel to fully quantify "the unleashing of forces," but it represented enough of a concern for him to delay the trial until after the 2016 election.

'DO THE RIGHT THING'

Trump found his scapegoat in his futile effort to overturn the election: his Vice President, Mike Pence. Pence was tasked with certifying the electoral votes. But Pence sought to fulfill his constitutional duties—which would mean confirming Biden as the election winner.

"I hope Mike is going to do the right thing . . . because if Mike Pence does the right thing, we win the election," Trump told his supporters during his January 6 speech.

As the mob descended on the Capitol, a gallows was constructed, and some insurrectionists chanted "hang Mike Pence." For choosing loyalty to the Constitution over loyalty to Trump, Pence faced threats on his life.

Trump University parallel: During Trump's May 27, 2016 campaign rally in San Diego, he also expressed frustration that a central figure—Judge Curiel—wasn't doing the "right thing" by dropping the Trump University cases. Much like Pence, Judge Curiel endured a wave of death threats after failing to do what Trump wished.

DOUBLING DOWN

Trump could have called off his followers during the Capitol insurrection. He could have asked for calm. But instead, he doubled down, seeking to inflame tensions further.

"Mike Pence didn't have the courage to do what should have been done to protect our Country and our Constitution, giving states a chance to certify a corrected set of facts, not the fraudulent or inaccurate ones which they were asked to certify previously. USA demands the truth!" Trump tweeted as the mob remained inside the Capitol. He later recorded a video message, telling the insurrectionists, "We had an election that was stolen from us" and "We love you, you're very special."

Trump reveled in the unrest, a chaos agent who embraced his ability to turn the temperature far past the boiling point.

Trump University parallel: Instead of tamping down his racist rhetoric against Judge Curiel in May and June 2016, Trump kept repeating it in numerous interviews, even as fellow Republicans criticized his attacks, magnifying the firestorm exponentially.

MOVE ON, EVENTUALLY

One day after the deadly Capitol siege and after vowing to "never give up" and "never concede," Trump released a video statement acknowledging the truth about the election. "Congress has certified the results, and a new administration will be inaugurated on January 20th," he said. He still wouldn't use the word *concede,* and despite the lip service, he never committed to the peaceful transfer of power to the President-elect, Joe Biden. Less than two weeks later, after Republican senators again failed to remove him following his second impeachment, Trump departed the White House for the final time.

Trump University parallel: Trump could have settled the Trump University cases at any point from 2010 on forward, and a modicum of contrition on his part could have allowed him to make the matter disappear years before he ran for office. A Trump University settlement— much like his commitment to the transfer of power to the incoming administration—didn't have to involve so much avoidable hardship and sadness or get dragged out for so long.

VOW TO RETURN

Trump has expressed interest in running for re-election in 2024, despite the fact that he will be 78 years old at the time of the election. "I am looking at it very seriously, beyond seriously," he told Fox News' Sean Hannity in April 2021, stating it was "too soon" from a legal standpoint to formally announce his run. The conman is always dangling a payoff, a master manipulator abusing his mark's loyalty and trust through the power of persuasion.

Trump University parallel: During the 2016 campaign, Donald Trump vowed to reopen Trump University, and suggested his adult children could run it. "After the litigation is disposed of and the case won, I have instructed my execs to open Trump U(?), so much interest in it! I will be pres," he wrote on Twitter. Thankfully, those plans have not materialized.

UNFINISHED BUSINESS

Joe Biden's inauguration on January 20, 2021, a sparse ceremony offset by barriers and armed guards following the deadly insurrection two weeks earlier, gave me a sense of optimism for the future. Biden, in his address, promised to represent all Americans, even those who didn't support his campaign for president. To unify a divided America.

"We must end this uncivil war that pits red against blue, rural versus urban, conservative versus liberal," he said. "We can do this if we open our souls instead of hardening our hearts. If we show a little tolerance and humility." This was a long way from the "American carnage" that Trump noted in his inaugural address four years earlier.

But there was still unfinished business with the former guy whose name appeared with mine on hundreds of legal filings. Ex-president Trump faced a treacherous legal path ahead, a minefield of challenges expected across numerous venues. And there was that outstanding report I'd made with the California Department of Justice, too. Accountability couldn't come soon enough.

CHAPTER 20

ACCOUNTABLE?

As Donald Trump's presidency was coming to a tragic, tumultuous end, I still had no answers about the report I made to the California Department of Justice in 2019 about Trump's hot-mic conversation.

I'd call or email every few months asking if there were any updates but I usually didn't get much insight or clarity on the status of the investigation. Of course, the COVID-19 pandemic didn't help—instead of working at a centralized call center, employees were operating remotely from home, so it wasn't easy to get the same person on the phone twice.

Was the case closed? Still active? Dormant? Would I ever know? I didn't know what to believe. But a December 2, 2020 phone conversation I had with a department employee left me baffled and hopeful.

"I don't even really know what I'm looking at here," the employee told me before putting me on hold, so the music blared through my earpiece.

If the case wasn't being pursued or wasn't active, I imagine that would have been easy to see. Instead, something—call it gut instinct, intuition, or just a sense of reading between the lines—told me that my report was being investigated and taken seriously. All I wanted was for someone to care.

CHALLENGES AHEAD

After leaving office, Donald Trump had lots of reasons to worry. The Office of the Presidency no longer protected him.

He found himself facing a wave of legal challenges and threats across numerous venues.

"Trump is possibly the most spectacularly terrible businessman of the past 40 years in America. He's like the exact opposite of Warren Buffett. Everything Trump touches turns to shit. He got lucky with that TV show. That's about it.

"It's all going to come crashing down in the next couple of years as all of these debts come due and his revenue streams dry up."

-TRISTAN SNELL, NEW YORK STATE ASSISTANT AG, 2011-2014

- A Manhattan DA's investigation into Donald Trump's personal and business finances—sparked by Michael Cohen's hush-money payouts ahead of the 2016 election—grew to encompass Trump's long-withheld tax returns after his Republican-padded Supreme Court in February 2021 ruled 9-0 that the documents could be turned over to investigators (so much for his hand-selected justices protecting him!). "A continuation of the greatest political Witch Hunt in the history of our Country," Trump whined in a fusillade of gibberish.

- An investigation by the New York State Attorney General's Office, which began in 2019 as a civil probe involving financial dealings, shifted to a "criminal capacity" by May 2021 and worked in tandem with the Manhattan DA investigation.

- Two grand juries in Georgia were investigating Trump's call for the Secretary of State to find him votes and overturn the state's election results. Fulton County DA Fani Willis was investigating Trump for racketeering, among other potential crimes, the same element that anchored my 2013 federal lawsuit against Trump.

- Washington, DC was investigating Trump's role in inciting the January 6 insurrection.

- Donald was facing dozens of lawsuits, including a defamation lawsuit by writer and fashion icon E. Jean Carroll, who claimed Trump raped her in a New York department store in the mid-1990s (Trump denied the accusation, shamefully stating that Carroll "wasn't my type"). Since the lawsuit was filed during his presidency, Trump argued that he should be shielded from the matter, then sought to have the government represent him.

- Massive amounts of debt—hundreds of millions of dollars—were also coming due in the next few years for The Trump Organization.

He needed to be held accountable somewhere, someway, somehow. Would it be my report? Or something else?

WAY TO GO, JOE!

The beginning of Joe Biden's presidency represented the first feeling that a new normal was approaching for the country and its pandemic response.

President Biden—oh, how pleasant that sounds—pushed for the country to give 100 million COVID-19 vaccine shots in his first 100 days in office, and when his administration quickly achieved that goal, the number was upped to 200 million.

It felt empowering to get the vaccine shots. In addition, it reduced the likelihood that I would suffer severe long-term side effects if I contracted COVID-19.

PARTY OF NOTHING

I could breathe easier again for a lot of reasons.

We didn't have to constantly worry about what Donald Trump was tweeting anymore. He was de-platformed from Twitter and other social media platforms for his role inciting the January 6 insurrection.

Things were quieter.

But even though Trump was out of our social media feeds didn't mean he was gone. The Republican party continued to rally around a twice-impeached one-term president who guided the party to lose the Senate and House. The GOP, sucked up by culture wars and cultism, didn't much care that insurrectionists stormed the Capitol, some of them carrying Confederate flags. Republicans pushed to block a congressional investigation into the insurrection's causes. The few Republicans who spoke out against Trump and the insurrection were put on notice—in Liz Cheney's case, she was stripped of her House Republican Caucus leadership role for not supporting the Big Lie that the election was stolen.

The Party of Lincoln completed its transformation into the Party of Trump. And pretty soon, it became the Party of Nothing.

'NO NEWS IS GOOD NEWS'

I had a phone conversation with a representative with the California DOJ on April 27, 2021, requesting an update on my PIU report.

"Unfortunately, I don't know the answer to that," the analyst told me when I asked if the investigation was closed. "I'll reach out to my manager to see if we know more information, but other than that, that's all the information that we can provide you at this time."

Hmm . . . .

I received a phone call from Casey Hallinan with the DOJ's Public Inquiry Unit two days later.

"Whether we investigate or don't investigate, we are unable to comment on the possibility of an investigation," she said in a voicemail message. "If a lawsuit is filed by our office, then it will become public information and you can find all the information on the website, but until then, there's nothing that anyone is going to be able to discuss with you.

"If you want to continue to follow up, you can watch our website for any press releases that may come about," she added.

Hmm . . . .

I still needed clarity, so I called the office again in early May about my report.

"Based on what I'm looking at, it looks like we're still going through the process," the rep told me. "Usually when we do say, 'Hey, there's nothing we can do about this, you're on your own,' or 'good luck, Godspeed,' that kind of thing, you'll get a letter from our office letting you know that. I don't see anything indicating any of that. So generally, when that happens, that usually means that our attorneys are still in the process, either vetting or maybe there's still an investigation going on. So in this instance, despite the timing and the fact you haven't really heard much from our office, I'd say no news is good news, because that means they're still working on it. Cause if it were over and done with, we would have informed you that we're not doing anything further. So if [Casey Hallinan] is telling you to keep an eye on the press section of our office, then chances are that there's a distinct possibility we might have something to show there. But as for how long that'll take, I can't tell you because those kinds of decisions aren't made at this level."

I received another call from the California DOJ that June, clarifying that they "aren't allowed to discuss" whether there is an investigation, even if a victim is inquiring, because it could compromise their efforts.

And so I would wait, again, in hopes of holding Donald Trump accountable a second time. By mid-2021, I still wasn't sure if anything would come of my report. But at the very least, someone was looking into it.

THE LONG WAIT

Allen Weisselberg bowed his bald head as he walked the longest walk of his life.

The Trump Organization CFO had largely stayed out of the spotlight himself—news outlets didn't even have usable wire image photos of the longtime exec, save for some scowling snaps from a 2017 press conference when he was spotted behind Donald Trump, Sr. and Jr.—but here was the money man on July 1, 2021, handcuffed and being perp walked to

Manhattan criminal court. The same money man who six years earlier had sat for a deposition in my lawsuit against Donald Trump.

The Manhattan DA's investigation into The Trump Organization bore fruit: the organization and Weisselberg face fifteen counts in total, alleging a scheme to defraud in the first degree. According to the grand jury indictment, between 2005 and 2021, Weisselberg and other Trump Organization executives were regularly paid "off the books" to avoid having to report the pay for tax purposes. Weisselberg's indirect pay, $1.7 million, came in the form of an apartment lease, utility bills, car payments, and private school for his grandkids "to be paid by personal checks drawn on the account of and signed by Donald J. Trump," according to the indictment. The payouts by Trump felt all too familiar when compared with the $500,000 checks he made out to himself from Trump University funds.

Investigators allege that The Trump Organization was using two sets of books—one to report to authorities, the other one secret. The charges represented a major blow to the company and its ability to do business.

I found it fitting that Weisselberg, who oversaw Trump University's finances and signed most of its checks, would find himself in handcuffs. And that the time frame over which this fraud occurred covered the entire life cycle of Trump University.

Allen Weisselberg's arrest was significant. But he wasn't Donald John Trump. And as Weisselberg claimed in his 2015 deposition, *he was acting on Trump's behalf.*

Days after the CFO's arrest, Trump criticized the charges in a sweaty stump speech, expressing how confusing and frustrating it is that "they go after good hardworking people for not paying taxes on a company car." This, from someone who's called himself "the king of the tax code."

There was a sense, with Weisselberg facing the music, that everything was finally imploding for Trump, that the walls were closing in, that this time it was all over. But people had felt that way about Trump many times before, too, and he always seemed to skate by.

Frustratingly, as I know too well, the path to justice against Donald Trump remains winding and long, even when there's a paper trail and video evidence. Cases take time to build. But time gave Trump the chance to work on his next con, one that could bring him lots of money, unchecked power, and four more years of immunity.

I can imagine it now: Donald Trump, arrested and free on bond, blaming a rigged system, pushing for another trial delay, and promising his supporters a road of opportunity ahead if he's reelected to a second illegitimate term as president.

"Success. It's going to happen to you," he'll say, and people will give him their money.

NOTES

This book relies on the author's personal notes and recollections, eight years of court filings, media coverage, and interviews with key sources such as Amber Eck, Tristan Snell, Sonny Low, and John Brown. Documents from the two federal Trump University lawsuits—*3:10-cv-00940-GPC-WVG Low v. Trump University, LLC et al* (the Makaeff/Low case) and *3:13-cv-02519-GPC-WVG Cohen v. Trump* (the Cohen case)—can be found on PACER (Public Access to Court Electronic Records) at https://pcl.uscourts.gov/.

While the Trump University legal saga, for all intents and purposes, is over, Donald Trump's own legal issues remain ongoing, with open investigations across numerous jurisdictions (including, as of this writing, the California Department of Justice). Writing anything about Trump, let alone a book, is akin to trying to hit a moving target. The news cycle races at warp speed with developments coming one after another, making it difficult to properly report on any one thing.

With all things Trump, there's still so much we don't know. The years ahead will hopefully provide more illumination and fill in the missing details. The information reported in this book pulls from a wide range of sources, documents, and news reporting, and we've noted those that provided significant contributions below.

CHAPTER 1: THE ART AND THE DEAL

The chapter relies heavily on the author's personal recollections and the details from his lawsuit, *3:13-cv-02519-GPC-WVG Cohen v. Trump*. To

view the Trump University promotional video, visit
https://www.youtube.com/watch?v=4q1N_B6Y4ZQ.

CHAPTER 2: LETDOWN

For more about the connections between Biff Tannen from *Back to the Future* and Donald Trump, read *"Back to the Future* Writer: Biff Tannen Is Based on Donald Trump" by Ben Collins of *The Daily Beast*, Oct. 21, 2015 at https://www.thedailybeast.com/back-to-the-future-writer-biff-tannen-is-based-on-donald-trump.

CHAPTER 3: THE BEGINNING

The Trump University application with the U.S. Patent and Trademark Office was first obtained by The Smoking Gun.com and published online on Aug. 26, 2004, at
http://www.thesmokinggun.com/documents/crime/donald-dean. *Doonesbury* cartoons by Garry Trudeau can be found at https://www.gocomics.com/doonesbury. Reporting by Joe Mullin and Jonathan Kaminsky, first for *The Sacramento Bee* and later, *Ars Technica*, has proven prescient and enlightening in terms of National Grants Conferences and Trump University—it was extremely helpful in piecing together the *why* behind Trump University going from an online-only to seminar-based operation. For more on their coverage, read "Trump University and the art of the get-rich seminar" published April 29, 2016 at https://arstechnica.com/tech-policy/2016/04/we-witnessed-the-birth-of-trump-university/. Trump's political donations to Greg Abbott are available at https://www.followthemoney.org/. Details from Tristan Snell, former Assistant AG for New York who investigated Trump University, were obtained in a May 4, 2021 phone interview. Other details were obtained from *The People of the State of New York v. The Trump Entrepreneur Initiative LLC*, filed in 2013.

CHAPTER 4: LEAD PLAINTIFF

The chapter relies heavily on the author's personal recollections and the details from his lawsuit, *3:13-cv-02519-GPC-WVG Cohen v. Trump*. The

Trump University playbooks were filed in court in May 2016. The "honey badger" video link Jason Forge sent the author to represent attorney Patrick Coughlin's relentless nature is available at https://youtu.be/4r7wHMg5Yjg.

CHAPTER 5: COHEN'S DEPOSITION

A transcript of the author's May 29, 2014 deposition—available at https://pcl.uscourts.gov/—serves as the basis for the chapter.

CHAPTER 6: CLASS CERTIFICATION

Judge Gonzalo Curiel's order granting motion for class certification, appointing class representative, and appointing class counsel in *Cohen v. Trump* was filed Oct. 27, 2014. The document is available on PACER.

CHAPTER 7: MEETING TRUMP

The chapter relies on the author's reflections of the March 2015 mandatory settlement conference and a personal conversation he shared with attorney Jason Forge.

CHAPTER 8: THE POLITICIAN

Judge Curiel's June 30, 2015 order allowing the author's counsel to ask Trump questions about his net worth under penalty of perjury was a bit of schadenfreude for Trump that may not have happened if he didn't grandstand and wildly overstate his riches. That order came weeks after Trump's infamous ride down the Trump Tower escalator and into the presidential race. Video from that speech can be viewed at https://www.youtube.com/watch?v=apjNfkysjbM&t=124s. Segments of transcripts from Allen Weisselberg's June 2015 deposition are available on PACER, but they are not easy to find. Document 123-2 in *Cohen v. Trump* was filed August 4, 2015 and Document 220-2 was filed June 3, 2016. For more information on Weisselberg's deposition, read "Allen Weisselberg, self-professed 'stickler' CFO at center of Trump criminal probe says he leaves 'legal side' of money flow to others" by Molly Crane-Newman and Nancy Dillon of the *New York Daily News* published on

April 24, 2021 at https://www.nydailynews.com/news/politics/us-elections-government/ny-trump-accountant-allen-weisselberg-becomes-key-figure-in-criminal-probe-20210425-4tce7nirrbepje4b3fw6cosk4m-story.html.

CHAPTER 9: TRUMP'S DEPOSITION

To view video clips from Donald Trump's Dec. 10, 2015 deposition, and to read about the context of his statements, visit "Donald Trump Wanted to Keep This Video Deposition Secret. We Got a Copy." by David Corn and *Mother Jones* published on Sept. 18, 2020 at https://www.motherjones.com/politics/2020/09/donald-trump-university-fraud-lawsuit-deposition-full-video/. Trump's deposition transcripts were filed in court in June 2016 and are available on PACER.

CHAPTER 10: THE HOT-MIC MOMENT

Video of Donald Trump's hot-mic conversation on Dec. 10, 2015 is available at https://www.motherjones.com/politics/2020/08/new-hot-mic-video-what-trump-told-his-lawyer-when-he-didnt-know-a-camera-was-rolling/ and a transcript of the conversation is available in the following pages.

CHAPTER 11: THE CAMPAIGN TRAIL

The chapter relies on many video clips, including the Feb. 25, 2016 Republican primary debate (https://www.youtube.com/watch?v=GasRDffe1Xg&t=5229s), the American Future Fund ad about Trump University (https://www.youtube.com/watch?v=uoSaJueQsuQ), Trump's Feb. 27, 2016 rally in Arkansas (https://www.youtube.com/watch?v=uO9AIqtWkAE&t=1123s), his appearance on *Fox News Sunday* (https://www.youtube.com/watch?v=VxMNsitws9Q&t=308s), and the March 3, 2016 Republican primary debate (https://www.youtube.com/watch?v=EfZ1GWehTNA&t=3611s).

CHAPTER 12: DELAY

The transcript from the May 6, 2016 pre-trial conference involving Judge Curiel—part of the Makaeff/Low case because it was scheduled for trial first—was a crucial document and weighs heavily on the chapter. Other sources of information include Donald Trump's May 27, 2016 speech in San Diego (https://www.youtube.com/watch?v=tl5CJy1Fijc&t=2325s), the article "Trump Says Judge's Mexican Heritage Presents 'Absolute Conflict'" by Brent Kendall of *The Wall Street Journal*, published June 3, 2016 (https://www.wsj.com/articles/donald-trump-keeps-up-attacks-on-judge-gonzalo-curiel-1464911442), Trump's interview with CNN's Jake Tapper (https://www.youtube.com/watch?v=eKwps5fjjCY), and segments about Trump University by *Late Night with Seth Meyers* (https://www.youtube.com/watch?v=5brIpJNaHRY) and HBO's *Last Week Tonight with John Oliver* (https://www.youtube.com/watch?v=cBUeipXFisQ). Andrew M. Harris of *Bloomberg* also reported on Donald Trump's comments about Judge Curiel to Republican leaders on June 5, 2016 in the article "Trump Says Muslim Judge Might Be as Biased as 'Mexican' Curiel": https://www.bloomberg.com/news/articles/2016-06-05/trump-says-u-s-allies-should-pay-in-full-for-american-defense.

CHAPTER 13: RUNAWAY TRAIN

CNN's interview with James Harris, the author's so-called "mentor for life," in 2016 remains stunning to watch: https://www.youtube.com/watch?v=84lUQFvHeDk. As is his YouTube video as James "Paradise" Harris predicting a real estate crash that didn't happen: https://www.youtube.com/watch?v=xGA061tmiGQ.

CHAPTER 14: DECISION

The chapter relies on the author's recollections and email and text records, as well as transcripts from court proceedings.

CHAPTER 15: HOLDOUT

Legal filings for *0:2017cv55635 Sherri B. Simpson, et al v. Trump University, LLC, et al* are available on PACER at https://pcl.uscourts.gov/. Video of the Ninth Circuit Court of Appeals hearing on November 15, 2017 is available at https://www.youtube.com/watch?v=5S57KbnOUqo&t=336s.

CHAPTER 16: ILLEGITIMATE PRESIDENT

The chapter relies heavily on the Mueller Report, available online at https://www.justice.gov/archives/sco/file/1373816/download. The SDNY's sentencing memo for Michael Cohen is also a key document (https://www.documentcloud.org/documents/5453401-SDNY-Cohen-sentencing-memo.html), while his disclosure to Congress that Trump speaks in code (https://www.youtube.com/watch?v=tFf7Za9lV-4) remains a crucial disclosure to understanding Donald Trump's mode of communication.

CHAPTER 17: THE WHISTLEBLOWER

The chapter is heavily based on the author's notes, emails, and phone records.

CHAPTER 18: ON THE RECORD

David Corn and *Mother Jones'* story about Donald Trump's hot-mic conversation on Dec. 10, 2015 is available at https://www.motherjones.com/politics/2020/08/new-hot-mic-video-what-trump-told-his-lawyer-when-he-didnt-know-a-camera-was-rolling/. Video clips from Trump's Dec. 10, 2015 deposition are available at https://www.motherjones.com/politics/2020/09/donald-trump-university-fraud-lawsuit-deposition-full-video/. Video from the Sept. 18, 2020 episode of *The ReidOut* is available online at https://www.youtube.com/watch?v=lC7LXNcGgM0.

CHAPTER 19: PARALLELS TO THE PAST

The chapter relies on a wide range of material pulling from many sources, including reporting from *I Alone Can Fix It: Donald J. Trump's Catastrophic Final Year* by Carol Leonnig and Philip Rucker.

CHAPTER 20: ACCOUNTABLE

The chapter relies on the author's recollections and notes, as well as a May 4, 2021 phone interview with Tristan Snell, former Assistant AG for New York who investigated Trump University. The indictment against The Trump Organization and Allen Weisselberg is available at https://s3.documentcloud.org/documents/20982368/new-york-v-trump-org-allen-weisselberg.pdf.

TIMELINE

2004: The Trump Organization files paperwork with the U.S. Patent and Trademark Office for Trump University.

2005: Trump University launches with online-only courses.

A New York State Education Department education official reached out to Trump University expressing concerns with their using the term "university."

2007: Trump University begins in-person seminars of its own.

2009: Art Cohen attends Trump University seminars and spends $34,995 for the Gold Elite membership. He quickly grows disenfranchised.

2010: Tarla Makaeff files a federal class-action lawsuit against Trump University covering anyone who purchased Trump University seminars from 2006 to the present. Trump University countersues, alleging defamation.

Trump University changes its name to Trump Entrepreneurial Initiative before shutting down.

2011: U.S. District Judge Irma Gonzalez denies Makaeff's anti-SLAPP motion.

Art Cohen learns of Makaeff's lawsuit and joins the class. The class for the Makaeff case covers residents in California, New York, and Florida.

The New York State Attorney General's Office investigation into Trump University intensifies behind Assistant AG Tristan Snell.

2012: Donald Trump is deposed by Rachel Jensen.

2013: The 9th Circuit Court of Appeals reverses Judge Gonzalez's decision on the Makaeff anti-SLAPP motion, clearing the way for Judge Curiel to later award Makaeff nearly $800,000 in legal fees.

New York Attorney General Eric Schneiderman sues Trump Entrepreneur Initiative LLC/Trump University, Donald Trump, and Michael Sexton in state Supreme Court in Manhattan and seeking $40 million, Art Cohen files a lawsuit against Donald Trump in federal court seeking a national class action under the civil RICO Act.

2014: The class is certified in the Makaeff case and Judge Curiel denies a motion to dismiss the Cohen case.

Art Cohen participates in a deposition hearing. A follow-up hearing is held the following year.

A nationwide class is certified in the Cohen case.

2015: Donald Trump announces he's running for president.

Trump sits for a deposition at Trump Tower on Dec. 10, 2015, during which time he's caught in a hot-mic moment discussing the case on a court video live feed.

2016: The start of the first federal Trump University trial is delayed from the summer until late November—after the presidential election.

Trump carries out his racist attacks against Judge Curiel and uses his platform on the campaign trail to criticize those trying to hold him accountable, including the lead plaintiffs.

Tarla Makaeff withdraws as lead plaintiff and is replaced by Sonny Low.

Trump secures the Republican presidential nomination and months later, an Electoral College win to become the next president.

The sides hammer out a $25 million settlement deal to avoid going to trial.

2017: Trump is inaugurated as the 45th U.S. President.

Sherri Simpson files an objection to the settlement, delaying distribution of the settlement money by nearly a year.

2018: The Ninth Circuit rejects Simpson's objection and affirms Judge Curiel's final approval order, clearing the way for the settlement money to be released.

2019: The final settlement money is distributed.

Art Cohen files a report with the California Department of Justice about the hot-mic conversation from Trump's 2015 deposition.

Donald Trump is impeached for the first time but the Republican-led Senate later votes against removal.

2020: Hundreds of thousands of Americans die amid the coronavirus pandemic.

Donald Trump is defeated in the presidential election by Joe Biden, but does not accept the results or properly commit to a peaceful transfer of power.

2021: Trump fuels a deadly insurrection at the U.S. Capitol on Jan. 6, delaying the Electoral College results certification.

Trump is impeached for the second time but the Senate votes against removal.

Trump leaves office to face an uncertain future, with legal threats emerging on multiple fronts.

TRANSCRIPT OF DONALD TRUMP'S HOT-MIC CONVERSATION WITH ATTORNEY DANIEL PETROCELLI, DECEMBER 10, 2015, AT TRUMP TOWER.

For the full video, visit https://www.youtube.com/watch?time_continue=274&v=iRX0Cz8hvMA &feature=emb_title.

DT: Donald Trump

DP: Daniel Petrocelli

STEN: Court stenographer

UMS: Unidentified male speaker

DJP: Dan Pfefferbaum

Following some idle chit-chat between Petrocelli, Trump, and a court stenographer in the room, Petrocelli and Trump's conversation picks up, at first centered around the day's schedule and the length of Trump's deposition. The talk quickly shifts to the case and Judge Curiel.

DJF: A little over four hours.

DT: I thought it was seven.

DP: Seven by the time we are finished here we'll only have two hours left, and we'll worry about it another time. Maybe when we're in LA next.

DT: Then like they make this personal . . . I had a corporation. You know everyone I ask who's a lawyer. . . they say, "how could it be so personal?"

DP: It's really, the judge did not (indecipherable)

DT: And you're shocked at that? Right?

DP: I am, that's what made me feel the judge had it in for you. But, let me take it (interrupted)

DT: But there is a reason for a corporation. Is there something you can do about it? Because if you could do that, we win the case.

DP: Exactly right, exactly right. You're the only reason why this case is going on because of that.

DT: What can you do about it?

DP: We have one more shot at it. . . (crosstalk) . . . he just denied the dismissal of the suit.

DT: And personal too?

DP: Against you personally.

DT: How can he do that? You know, I've got hundreds of cases and I never get sued. . .

DP: Because they are saying you are personally involved in making false statements but they can't prove that. That's the only reason.

DT: So could you now, at the end of all depositions, go and ask for the judge again because I declared. . .

DP: I'm going to have to think about it.

DT: Is he an asshole, or does he just want me in his courtroom?

DP: Latter, I think.

DT: You really think so? You know him a little bit?

DP: I do. He's a, he's a average judge. He's not nuts. He's on the wrong side of the aisle too, that's not helping.

DT: What about the Spanish thing? The first judge . . . she would have thrown it out . . . Do you know who it is?

DP: I heard of her, yeah. She's about ready to retire.

DT: Then I got this guy, NOTHING.

DP: That's why you have to strike when the iron's hot.

DT: That's happened a few times to you over the years where . . . you've got a problem with the judge, then you've got a problem.

DP: For sure.

DT: How do you think we win in this case?

DP: If we had to try this case, I think we would win this case. I think you're a big reason why, because I think the jurors like you . . . You're being honest.

DT: You think it's an easy win?

DP: Um, not a slam dunk. I've had easier cases. But I'd put it at like, about 50 percent.

DT: . . . And by the way, the only good ruling we did get is that they have to try their damages separately, right?

DP: Yeah, we won that.

DT: Doesn't that kill them? They got to bring separate cases for everybody to get damages?

DP: Yeah, that's just getting played out right now.

DT: But isn't that a great win for us?

DP: It's a significant win. The judge doesn't know what to do with this case.

DT: Did he make a wrong decision?

DP: He made the wrong decision certifying this as a class action.

DT: If we had it decertified we'd essentially walk away.

DP: Oh yeah, then it's over.

DT: Didn't we almost have it decertified by him doing that?

DP: He had it half-decertified, exactly, because now everybody's gotta come in and prove their own individual damages . . .

DT: Where are these people, I'm surprised they're not here (pointing across the table)

Trump and Petrocelli turn to Dan Pfefferman, one of my attorneys, who was located in the room at the time.

DP: Hey Dan, want to get your colleagues?

DJP: Sure.

DT: We actually waited 10 minutes by the way.

DJP: We were here half an hour at lunch . . .

Pfefferman steps out of the room looking for Jason Forge and Rachel Jensen, while Trump and Petrocelli continue talking. Trump is speaking in hushed tones.

DP: I know exactly what. . .

DT: . . . Go in there and say that thing about him. You understand?

DP: I'll give it a shot.

DT: You'll give it a shot?

DP: I'll see what I can do.

DT: And the other thing is. . . we'll wait.

DP: Let's wait, we'll talk separately.

DT: Will you have a better shot after this?

An interruption by the court reporter causes Trump and Petrocelli to pause their conversation.

DT: So you have a better chance. . .

DP: I'll give it a shot.

DT: Then boom (waving his hands) maybe you get lucky.

As Petrocelli asks about the video equipment for the deposition, Trump calls to someone off-camera, "Keith"—believed to be his longtime handler Keith Schiller.

DT: Hey Keith, Keith, any calls upstairs? Just check . . . just check with the phone.

UMS: Yeah.

DT: I've had some crazy cases. I can't say this is the worst of 'em. I've had some crazy cases . . . This is one that should be . . . (indecipherable)

UMS: Pete Bevaqua, he said he'll talk tomorrow, he just wanted to catch up.

DP: Do you know where the rest of these lawyers are?

UMS: Haven't seen them. They might be in the back end room. Want me to go get them?

DP: Yeah, we'd like to get rolling.

DT: I think we should put on the record we've been waiting for 10 minutes – they'll say we left and then we came back . . .

DP: When did we start our break? (directing question to court stenographer)

STEN: Let me see . . .

DT: We were gone for 5 minutes.

DP: What time do you have now?

STEN: 4:08

DP: What is it?

STEN: 4:08

DP: We were back by 3:58

DT: It's 5 after 4.

DP: No, its 8 after 4.

DT: It is?

STEN: Well, it' s only 4:05. It's 5 after, my computer is a little fast. Would either of you like a nut? (*the stenographer offers a bag of nuts*)

DT: No thank you, darling . . . our man Barrack, the *Ba-rock*.

DP: He's got a new bride, couple new kids.

DT: What's that all about? When did he get married?

DP: Got married, ah, about a year ago.

DT: Is she beautiful?

DP: Yeah, young. She's 38, 37.

DT: How old is he, 65?

DP: I think he's like 67.

DT: He gets a kick out of this, can you believe this, sitting here with this bullshit? (making numerous gestures)

DP: With everything on your mind, I don't know how you're doing this. I really feel bad for you.

UMS: They're having a problem with the printer. They'll be here in two minutes.

Petrocelli and Trump discuss their waiting for the other attorneys to return. Trump returns the conversation to Petrocelli's claim that the case was a 50-50 shot.

DP: You never go above 70 percent in a case

DT: Even if it's a lock.

DP: Yeah . . . X-factor.

DT: You mean even if you think you got a lock, you're not going to tell the client, 100 percent.

DP: I have never gone above 75 percent

DT: When people ask, "So, what are the chances of you getting the nomination?" I say 50 percent, even though I'm at 40. You understand? . . . I don't want to say, "Oh, I'm going to get it."

DP: It's the smart bet, sir.

Trump asks again about his chances at winning the case.

DT: This is one of the stronger cases, right?

DP: I would rate this above average. I've had stronger cases, and I've had weaker cases. I think the guys under you sort of let you down, a little sloppy.

Trump and Petrocelli continue talking about Trump University and the case, often in indecipherable tones, and Trump brings up the Better Business Bureau.

DT: Better Business Bureau gave it an A . . . (following complaints BBB) gave it a D. Know what that is? It's a kill for you. (shaking his head) He calls them up, "we're gonna sue you" . . . An A, got the D removed.

DP: For the university?

DT: Yeah . . . . My guy upstairs, Alan Gartner type, he's tough, gave them a call.

DP: Works for you upstairs?

DT: Yeah.

As the other attorneys come into the room, Trump and Petrocelli say they will continue their conversation later as they prepare to continue the deposition.

TRUMP'S 6DS

Trump University showed Trump's six Ds on display:

DECEIVE—DEFRAUD—DENY—DEFLECT—DODGE—DELAY

DECEIVE

Trump University's promotions were full of blatant lies. Trump University, in fact, was not a university and did not feature Trump's secrets.

DEFRAUD

Students lost thousands of dollars, in some cases their life savings, while Trump wrote himself checks for over $5 million for personal gain.

DENY

Trump denied that Trump University students were dissatisfied with the services despite requests for refunds and complaints to the BBB.

DEFLECT

Trump attacked students who complained about poor services. He promoted a 98% "approval rating" that was unrelated to the services provided.

DODGE

Trump blamed others for the poor performances of mentors and so-called professors for lack of real estate experience.

DELAY

Instead of negotiating a settlement in good faith, Trump prolonged litigation with endless motions, appeals, and counter-suits, and used hostility and his national platform to get the trials pushed until after the 2016 election. The delay enabled his bid for the presidency to succeed.

ACKNOWLEDGMENTS

Art Cohen

Before this book came the Trump University settlement, which would not have been secured without the legal acumen and determination of my counsel, especially Amber Eck, Jason Forge, and Rachel Jensen. My fellow lead plaintiffs (Tarla Makaef, Sonny Low, John Brown, and J.R. Everett) showed so much courage to fight alongside me to help win the $25M settlement for all students.

This book would not have happened without Rob Price, President and Sarah Duckworth, Director of Author Relations of Gatekeeper Press, and their publishing team. Rob and Sarah went the extra length to help ensure the highest quality publishing possible.

To David Corn with Mother Jones, who never wavered in his efforts to publish elements of my story in August and September 2020.

A special thanks for Amber Eck, John Brown, and Sonny Low, as well as Tristan Snell, former assistant NY Attorney General, for sharing their insights and perspectives for this book.

My heartfelt thanks to Zimin Cohen, who spent many hours helping me design the book's cover.

To my college friend Seth Grenald, who took the extra time and effort to review early drafts and make recommendations along the way.

To the friends who gave me their support and feedback during the past two-plus years putting this memoir together—Steven Azar, Pat Canada,

John Haggis, Aaron Jarson, Yuval Minkowski, Egle Petrov, and Sergey Petrov.

To my wife, children, brother, and mother-in-law whose moral and emotional support during the past two-plus years helped make finishing this writing endeavor possible.

And finally, to Dan Good, whose partnership in writing this book was essential to telling the story in the most compelling and informative manner. Dan's journalism experience helped me navigate through the elements of the book publishing world. His unwavering ability to uncover critical information embodied the definition of a great investigative Journalist. Dan understood early on how important it was to publish my story—his dedication made it possible.

Dan Good

To the lawyers and journalists and family and friends who've helped to shape this book's progress—your impacts have been meaningful and significant.

To my parents and Suzy and Dean, your support means everything to me.

To Art, I'm honored to have teamed up to tell your story. You and other Trump University victims endured so much suffering, and waited so long, in search of closure. Your efforts are commendable. I cherish this collaboration and the friendship that's developed from it.

CPSIA information can be obtained
at www.ICGtesting.com
Printed in the USA
BVHW040757181021
619198BV00004B/7/J